The Challenge of Independent Colleges

THE CHALLENGE OF INDEPENDENT COLLEGES

Moving Research into Practice

EDITED BY
Christopher C. Morphew
and
John M. Braxton

Johns Hopkins University Press
BALTIMORE

© 2017 Johns Hopkins University Press
All rights reserved. Published 2017
Printed in the United States of America on acid-free paper
9 8 7 6 5 4 3 2 1

Johns Hopkins University Press
2715 North Charles Street
Baltimore, Maryland 21218-4363
www.press.jhu.edu

Library of Congress Cataloging-in-Publication Data

Names: Morphew, Christopher C., 1967–, editor. | Braxton, John M.,
    editor.
Title: The challenge of independent colleges : moving research into
    practice / edited by Christopher C. Morphew and John M. Braxton.
Description: Baltimore : Johns Hopkins University Press, 2018. |
    Includes bibliographical references and index.
Identifiers: LCCN 2017012952 | ISBN 9781421424316 (hardcover :
    acid-free paper) | ISBN 9781421424323 (electronic) | ISBN
    1421424312 (hardcover : acid-free paper) | ISBN 1421424320
    (electronic)
Subjects: LCSH: Private universities and colleges—United States—
    Administration. | Education, Higher—Aims and objectives—United
    States.
Classification: LCC LB2341 .C4728 2018 | DDC 378/.040973—dc23
    LC record available at https://lccn.loc.gov/2017012952

A catalog record for this book is available from the British Library.

*Special discounts are available for bulk purchases of this book. For
more information, please contact Special Sales at 410-516-6936 or
specialsales@press.jhu.edu.*

Johns Hopkins University Press uses environmentally friendly book
materials, including recycled text paper that is composed of at least
30 percent post-consumer waste, whenever possible.

Contents

Foreword

Like other higher education institutions, small and mid-sized private, nonprofit colleges and universities—also known as independent colleges—are facing many difficult-to-answer questions. The most vexing questions include, What are the most effective strategies for promoting students' access and affordability, assessing student learning outcomes, and ensuring students' success? How can an institution promote equity in opportunity and outcomes, recognizing the changing demographic characteristics of the US population? How can and should emerging technologies be leveraged to improve teaching and learning? What are the most appropriate components of the curriculum? What is the ideal composition of the faculty and what is the faculty's role in academic governance? How can and should an institution adapt to reflect changes in the demographic, economic, and global environment in which it operates? How can an institution achieve its mission in the context of finite fiscal resources and other external pressures? How can institutional leaders ensure that the benefits of higher education continue to exceed the costs?

Although many studies inform understanding of these and other questions, existing research has at least three limitations. First, relatively few studies focus specifically on small and mid-sized independent colleges and universities. Independent colleges are an important but understudied sector of higher education. In 2016, the 653 four-year colleges and universities that are members of the Council of Independent Colleges (CIC) were one-fifth of the nation's 3,026 four-year colleges and universities. According to data reported in IPEDS (The Department of Education's Integrated Postsecondary Education Data System), the CIC institutions enrolled nearly 1.8 million students, or 13 percent of the total enrollment in four-year colleges and universities in fall 2015, with a median enrollment of 1,880 students.

Second, even when available, research often includes insufficient consideration of the distinctive characteristics of this sector. Independent colleges and universities differ from institutions in other sectors in terms of their academic missions, pedagogical approaches, organizational structures, campus cultures, business models, and student outcomes. To be useful to campus leaders and faculty members, research must consider the unique institutional contexts of these institutions and recognize the ways that the characteristics of these institutions influence both the framing of the questions that need to be addressed and the appropriate answers to these questions.

Third, even when available and relevant, existing research on independent colleges and universities is frequently underutilized by administrators and faculty members. Campus leaders may be unaware of the availability of relevant research and/or lack easy access to relevant research findings.

With the goal of improving the production of relevant high-quality research by scholars and its use by private college leaders, CIC agreed to partner with members of the Association for the Study of Higher Education (ASHE). CIC is an association of 755 nonprofit independent colleges and universities and higher education affiliates and organizations that has worked since 1956 to support college and university leadership, advance institutional excellence, and enhance public understanding of private higher education's contributions to society. ASHE is a scholarly association of about 2,000 academics, graduate students, and others who are engaged in research about higher education. With the high share of its members who are graduate students, ASHE also plays a role in shaping the direction of the next generation of higher education research.

Initiated in August 2014 by Laura Perna when she was president-elect of ASHE, the ASHE-CIC collaboration was part of a larger initiative funded by the William T. Grant Foundation. Each of the five collaborations that was part of this initiative was designed to advance the production of high-quality research on important issues facing higher education policy and practice and to improve connections between the creators and users of higher education research.

Through a series of in-person and virtual meetings, the ASHE-CIC collaboration worked diligently for more than two years to develop a shared understanding of the important researchable questions that leaders of independent colleges need to address. This collaboration also has generated improved understanding of ways to productively connect research and practice.

Members of the ASHE-CIC collaboration discussed insights gained through their work in a well-received presidential session at the ASHE Conference in Denver, Colorado, in November 2015. Entitled "Beyond Research to Practice: Institutionalizing Collaboration between ASHE Researchers and Smaller Private Institutions," this presidential session shared with ASHE members insights about the gap that exists between research and practice at smaller private colleges and universities. A subsequent presidential session at the ASHE Conference in Columbus, Ohio, in November 2016 featured ASHE scholars addressing the question, "Is My Work Making a Difference for Independent College and University Leaders? Seriously," with senior leaders of CIC colleges providing responses.

This volume is a useful and lasting product of the ASHE-CIC collaboration. We believe that higher education scholars and leaders of small and midsized independent colleges will find this volume to be a useful resource for improving institutional practice, defining new areas of research, and bridging the research and practice divide.

Together, the chapters in this volume address the limitations in research that we outline above. The chapters address critical and timely questions—and they do so recognizing the perspectives, contexts, and characteristics of independent colleges. The volume also signals the utility of connecting research and practice, as it includes chapters written by well-regarded scholars in higher education and reactions to these chapters from leaders of independent colleges. In short, this collection offers helpful research-based insights into the difficult problems facing leaders at independent institutions and sheds important light on the gaps between research and practice at these institutions. This published volume will enable others to benefit from the learning achieved through the collaboration's efforts.

This volume makes valuable contributions to research and practice because of the outstanding contributions of those involved. We are grateful that Christopher Morphew, professor and executive associate dean for research and innovation in the College of Education at the University of Iowa; Harold V. Hartley III, CIC senior vice president; and Hollie Chessman, CIC director of research projects, agreed to represent ASHE and CIC, respectively. Christopher, Hal, and Hollie have provided excellent leadership over all aspects of the collaboration. They ably identified collaboration participants (for example, ASHE scholars with interest in the private college sector, scholar-practitioners at independent colleges), guided members of the collaboration toward identifying shared goals, and worked to ensure achievement of the collaboration's self-identified goals in a timely manner. We also appreciate the contributions of John Braxton who, along with co-chairs Christopher, Hal, and Hollie, rendered invaluable service as a coeditor of this publication.

We also want to thank the ASHE members who authored chapters in this volume and the CIC campus leaders who provided insightful reactions to the chapters. Contributors to the volume include an impressive array of higher education scholars at various career stages and institutions, as well as presidents and provosts from nine different CIC institutions. This volume also provides a solid foundation for continued meaningful connections between research and practice into the future. We hope that the relationships developed between researchers and practitioners through this ASHE-CIC collaboration continue. This volume clearly demonstrates the utility of intentional efforts to bridge our too-often-separate research and practice communities.

Laura Perna
James S. Riepe Professor
University of Pennsylvania
Past-President, ASHE

Richard Ekman
President
Council of Independent Colleges

Preface

CHRISTOPHER C. MORPHEW

This book is different from other higher education publications because it's part of an attempt to bridge a research-to-practice divide and connect the work of higher education scholars with the realities of campus leaders who confront complex problems every day. That divide doesn't exist because higher education scholars don't care about what goes on at the campus level. They do care. Neither does the divide mean that campus leaders aren't smart enough to read and make sense of the work of higher education scholars. They are plenty smart. Rather, the divide reflects that the vast majority of published work on the subject of higher education can be broken into one of two camps, the scholarly or the practical.

The typical scholarly publication is a journal article that follows a standard recipe: a statement of the problem plus a robust literature review, followed by a dry discussion of the study's data sources and methodology and, finally, a discussion of the study's findings. The goal is probably generalizable findings, as well as methodological or conceptual additions to existing research. There may be an "implications for practice" section, but it's largely an afterthought, probably a function of a reviewer's nudge. The practical publication (probably a book-length manuscript), conversely, might be authored by a campus leader describing a problem and its consequences for a specific sector of higher education. This work isn't devoid of data or useful findings; there might be robust case studies, for example. The goal of this publication is to bring an important problem into focus and advocate for a specific solution or increased attention to that problem.

The author of the scholarly journal on higher education is likely a member of the Association for the Study of Higher Education (ASHE), a leading professional association for higher education researchers. The campus leader authoring the book just might be a member of the Council of Independent Colleges (CIC), a membership group of more than 700 smaller private colleges that has worked to represent the interests and needs of its member campuses since 1956.

You can learn a lot from reading both types of publications. One of the things you'll learn is that the scholars and campus leaders authors are focused on similar issues but write with different goals and audiences in mind. For example, issues of access may be central to the publications penned by both scholars and campus leaders. The scholar, however, is focused on what she can add to the existing literature on the subject, perhaps as a result of newly available data or the application of an emerging conceptual framework. The campus leader is concerned, meanwhile, about access because her campus is struggling with how to juggle a growing discount rate and a mission that includes educating the region's neediest students. The scholar finishes with "directions for future research," while the campus leader might finish with a call to action.

ASHE and CIC are partners in an effort to bridge this divide because the leaders of both groups think it's important (and possible) to produce scholarship relevant to the everyday problems faced by smaller, private colleges. Toward that end, this book is organized in a way that juxtaposes what we know about topics central to the health and mission of independent colleges with what's happening on these campuses. Specifically, the editors asked ASHE scholars to contribute chapters that describe what the literature can tell us about a core issue of particular importance to independent higher education (e.g., public purposes and benefits of using technology to improve learning) and the specific challenges and opportunities that face these campuses. What can independent colleges do to remind the public that they have a historic and continuing mission that is central to an engaged, democratic society? What is their potential market advantage in employing new technologies to improve student learning? Then, we asked presidents or provosts on nine CIC campuses to read these chapters and react to the utility of what they read. What did they learn? What knowledge do they wish the chapter would have contained, given the current challenges on their campus? Can they use these ideas to solve puzzles on their campuses? Although we asked the scholars to go through several edits of their chapters, you will read the chapter reactions largely unvarnished (save for a few minor edits) because we thought it important for the reader to read the uncensored views of campus leaders.

In the concluding chapter, my coeditor John Braxton and I return to wrap things up. Our message is that the research-to-practice bridge has some significant support but needs more construction. We're optimistic that this volume will demonstrate that scholars and campus leaders are on the same page and share similar goals. More work is needed to be accomplished by both communities if we're to figure out how to improve what's happening on private college and university campuses as a result of empirical research.

Acknowledgments

The editors thank past ASHE Presidents Laura Perna and Scott Thomas for their leadership on the ASHE W. T. Grant collaborations. The ASHE-CIC collaboration is part of that collaboration and indicative of Laura and Scott's efforts to make the work of ASHE more relevant to practitioners. Thanks also to the leadership at the Council of Independent Colleges, including President Richard Ekman and Senior Vice President Harold V. Hartley III, who were great to work with throughout this process. Current and former CIC staff members, including Hollie Chessman, Jesse Rine, and Natalie Pullaro Davis, provided important support to the project as well and deserve our thanks.

The Challenge of Independent Colleges

An Overview of the Independent College Sector

HAROLD V. HARTLEY III

The residential liberal arts college is a distinctively American form of higher education that was dominant in the United States from its founding through the nineteenth century and that continues to play a vital role in postsecondary education today.[1] As the landscape has changed and higher education has evolved, so too have small and mid-sized, private not-for-profit (i.e., independent) colleges and universities. What are the differentiating characteristics of independent colleges? How are these institutions of higher education adapting to changing student demographics and economic conditions? In what ways are independent colleges and the education they provide misunderstood? How might these conditions shape a research agenda that would usefully inform education policy and help independent colleges adapt and thrive as a vital segment of American higher education?

The Council of Independent Colleges (CIC) has long sought to address these questions. Founded in 1956, CIC is a national association of more than 750 independent colleges and universities and affiliated organizations working together to support college and university leadership, advance institutional excellence, and enhance the contributions of independent higher education to society. The 653 member four-year colleges and universities are diverse and range from a small number of highly selective and wealthy colleges to many more that have regional application pools and modest endowments. The CIC membership includes institutions with ties to religious denominations, with no religious affiliation, that are historically black institutions or women's colleges, and that are located in either urban or rural settings. While many of these institutions in recent years have diversified their educational offerings to include professional fields and graduate degrees, all remain committed to an undergraduate academic core rooted in the liberal arts. As tuition-dependent institutions, they also are quite entrepreneurial, continually seeking ways to enhance their educational programs, institutional performance, and market position. CIC's services to member institutions emphasize leadership development and academic program improvement. Although headquartered in Washington, DC, CIC leaves lobbying activities to other associations.

At the invitation of the Association for the Study of Higher Education (ASHE), CIC and ASHE have embarked on a collaboration to bring renewed focus to the study of the independent college sector and to bridge the research-to-practice gap. All too often higher education research overlooks smaller private colleges and universities as a population of interest or fails to differentiate results of this sector in research findings. Moreover, results that are relevant to the independent college sector are often overlooked by independent college administrators and faculty members. Given the challenging environment faced by independent colleges, what can be learned by the resiliency of this segment of American higher education and how can targeted research studies improve its effectiveness? This volume is an important step in a joint effort by ASHE and CIC to increase the quantity and quality of pertinent research about the independent college sector and to increase the use of empirical evidence in decision making by independent college leaders.

Understanding the Independent College Sector

The independent colleges and universities that constitute the CIC membership are often characterized as small and mid-sized. Member institutions represent roughly a quarter of all four-year colleges and universities in the United States and the approximately 1.8 million students attending CIC institutions make up 13 percent of the total four-year student enrollment. More than half (58 percent) of the CIC institutions have enrollments of 2,000 or fewer students. By type of degree offered, nearly half (47 percent) are baccalaureate colleges and another 44 percent are master's level institutions. Only 6 percent of the CIC membership is classified as doctoral-granting institutions. The majority of CIC colleges and universities serve traditional-aged student populations with two-thirds (67 percent) of the CIC undergraduate enrollment under the age of 22.[2]

Traditional, residential, undergraduate, small size, small classes, rooted in the liberal arts, close student-faculty relationships, a co-curricular program that supports classroom learning, tuition dependent—these are characteristics that typify the independent colleges CIC serves. Empirical research has consistently found that many of these characteristics yield better learning outcomes and a greater likelihood of persistence to degree.[3] Yet frequently, independent colleges are caricatured as expensive, exclusive, and elitist, as well as outmoded or irrelevant and resistant to change.

To ground the assertions of the positive attributes of independent colleges in reliable evidence and to debunk the prevailing myths about these institutions, more than a decade ago CIC initiated research to document the quality and value of the education provided by its member colleges and universities and in the process to help its members make data-informed decisions in light of the challenges faced. Much of the empirical evidence has been published in a special section on the CIC website called "Making the Case" (www.cic .edu/MakingtheCase). In addition, CIC periodically has published reports and briefs on particular issues, such as addressing myths about student debt (www .cic.edu/StudentDebt).

More recently, CIC redoubled its efforts to make its case by launching a public information campaign, Securing America's Future: The Power of Liberal Arts Education (www.cic.edu/LiberalArts), to promote the effectiveness and contributions of private liberal arts colleges and universities and the importance of the liberal arts as fields of study. Activities have included a national symposium on the liberal arts held in September 2015, a website for prospective students and their parents (www.LiberalArtsPower.org), and a social media campaign featuring Twitter avatars Libby and Art (@SmartColleges and #LiberalArtsPower). In addition, CIC undertook the Project on the Future of Independent Higher Education (www.cic.edu/IndependentFuture) to explore fresh approaches to higher education and new college business models and to examine the distinctive characteristics and missions of independent colleges that have enabled them to offer a high-quality education for so many years. During the 2016–17 academic year, CIC held eight workshops around the country to bring together campus teams of presidents, chief academic officers, faculty leaders, and others to help member colleges and universities prepare for the future more effectively (www.cic.edu/SecuringWorkshops). Generous support for these initiatives has been provided by Arthur Vining Davis Foundations, Carnegie Corporation of New York, Endeavor Foundation, Jessie Ball DuPont Fund, Gladys Krieble Delmas Foundation, Teagle Foundation, Lumina Foundation, and the TIAA Institute.

In 2016, CIC launched *Digest of Recent Research*, a series with support from the Spencer Foundation intended to highlight timely research from scholarly journals and other publications with a focus on findings relevant to presidents and other leaders of independent colleges and universities (www.cic.edu/ ResearchDigest). Edited by John M. Braxton, professor of higher education at Vanderbilt University, each *Digest* offers a brief summary of selected articles that includes a discussion of the findings and implications for action by the leadership of independent colleges and universities.

What follows is a summary of the key research findings generated and gathered by CIC that address the topics of the affordability of an independent college undergraduate degree, the accessibility of these institutions to diverse students and their success in the timely graduation of these students, the quality and relevance of an education grounded in the liberal arts, and the superior outcomes of undergraduate education at an independent college. Given the pressing national priority to increase the number of college graduates, it is important to understand the key role that independent colleges play and to give due attention in the research literature to this vital segment of American higher education. This summary also identifies challenges faced by independent colleges that will be taken up in subsequent chapters in this volume and forms the basis for future research that would benefit this sector.

Affordable for Students and Families

Much has been written about the affordability of higher education in general and of private colleges in particular. Because public colleges and universities receive considerable state subsidies, they are able to charge tuition and fees that are far below the actual cost per student to the institution. To make up for this difference, independent colleges typically provide generous grants from institutional sources to their students. Four out of five students (82 percent) enrolled at private four-year institutions receive institutional grants compared with slightly more than half that share (45 percent) of students enrolled at public four-year institutions and only one in three students (34 percent) at for-profit four-year institutions.[4]

In 2016–17, the average published tuition and fees at a private, four-year college or university for a full-time undergraduate student was \$33,480, but the average "net price"—the amount students and their families actually pay after grant aid from all sources (federal, state, and institution) and federal tax credits—was only \$14,190, or approximately 42 percent of the "sticker price." Furthermore, over the past decade (from 2006–7 to 2016–17), published tuition and fees have risen much faster at public institutions (41 percent increase) than at private institutions (27 percent increase).[5]

When comparing a matched set of public and private four-year nondoctoral colleges and universities, Zumeta and Huntington-Klein[6] found that the total cost after grants per four-year degree (based on out-of-state charges at public institutions) was on average $57,428 at publics versus $62,566 at privates. Moreover, since students at independent colleges on average graduate in four years at nearly twice the rate at public institutions (52.7 percent at private, nondoctoral institutions vs. 27.1 percent at public, nondoctoral institutions), they limit the number of years needed to pay for their education and are able to enter the job market or graduate school sooner than their peers at public institutions, thereby increasing opportunities for lifelong earnings.[7]

Another measure of affordability is the level of debt incurred by college graduates. Nearly half (48 percent) of the graduates of private four-year colleges and universities had less than $20,000 in debt, with one quarter (26 percent) having no federal educational debt at all upon graduation.[8] The average debt of a graduate with a baccalaureate degree from a four-year independent college in 2013–14 was $19,300—down from $19,900 the year before and the same level as in 2006–7—compared with $15,200 for a public college graduate—up from $15,000 the previous year and $12,000 in 2006–7.[9] Moreover, the default rate on federal student loans in fiscal year 2012 was 6.5 percent among all borrowers at private four-year institutions versus 7.3 percent of borrowers at public institutions and 14.0 percent at for-profit institutions.[10] By these measures, an independent college education is more affordable than frequently portrayed, and for those students who must finance some of their educational costs, the level of debt is manageable.

While much attention has been given to the estimated $1.3 trillion total amount of outstanding student debt, it is important to recognize that approximately 40 percent of that total is graduate student debt.[11] According to data from the US Department of Education's Federal Student Aid Data Center, only 15 percent of all federal student loans in 2014–15 went to students enrolled at CIC member colleges and universities, consistent with the share of total enrollment. Moreover, 37 percent of these loans went to finance graduate study.[12]

Efforts to keep independent colleges affordable are not without cost. Rising tuition discount rates, shrinking pools of eligible high school graduates, increased operating costs, especially for personnel, and modest endowments all limit the ability of independent colleges to provide an affordable education to students from all economic backgrounds. Because of these pressures, Moody's recently predicted that the number of closures for independent colleges would triple in four years, and the number of mergers would double.[13] Despite these pressures, an analysis of the financial health of independent colleges over the most recent years for which data are available indicates that 67 percent of institutions have maintained or increased their financial stability.[14]

What will it take to keep an independent college education affordable, especially for low-income students, into the future?

Access and Success for Diverse Students

Overall, the enrollment of underrepresented students by race/ethnicity, income status, and parental education at independent colleges is comparable to that at four-year public institutions. In other words, public institutions are not significantly more diverse by these demographic characteristics than are private institutions. For example, 12 percent of students enrolled at CIC member colleges and universities are African American compared with 11 percent at four-year public institutions. Similarly, Hispanics make up 9 percent of the enrollment at CIC institutions versus 14 percent at publics. In all, 39 percent of CIC students are students of color versus 44 percent of public students.[15]

Students enrolled at smaller private colleges are more diverse than those at larger public universities when measured by the level of income or educational attainment of their parents. With regard to enrollment by parental income of dependent students, one-third (33 percent) of students enrolled at nondoctoral independent four-year colleges and universities are low-income (families with incomes less than $40,000) compared with 27 percent at public doctoral institutions. At the other end of the income spectrum, students from families making $120,000 or more per year make up 17 percent of the enrollments at private nondoctoral colleges versus 25 percent at public doctoral universities.[16] Similarly, a higher proportion of first-generation students (where neither parent had ever enrolled in college) are enrolled at independent nondoctoral colleges (17 percent) than at public doctoral universities (15 percent).[17]

Not only are smaller private colleges as diverse as their larger public counterparts, they graduate underrepresented students at higher rates. For example, the four-year graduation rates for African American students enrolled at independent nondoctoral colleges are double that at nondoctoral public institutions and a third again as high as at doctoral public institutions (30 percent vs. 13 and 21 percent). The comparative four-year graduation rates of Hispanic students are even higher at nondoctoral private colleges when compared with nondoctoral and doctoral public institutions (36 percent vs. 15 and 24 percent).[18]

The four-year graduation rates of low-income and first-generation students also are higher at independent colleges compared with public institutions—and also more than double the rate when comparing nondoctoral private with nondoctoral public institutions. For low-income students, the four-year graduation rate is 23 percentage points higher at private nondoctoral (36 percent) versus public nondoctoral (13 percent) and 14 points higher than public doctoral (22 percent) institutions. Similarly, the four-year graduation rate of first-generation students is 24 percentage points higher at nondoctoral private colleges (42 percent) when compared with nondoctoral public institutions (18 percent) and 16 points higher when compared with doctoral public institutions (26 percent). In fact, first-generation students are just as likely to complete their undergraduate degrees in four years at independent colleges (42 percent) as they are in six years at public nondoctoral institutions (41 percent).[19]

How can independent colleges maintain a strong track record of serving underrepresented students?

Educational Quality

Part of the reason for the comparative academic success of independent colleges is their primary focus on undergraduate education instead of a strong emphasis on graduate education and scholarly research. In addition, smaller private colleges are more likely to provide educational environments closely aligned with better student outcomes. A recent report by the Center for Post-secondary Research at Indiana University[20] reaffirmed long-standing findings that students at nondoctoral independent colleges are more likely than students at public institutions to experience academically challenging settings, closer student-faculty interactions, effective teaching practices, and supportive learning environments. Furthermore, private college students are more likely to participate in two or more "high impact practices,"[21] resulting in higher levels of retention and student learning. Students enrolled at independent colleges also are more likely to experience a curricular and co-curricular emphasis on values and ethics. In short, the report concluded, "the traditional, residential liberal arts college provides a more effective learning environment for today's students."[22]

Another study found that the overall benefit from educationally enriching practices at independent colleges extends to first-generation and low-income students.[23] For example, nearly half of low-income students (48 percent) enrolled at private nondoctoral colleges reported that they never had a large class, compared with less than a third (29 percent) at public nondoctoral institutions. The results were similar for first-generation students: 47 percent at private nondoctoral colleges indicated never having a large class versus 33 percent at public nondoctoral institutions (and only 10 percent at public doctoral universities). Comparably strong results for first-generation and low-income students were found for other features of a personalized academic environment: discussing academic matters with faculty members outside of class, meeting informally with faculty members, and never having graduate students as instructors.[24]

Independent colleges also excel at enrolling and graduating students in STEM (science, technology, engineering, and mathematics) fields, an area of critical national need to maintain American global competitiveness. Private nondoctoral colleges enroll similar proportions of students in STEM and health-related majors as at public nondoctoral institutions (21 vs. 20 percent, respectively).[25] Furthermore, students majoring in STEM fields are much more likely to graduate and to do so on time at private nondoctoral colleges. Among those who obtained a bachelor's degree in a STEM field, four in five (80 percent) did so in four years or less at private nondoctoral colleges compared with just over half (52 percent) at public doctoral institutions and one-third (34 percent) at public nondoctoral institutions.[26] Many smaller independent colleges outperform much larger research universities in sending their graduates on to obtain doctorates in STEM fields. For example, Allegheny College, with an enrollment of just over 1,800 undergraduate students, sent 25 students on to earn doctorates in chemistry between 2006 and 2010, a comparable number to two research universities also in western Pennsylvania: 30 from the University of Pittsburgh (over 17,400 undergraduates) and 25 from Carnegie Mellon University (over 5,400 undergraduates).[27]

One of the challenges of their smaller size and limited resources is the ability of independent colleges to offer a wide range of academic majors. Some have established online programs as a cost-effective means of expanding educational offerings.[28] Other CIC institutions are making use of online instruction to address an entirely different problem: how to keep upper-level courses that are essential for liberal arts majors strong and viable.[29] Another approach, consistent with a broader trend in American higher education, is to use contingent faculty members to expand academic programs, but as Morphew, Ward, and Wolf-Wendel[30] report, these part-time and non-tenure-track instructors frequently do not have the same level of orientation to institutional mission or support for faculty development, which raises questions about their ability to maintain the same academic quality as full-time faculty members.

What approaches are most likely to help independent colleges maintain the high quality of their educational offerings?

Assessment of Student Learning

Contrary to the widely held view that colleges and universities are resistant to efforts to assess educational quality and be transparent about learning outcomes, independent colleges have been at the forefront of efforts to improve the quality of student learning. CIC has long been a national leader of voluntary assessment initiatives while at the same time advocating for institutional autonomy.[31] In 2001, CIC was the first national presidential association to urge its members to use the National Survey of Student Engagement (NSSE). To date, approximately 92 percent of CIC colleges and universities have used NSSE to assess student engagement. In 2002, CIC partnered with the Council for Aid to Education to develop and use the Collegiate Learning Assessment (CLA), and by 2005 CIC was running the largest consortium in the country with 33 colleges and universities using the CLA to improve student learning,[32] an effort that continued through 2012 with as many as 57 institutions.[33]

Since 2004, CIC has prepared annual benchmarking reports so that its member institutions are able to ground institutional planning and decision making with reliable comparative data. CIC's Key Indicators Tool (KIT) provides a customized benchmarking report for each CIC member institution, with 20 indicators of institutional performance in four key areas: (1) student enrollment and progression, (2) faculty composition and compensation, (3) tuition revenue and financial aid, and (4) financial resources and expenditures (www.cic.edu/KIT). CIC's Financial Indicators Tool (FIT) is the first national benchmarking report to provide comparative data on four financial indicators measuring resource sufficiency, debt management, asset performance, and operating results, along with a fifth composite indicator, the Composite Financial Index[34] as an overall gauge of financial health (www.cic.edu/FIT).

Consistent with its emphasis on institutional autonomy while encouraging evidence-based decision making and curricular reform, in 2011 CIC was the first national association selected to test the Lumina Foundation's concept of the Degree Qualifications Profile (DQP). A consortium of 25 independent colleges spent two years using the DQP to define what students should learn, understand, and know at the undergraduate degree level and to demonstrate the quality of their academic programs by using their own measures of student learning outcomes without the intrusion of state or federally mandated standards.[35]

What strategies should independent colleges and universities consider to continuously improve student learning and make learning outcomes transparent?

Postgraduate Outcomes

Despite much recent criticism of the value of a liberal arts education by pundits and politicians,[36] a significant body of evidence indicates that independent college graduates with liberal arts backgrounds have better outcomes than other graduates. In addition to higher graduation rates and shorter time-to-degree, graduates with liberal arts majors are as likely to be employed as graduates in other majors. For example, Carnevale and Cheah[37] found that, even during the height of the recession, the unemployment rate for graduates in anthropology and archaeology (12.6 percent) was similar to that of architects (12.8 percent). In addition, while students majoring in liberal arts disciplines may begin employment with a lower annual salary than graduates in other fields, over time the earnings gap closes. For example, right out of college, humanities and social sciences majors on average earn less per year than professional and pre-professional majors ($26,271 versus $31,183); but by the time these graduates reach their peak earning years (ages 55–60), those who majored in the humanities and social sciences are earning more ($66,185 versus $64,149).

A major factor in the employment and earnings success of independent college graduates is the value employers place on an education in the liberal arts. An overwhelming majority of employers (80 percent) surveyed in 2013 by Hart Research Associates agreed that, regardless of major, every college student should acquire broad knowledge in the liberal arts and sciences.[38] Moreover, nearly all employers surveyed (93 percent) agreed that "a candidate's demonstrated capacity to think critically, communicate clearly, and solve complex programs is *more* important than his or her undergraduate field of study."[39]

Overall, independent college graduates indicate that they are more likely to achieve measures of a successful life and attribute it to the college education they received. A survey of 1,000 college graduates conducted by Richard Detweiler[40] compared findings of liberal arts college alumni with those who graduated from other types of institutions. Liberal arts graduates were 25 to 90 percent more likely to report being personally fulfilled in their lives. They also were 25 to 45 percent more likely to have become leaders in their communities or professions and 27 to 38 percent more likely to be lifelong learners. In addition, alumni of liberal arts colleges were 25 to 60 percent more likely to report volunteer involvement, giving to nonprofit groups, and other altruistic characteristics.[41]

How can independent colleges continue to ensure strong postgraduate outcomes in spite of the demographic, financial, and technological challenges they face?

Innovative and Entrepreneurial

Another charge frequently leveled against independent colleges is that they are tradition-bound institutions resistant to change and wedded to an antiquated business model that cannot be sustained given current economic conditions and shifting student demographics. A survey of independent college presidents conducted in 2014 by Hearn and Warshaw[42] dispelled this myth when they found to the contrary that every institution reported deploying some form of revenue enhancement or cost-containment strategies, or both, many doing so aggressively. The authors found that on average institutions had undertaken 15 substantive change initiatives or innovations over the previous five years to address the economic and enrollment challenges they faced. Their report concluded, "The image of the hidebound college steadfastly resisting reform is nowhere to be seen."[43]

Popular strategies used by independent colleges to contain costs included leaving open faculty positions unfilled (64 percent), freezing salaries (61 percent), reducing other staff (61 percent), restructuring or closing academic programs (57 percent each), and outsourcing operations (49 percent). The most frequent revenue enhancement measures undertaken were opening new undergraduate programs (83 percent) and graduate programs (74 percent), making changes to campus approaches to fundraising (70 percent), and expanding online courses and programs (65 percent). Other initiatives and innovations included changes to admissions strategy (77 percent) and financial aid practices (71 percent), expansion of athletic programs and facilities (62 percent), and increased international student recruitment (58 percent).[44]

Despite the significant efforts to make changes to business and delivery models, college and university presidents indicated that these reforms were congruent with the missions of the institutions they were leading. Nearly two-thirds of the presidents (63 percent) reported that the change efforts were helping them preserve the mission of their institutions while another third (34 percent) viewed the initiatives as an expansion of, not a departure from, the institutional mission. Moreover, presidents found trustees and senior administrators to be largely in favor of their change strategies, with even moderate acceptance among the faculty.[45]

A further study by Morphew and colleagues[46] examined the changing roles and composition of the faculties of independent colleges. Consistent with the trend across American higher education, independent colleges have seen a significant decline in full-time faculty appointments, from 64.8 percent in 2000 to 51.6 percent in 2012 (although to levels that remain higher than other types of colleges and universities). The increased use of contingent faculty members —part-time and non-tenure-track—at independent colleges was found to be largely confined to adult, online, and graduate programs, especially in expanding fields such as professional programs and the health sciences.[47] These findings suggest that the use of contingent faculty members in independent colleges is strategic and entrepreneurial, providing campus leaders flexibility in adapting academic offerings to changing market conditions.

What areas are most promising for future innovation and entrepreneurial approaches as independent colleges seek to be responsive to external conditions?

Recommendations for Future Research

Small and mid-sized private not-for-profit colleges and universities are a vital and distinctive sector of American higher education. These independent colleges have played an important role in preparing future leaders in business, industry, and the nonprofit and public sectors since the founding of our nation. Despite predictions of imminent demise by some pundits, independent colleges are certain to have an essential future in serving national needs to prepare an educated citizenry for many years to come.

Although frequently overlooked due to their small size and diverse characteristics, independent colleges deserve greater attention by scholars and should be more frequently included in research studies. Too many studies focus on large research universities at one end of the higher education spectrum or on community colleges at the other end to the exclusion of perhaps the most educationally robust and effective sector: independent colleges. Much can be gained for all of higher education by better understanding the distinctive features of the learning environments and student outcomes of independent colleges. More widespread inclusion of independent colleges in research studies would also likely result in more attention paid to this overlooked sector by policy-makers and foundation leaders. But most importantly, an increase in practical, actionable research findings would provide valuable guidance to faculty members and administrators of independent colleges, enabling them to make more effective choices as they lead their institutions in today's challenging environment. The chapters in this book by ASHE scholars seek to address these issues directly, and the responses by presidents and chief academic officers of independent colleges and universities provide important insights from practitioners about the relevance of existing research and the need for further study.

This volume represents an important step forward in focusing the attention of the higher education research community on the importance of studying independent colleges and in closing the research-to-practice gap. Together, ASHE and CIC have collaborated to bring together some of the best scholars of higher education with some of the strongest leaders of independent colleges to identify key topics and model an approach to scholarship that not only generates new knowledge but will yield research-informed practice. It is an important development that is sure to be embraced by the membership of both organizations.

NOTES

1. Thelin, "A Crucible Moment."
2. Council of Independent Colleges, "2016 CIC Institutional Members Profile."
3. Astin, *Four Critical Years*; Astin, *What Matters in College*; Pascarella and Terenzini, *Findings and Insights*; Pascarella and Terenzini, *A Third Decade of Research.*
4. Snyder, de Brey, and Dillow, "Digest of Education Statistics 2015. "
5. College Board, *Trends in Student Aid.*
6. Zumeta and Huntington-Klein, "Cost-Effectiveness of Undergraduate Education."
7. Council of Independent Colleges, "Expanding Access and Opportunity."
8. Council of Independent Colleges, "Student Debt."
9. Ibid.
10. US Department of Education, "Comparison of FY 2013."
11. Delisle, "Graduate Student Debt Review."
12. Council of Independent Colleges, "Reframing Student Debt Totals."
13. Schwarz and Nelson, "Moody's."
14. Council of Independent Colleges, "Financial Stability of Independent Colleges."
15. Council of Independent Colleges, "2016 CIC Institutional Members Profile."
16. Cahalan and Perna, "Indicators of Higher Education Equity."
17. Council of Independent Colleges, "Expanding Access and Opportunity."
18. Zumeta and Huntington-Klein, "Cost-Effectiveness of Undergraduate Education."
19. Council of Independent Colleges, "Expanding Access and Opportunity."
20. Gonyea and Kinzie, "Independent Colleges and Student Engagement."

21. Kuh, "High-Impact Educational Practices."
22. Gonyea and Kinzie, "Independent Colleges and Student Engagement," 4.
23. Council of Independent Colleges, "Expanding Access and Opportunity."
24. Ibid.
25. Zumeta and Huntington-Klein, "Cost-Effectiveness of Undergraduate Education."
26. Council of Independent Colleges, *Strengthening the STEM Pipeline.*
27. Ibid.
28. Clinefelter and Magda, *Online Learning.*
29. Brown and Marcum, "CIC Consortium."
30. Morphew, Ward, and Wolf-Wendel, "Changes in Faculty Composition."
31. Council of Independent Colleges, "CIC Statement on Assessment."
32. Council of Independent Colleges, "Evidence of Learning."
33. Paris, "Catalyst for Change."
34. Tahey et al., "Strategic Financial Analysis."
35. Grimes, "Defining Outcomes, Demonstrating Quality."
36. See Stratford, "In GOP Debate."
37. Carnevale and Cheah, "Hard Times 2013."
38. Association of American Colleges and Universities, "It Takes More than a Major."
39. Ibid., 4.
40. Jaschik, "Making the Case."
41. Ibid.
42. Hearn and Warshaw, "Mission-Driven Innovation."
43. Ibid., 3.
44. Ibid.
45. Ibid.
46. Morphew, Ward, and Wendel-Wolf, "Changes in Faculty Composition."
47. Ibid.

REFERENCES

Association of American Colleges and Universities. "It Takes More than a Major: Employer Priorities for College Learning and Student Success." Washington, DC, 2013. https://www.aacu.org/sites/default/files/files/LEAP/2013_EmployerSurvey.pdf. Accessed February 18, 2016.
Astin, Alexander W. *Four Critical Years.* San Francisco: Jossey-Bass, 1977.
———. *What Matters in College: Four Critical Years Revisited.* San Francisco: Jossey-Bass, 1993.
Brown, Jessie, and Deanna Marcum. "CIC Consortium for Online Humanities Instruction Evaluation Report for Second Course Iteration." Unpublished report. Washington, DC: Council of Independent Colleges, 2016.
Cahalan, Margaret, and Laura W. Perna. "Indicators of Higher Education Equity in the United States: 45 Year Trend Report." Pell Institute for the Study of Opportunity in Higher Education, 2015. https://eric.ed.gov/?id=ED555865. Accessed February 19, 2016.
Carnevale, Anthony P., and Ban Cheah. "Hard Times 2013: College Majors, Unemployment and Earnings." Washington, DC: Georgetown University Center on Education and the Workforce, 2013.
Clinefelter, David, and Andrew Magda. *Online Learning at Private Colleges and Universities: A Survey of Chief Academic Officers.* Washington, DC: The Learning House, 2016.

College Board. 2016. *Trends in Student Aid*. Washington, DC.

Council of Independent Colleges. "CIC Statement on Assessment: Leadership for Student Learning Assessment and Accountability." 2012. https://www.cic.edu/r/r/Documents/CIC-Statement-on-Assessment.pdf#search=statement%20on%20assessment. Accessed February 18, 2016.

———. "Evidence of Learning: Applying the Collegiate Learning Assessment to Improve Teaching and Learning in the Liberal Arts College Experience." Washington, DC: Council of Independent Colleges, 2008.

———. "Expanding Access and Opportunity: How Small and Mid-Sized Independent Colleges Serve First-Generation and Low-Income Students." Washington, DC: Council of Independent Colleges, 2015.

———. "The Financial Stability of Independent Colleges and Universities." Washington, DC: Council of Independent Colleges, forthcoming.

———. "Reframing Student Debt Totals." 2nd ed. Washington, DC: Council of Independent Colleges, 2016. https://www.cic.edu/resources-research/research-studies-reports/reframing-student-debt. Accessed January 27, 2017.

———. "Strengthening the STEM Pipeline: The Contributions of Small and Mid-Sized Independent Colleges." Washington, DC: Council of Independent Colleges, 2014.

———. "Student Debt: Myth and Facts" 3rd ed. Washington, DC: Council of Independent Colleges, 2016. https://www.cic.edu/r/r/Documents/Student-Debt-Fact-Sheet.pdf. Accessed January 27, 2017.

———. "2016 CIC Institutional Members Profile." Washington, DC: Council of Independent Colleges, 2016.

Delisle, Jason. "The Graduate Student Debt Review: The State of Graduate Student Borrowing." Washington, DC: New America Foundation, 2014.

Gonyea, Robert M., and Jillian Kinzie. "Independent Colleges and Student Engagement: Descriptive Analysis by Institutional Type." Washington, DC: Council of Independent Colleges, 2015.

Grimes, Terry. "Defining Outcomes, Demonstrating Quality: The CIC Degree Qualifications Profile Consortium." Washington, DC: Council of Independent Colleges, 2014.

Hearn, James C., and Jarrett B. Warshaw. "Mission-Driven Innovation: An Empirical Study of Adaptation and Change among Independent Colleges." Washington, DC: Council of Independent Colleges, 2015.

Jaschik, Scott. "Making the Case for Liberal Arts Colleges." *Inside Higher Ed*, January 9, 2017. https://www.insidehighered.com/news/2017/01/09/research-documents-life-impact-attending-liberal-arts-college. Accessed January 27, 2017.

Kuh, George D. "High-Impact Educational Practices: What They Are, Who Has Access to Them, and Why They Matter." Washington, DC: Association of American Colleges and Universities, 2008.

Morphew, Christopher C., Kelly Ward, and Lisa Wolf-Wendel. "Changes in Faculty Composition at Independent Colleges." Washington, DC: Council of Independent Colleges, 2016.

Paris, David C. "Catalyst for Change: The CIC/CLA Consortium." Washington, DC: Council of Independent Colleges, 2011.

Pascarella, Ernest T., and Patrick T. Terenzini. *How College Affects Students: Findings and Insights from Twenty Years of Research*. San Francisco: Jossey-Bass, 1991.

———. *How College Affects Students: A Third Decade of Research*. Vol. 2. San Francisco: Jossey-Bass, 2005.

Schwarz, Emily, and John C. Nelson. "Moody's: One-Third of US Colleges Facing Falling or Stagnant Tuition Revenues." *Moody's Investor Services*, January 10, 2013. https://www.moodys.com/research/Moodys-One-third-of-US-colleges-facing-falling-or-stagnant—PR_263437.

Snyder, Thomas D., Cristobal de Brey, and Sally A. Dillow. "Digest of Education Statistics 2015 (NCES 2016-014)." Washington, DC: National Center for Education Statistics, Institute of Education Sciences, US Department of Education, 2016.

Stratford, Michael. "In GOP Debate, Rubio Again Criticizes Philosophy." *Inside Higher Ed*, November 11, 2015. https://www.insidehighered.com/quicktakes/2015/11/11/gop-debate-rubio-again-criticizes-philosophy.

Tahey, Phil, Ron Salluzzo, Fred Prager, Lou Mezzina, and Chris Cowen. "Strategic Financial Analysis for Higher Education: Identifying, Measuring and Reporting Financial Risks (7th Ed.)." New York: KPMG, Prager, Sealy, and Attain, 2010.

Thelin, John R. "A Crucible Moment: College Learning and Democracy's Future." In *Meeting the Challenge: America's Independent Colleges and Universities since 1956*, 3–35. Washington, DC: Council of Independent Colleges, 2006.

US Department of Education. "Comparison of FY 2013 Official National Cohort Default Rates to Prior Two Official Cohort Default Rates." Washington, DC: Office of Federal Student Aid, 2016. https://www2.ed.gov/offices/OSFAP/defaultmanagement/schooltyperates.pdf.

Zumeta, William, and Nick Huntington-Klein. "The Cost-Effectiveness of Undergraduate Education at Private Nondoctoral Colleges and Universities: Implications for Students and Public Policy." Washington, DC: Council for Higher Education, 2015.

1

Public Purposes and Benefits of Independent Higher Education

BARRETT TAYLOR AND DAVID WEERTS

Independent not-for-profit higher education is a critical sector within America's diverse portfolio of postsecondary education. In this chapter we explore the public purposes of independent higher education and its broad benefits to society. Drawing on past and contemporary research, we discuss opportunities and challenges for independent colleges as public-serving entities that promote democratic purposes. We conclude by offering ways in which scholarship may offer responses to the challenges of the independent college.

Defining the Public Good

As Chambers[1] and others have noted, defining the "public good" is complex and, at times, arcane. Indeed, it is possible that the public good should not be defined by scholars but rather through participatory democratic processes.[2] While we find much to commend this view, a working definition of the public good is essential as a guide for our analysis.

Traditional understandings of the public good contrast these benefits with the private good.[3] The private good primarily benefits an individual and is most readily seen in higher wages, longer life expectancies, and better life prospects.[4] To be sure, "positive externalities" and/or "spillovers" from private goods may entail benefits for the broader society. For example, higher-earning citizens make larger contributions to government tax coffers, and healthier individuals make fewer demands upon publicly subsidized medical infrastructure.[5] In general, however, these indirect public benefits are seen as distinct from the public good itself, which is understood as a benefit to society as a whole rather than as the by-product of individuals' own gains.[6]

Independent Colleges in Context: Serving Public Interests

Independent colleges have long made important contributions to the public good. Indeed, independent colleges initially flourished in the United States due to the distinct historical context that emphasized their public contributions and so allowed independent institutions to proliferate.[7] While these independent colleges are now considered "private" in governance and leadership, they have long held public purposes. For example, the early colonial colleges had the central social function of educating the colonies' and, later, the country's leadership.[8] Graduates pursued careers in public affairs alongside work in pulpits.[9] This close integration of church and public affairs was viewed as symbiotic in the early decades of the nation.[10] According to historian Tom Dyer,[11] antebellum colleges— that is, colleges established prior to the American Civil War—demonstrated a powerful emphasis on democracy and access to higher education. As such, they became leading institutions in the development of the nation.

In recognition of these public purposes, from the colonial period onward independent colleges have received financial support from public sources.[12] Today, this support is primarily manifested in indirect ways. Most significantly, independent colleges receive portable federal—and, in some cases, state— student financial aid, which facilitates enrollment.[13] Two notable examples of state-level aid are seen in Pennsylvania and Minnesota, both of which offer student financial assistance to support their robust public and private systems of higher education.[14] In these states and others, policymakers value independent colleges' contributions to the public good enough to partially fund their operations.

Federal tax policies are also favorable in supporting private investment in independent colleges. Both gifts to independent colleges and investment gains are exempt from taxation,[15] thereby providing donors with a publicly financed incentive to support independent colleges. Such incentives may be difficult to observe because forsaken tax receipts are less obvious than public expenditures. Nonetheless, these contributions can be sizable. Richard Vedder,[16] for example, calculated that Princeton University received approximately $54,000 per student due to federal tax exemptions and other indirect contributions to campus operations. While very few institutions hold endowments in the stratosphere of Princeton's, these subsidies in the aggregate represent substantial public investment in independent higher education.

These figures suggest that, historically, policymakers have placed great value in the public purposes of independent higher education. Yet this esteem for independent colleges—even for higher education as a whole—may be waning. Indeed, by many measures public officials are increasingly skeptical of the broad benefits of higher education. Direct financial support for higher education has retreated even as oversight has increased.[17] Both policymakers and students increasingly view higher education as a private good, meaning primarily an investment in individuals' future earnings and benefits. This has prompted outcry against rising tuition and loan indebtedness.[18] In addition, shifts away from traditional areas of instruction and into fields such as business administration that are more intuitively linked to high-salaried positions after graduation have been widely chronicled.[19] Higher education in the United States has always entailed benefits for individuals,[20] yet this shift in emphases toward the private good and away from the mixture of public and private benefits is notable. The public purposes of independent higher education, while long taken for granted, merit close inspection amid these changes.

Independent Colleges and the Public Good

It is one thing to assert that policymakers have historically valued the ways independent colleges contribute to the public good. It is another to enumerate those contributions. In the context of declining faith in the public value of higher education generally, a clear articulation of these contributions is of great importance.

Educating the "Whole Person"

One of the key ways higher education contributes to the public good is by educating citizens for participation in democratic society.[21] Independent colleges are especially well positioned to contribute in this way. Equal training for citizens is often, and somewhat intuitively, linked to general education in the liberal arts fields. Teaching in these areas has long been a signature element of independent colleges[22] and so has been central to how these organizations contribute to the public good. Readings[23] casts the traditional liberal arts core as the repository of national values and identity. A central concern in his work was transforming such a core to reflect a more diverse student body without abandoning the shared principles of democratic participation. Independent colleges often have been at the vanguard of these efforts, perhaps because instruction in the humanities is an endeavor to which independent colleges traditionally have been committed.[24]

Further, independent colleges have tended to engage in "whole person" formation outside the classroom. This means that many independent colleges have developed a suite of extra- and co-curricular activities that promote learning in residence halls, student activities, and other settings.[25] On balance, this holistic emphasis has encouraged students to understand the consequences of formal learning for practical living in order to contribute to the public good after graduation.[26]

In aggregate, then, independent colleges' contributions to the public good tend to be framed within a student-focused liberal arts tradition. Independent colleges, in other words, tend to emphasize both general education in traditional liberal arts fields, and to do so in the context of broader "whole person" formation. As a result, independent colleges articulate rich narratives about serving humanity, enrich the democratic spirit, create global citizens, and broadly serve society. In doing so, they signal their distinct roles to an audience that includes legislators, alumni, trustees, students, and prospective students.[27]

This conceptualization of the public good differs from that found at most regional public universities and research institutions. These institutions tend to position their public good contributions in ways that are more place-bound and economic in nature. For example, regional public institutions increasingly position their teaching and research activities in ways that serve local workforce needs. Meanwhile, research universities typically frame their public contributions as creating innovative products or industries to bolster job creation.[28] Independent colleges that focus on developing the whole person make distinctive contributions that complement the efforts of public institutions.

Civic Agency and the Independent College

Consonant with developing the whole person, many independent colleges emphasize training leaders for lives of service and civic engagement. Such an emphasis also constitutes a public good, as it nurtures democratic values and commitments among future generations of leaders. These commitments are evident on two fronts: training for professions and fostering pro-social civic behaviors.

First, professional careers—such as medicine, law, and the faculty—are traditionally understood to be altruistic endeavors that benefit society as a whole. Through extensive years of training, a professional earns wide discretion over complex work, such as the diagnosis and treatment of illness. In exchange for society's trust, the professionals use their discretion to serve the interests of patients, clients, or students rather than to enrich themselves.[29] From this perspective, professionals act as stewards of the public good and not exclusively for their own self-interest. Independent colleges have historically served as fertile training grounds for future professionals and civil servants,[30] a role that persists to this day.

Second, independent colleges are also at the forefront of civic learning movements that promote engagement in communities and, more broadly, society. Civic learning programs promote experiences that teach students how social systems work and offer opportunities to promote change. Examples include community-based service and research, civic pedagogies and collective civic problem solving, and diversity programs that promote learning across differences.[31] A 2012 report entitled *A Crucible Moment: College Learning and Democracy's Future* gave national attention to how students are educated in relation to civic competencies, knowledge, values, and collective action. The report, authored by staff of the Association of American Colleges and Universities (AAC&U), called on US educators to "reclaim and reinvest in the fundamental civic and democratic mission of schools and of all sectors within higher education."[32] The AAC&U has served as a champion for civic learning nationally, and the majority of its 1,300 members are independent colleges. Similarly, National Campus Compact, the American Democracy Project, and other civic-oriented organizations have robust independent college participation and lead the way in promoting civic action. For example, Augsburg College in Minneapolis, Minnesota, is well known for its emphasis on the civic learning view of the public good. Through the Sabo Center for Democracy and Citizenship, Augsburg brings together experiential education with the "public work" view of citizenship to create robust civic learning experiences for its students. The college has received national recognition for its innovative practices, including multiple mentions as a top school for service learning by *U.S. News and World Report* and the 2010 Presidential Award for Community Service, the highest honor in the annual President's Higher Education Community Service Honor Roll.[33]

Civic and Theological Traditions of Independent Colleges

Although many institutions are nonsectarian, substantial numbers of independent colleges draw on their long-standing religious traditions to shape civic learning and community commitments on their campuses. These traditions set them apart from secular institutions that traditionally frame their public contributions through economic or social justice/equity–oriented perspectives.[34] Faith-based institutions are distinct in that they are anchored in religious understandings of the human condition, which in turn guides their teachings about human dignity, purpose, and relationships with others. For example, many colleges rooted in the Abrahamic traditions (Christianity, Judaism, and Islam) view human beings through the *imago Dei*, meaning that humans are made in the image of God. Because of its emphasis on service and stewardship, this view of humanity provides a basis for the formation of students that pursue purposes and meanings that transcend the self. Such notions are linked to the classical notion of human flourishing, which promotes living to one's full potential and pursuing loving relationships and generosity toward others.[35]

Religious thought therefore guides the ways in which many independent colleges carry out their visions of civic life. In his book *The Purposeful Graduate*, Tim Clydesdale[36] found widespread success among vocational programs as they contributed to civic engagement, intellectual development, and goal setting at campuses participating in the Lilly Endowment's initiative, Programs for the Theological Exploration of Vocation. Clydesdale concludes that these vocational programs work because they are anchored in a mission-oriented mindset and emphasize individual and community formation. In other words, contributions to the public good are both profound and distinctive due to the emphasis on vocation and "calling" found within many faith-based independent colleges. As an example, operations such as Messiah College's[37] Agapé Center for Service and Learning draw on the institution's Anabaptist heritage to emphasize the cultivation of a student's service identity within a setting that is both explicitly religious and focused on redressing injustice in society.

Serving the Underserved: Demographics of Independent Colleges

The contributions that we have identified in the previous subsections tend to revolve around the distinctive qualities of independent colleges. By emphasizing general education, whole person formation, preparation for professional training, and a variety of civic learning initiatives that often are couched within religious commitments, independent colleges contribute to the public good in ways that complement the efforts of other institutions. However, independent colleges contribute to the public good in quantitative ways as well. Although often small in size, these institutions draw impressively large shares of their enrollments from traditionally underserved populations.

In the twentieth and early twenty-first centuries, college enrollment expanded dramatically,[38] and the swelling demand for higher education strained the capacities of many states. During that period, independent higher education offered an efficient avenue to expand access for a growing and increasingly diverse student population.[39] Indeed, according to figures tabulated by the National Center for Education Statistics (NCES), independent colleges are by some measures more diverse than their public counterparts. For example, a little more than 13 percent of students at independent four-year colleges in 2008 identified as black. This figure compares favorably with that of lower-priced public campuses (i.e., non-research university four-year institutions) and in part reflects the long-standing commitments of historically black colleges and universities (HBCUs) and other minority-serving institutions (MSIs). By contrast, less than 10 percent of students at public research universities were black.[40] Beyond simply enrolling traditionally underrepresented students, however, independent colleges often provide these individuals with high-quality educations.[41] By enrolling substantial numbers of underrepresented students in strong academic programs, independent colleges make important contributions to the public good by fostering broad participation.

Challenges for the Independent College Sector

Independent colleges may be praised for educating the whole person in a way that is likely to yield better educational outcomes,[42] but this form of education is notoriously costly and they face many financial challenges. Independent colleges often operate at a diseconomy of scope, meaning that they try to do many different things at once. Colleges could more easily control costs if they focused solely on instruction, but "whole person" formation—and therefore contributions to the public good—would suffer if extra- and co-curricular programs were deemphasized. Independent colleges also tend to operate at a diseconomy of scale, meaning that they typically choose to remain small in size. Enrolling a few dozen additional students might reduce per-student costs but also would increase average class size, decrease relative access to valuable co-curricular opportunities, and otherwise diminish independent colleges' contributions to the public good. The result may be that, relative to other higher education types, independent colleges face a particularly difficult task when seeking to maintain quality while managing costs.[43]

Resources are not limited to money; virtually all colleges and universities, including independent colleges, would welcome additional revenues.[44] However, because the vast majority of faculty members are trained in a different institutional context (i.e., the research university), independent colleges also face difficulties when identifying, recruiting, and retaining faculty members.

These two challenges can press colleges to change their missions in an effort to remain solvent. In the direst of cases, such decisions can exchange long-term health for short-term solvency.

Financial Challenges

Higher education costs are rising persistently across institutional types. Key factors in rising costs include the labor-intensive nature of higher education and the relatively slow growth of productivity over time (i.e., colleges and universities tend to prefer to produce a "better" education rather than a greater number of educated individuals).[45] With their traditional emphases on general education and whole person formation, independent colleges are perhaps particularly prone to these elements of "cost disease."

Rising costs can complicate the recruitment of students during a time when tuition prices are increasingly scrutinized by the American public. As the economic and political landscape changes, some independent colleges are particularly vulnerable to these competitive pressures, as evidenced by declining market share and susceptibility to closure.[46] In his study of financial sustainability of small independent colleges, James M. Hunter[47] explains that such institutions "do not have the enrollment volume, endowment strength and reputation and clout to resist internal and environmental fluctuations or competition."

While policymakers seem willing to continue to fund independent colleges through sources such as student financial aid and tax exemptions, these funding mechanisms can seem unpredictable.[48] That is, policymakers are generally unwilling to provide independent colleges with direct support; instead, colleges must compete to secure public funds. A college must enroll students to benefit from student financial aid and must control generous endowment holdings to benefit substantially from tax exemptions. More explicitly, Fred Thompson and William Zumeta[49] suggest that some public policies—such as large tuition price differences between private and public institutions and, in some states, low levels of public funding for student aid—threaten the health of independent colleges. A recent political challenge is the push for free community college, which some sector leaders suggest will divert support from small independent colleges that serve similar populations of low-income students.[50]

Hiring and Retaining Faculty Members

As mentioned previously, independent colleges make important contributions to the public good through instructional and co-curricular activities undertaken in a distinctive setting that emphasizes the whole person. This institutional context differs sharply from those from which most faculty members earn their terminal degrees. The overwhelming majority of doctorates—particularly in the sciences—are conferred by research universities.[51] Such programs tend to train faculty members to develop research skills.[52] By contrast, independent colleges, while conducting important scholarly activities, generally emphasize the importance of teaching over research. One common result is that terminal degree-holders who join the faculties of independent colleges may find that their training and skills need to be adapted to succeed in their new settings.

From the point of view of campus decision makers, this means that identifying faculty members can be a daunting and recurring challenge. When candidates for terminal degrees seek to distinguish themselves through their research and scholarly activities, how is an independent college to identify the individuals who are most committed to whole person education? Such challenges can be particularly acute for independent colleges—such as evangelical Christian colleges and HBCUs[53]—whose distinctive missions differ from the broad, all-encompassing missions of other institutional types.

Once faculty members have been recruited to an independent college, they must be retained in order to continue contributing to that college's operations. Here, too, independent colleges face many challenges. According to 2011–12 figures compiled by the College Board,[54] only about 44 percent of faculty were tenured at independent four-year colleges. This is the lowest percentage of tenured faculty members for any institutional type included in the survey, falling notably below the rates at public four-year (65 percent) and two-year (48 percent) institutions. To be sure, positions that do not offer the benefits of tenure likely increase institutional flexibility and so can be useful when responding to the financial pressures identified above. At the same time, such a strategy may simply replace financial strain with human resource problems, as the relatively modest number of tenure lines is likely to make it difficult to recruit and retain highly skilled faculty members.

Further difficulties emerge when considering the relatively low rates of compensation typically offered by independent colleges. According to data collected by the American Association of University Professors (AAUP),[55] faculty at independent colleges earn much lower salaries than do their peers at other types of institutions. The average salary across ranks at independent baccalaureate colleges was $83,715 in 2014, and the average faculty member at an independent master's college/university lagged behind even this figure at $81,924.

By contrast, faculty across ranks at doctoral institutions netted an average salary in excess of $100,000. These pay gaps may become even more striking for mission-focused independent colleges such as HBCUs, where salaries are typically lower than those of predominantly white institutions.[56]

What is more, the gaps between independent colleges and other institutional types appear to be widening over time. This occurs because salaries for faculty members at independent colleges tend to grow more slowly than do those at other institutional types. From 2013 to 2014, faculty members across ranks received raises of less than 2 percent at independent master's and baccalaureate colleges. By contrast, faculty at doctorate-granting universities received average increases of 2.3 percent, with full professors at those institutions netting 3 percent raises.[57] With a shrinking share of positions on the tenure track, lower starting salaries, and smaller raises, it is no wonder that independent colleges often struggle to identify, recruit, and retain faculty members who can contribute to their educational missions.

Cultural Challenges

Membership in mainline Christian denominations has declined in recent years.[58] In light of this reality, some religiously affiliated independent colleges are challenged in reconciling their faith traditions to an increasingly secular American society. For example, cultural, political, and legal shifts in the United States have changed traditional views about sexual identity and marriage in ways that may conflict with orthodox teachings. In response, some faith-based colleges have successfully filed for Title IX exemption to maintain their historic creeds and policies.[59] Such commitments have fueled politically contentious debates about whether such colleges should be eligible for public funding.[60] As the broader society accepts and celebrates these social changes, some faith-based independent colleges may face hurdles in connecting with a public with distinctively different values.

Another tension is evident in how some institutions' teachings about the origin of the universe may conflict with widely held views among scientists. Studies suggest that conservative Christian traditions are most likely to be those that reject climate change science and associated policies.[61] Despite this general pattern, some Christian colleges have been champions of the environmental stewardship movement and have drawn on their theological heritage to lead efforts for sustainability. For example, some campuses affiliated with the Council of Christian Colleges and Universities (CCCU) have robust commitments to "creation care," a set of beliefs and practices emphasizing stewardship of the earth and life upon it.[62] A given campus's particular variant of Christian practice is likely to shape an understanding of mission and the public good in ways that may distinguish that college from other equally devout organizations.[63] As such, there is no "one size fits all" in understanding political allegiances among faith-based independent colleges.

Pressures of "Mission and Money"

The financial, personnel, and—in some cases—doctrinal challenges may strain the missions of independent colleges. In extreme cases, the necessity of managing finances and retaining personnel may prompt independent colleges to abandon their historic missions in the pursuit of short-term revenue gains. As government trust in higher education wanes and taxpayer contributions to education seem under fire, decision makers on private campuses may face pressure to reduce emphasis on their public-facing missions in favor of securing resources immediately. At Indiana Wesleyan University,[64] for example, Fall 2013 enrollment swelled to nearly 15,000 students, but only about 3,000 of them pursued face-to-face studies on the institution's historic campus. While we know nothing of the decision making that led the campus to this enrollment profile, that university's expanding online profile at least hints at the possible eclipse of traditional forms of education by newer educational modes.

This pattern, in which pressures to secure financial and human resources prompt shifts in organizational mission, often has been observed among nonprofit organizations such as hospitals.[65] As a group, independent colleges are certainly prone to these pressures. Indeed, David Breneman's[66] classic study of liberal arts colleges concludes that the majority of these organizations were likely to abandon their missions. Liberal arts colleges, in Breneman's account, were poised to adapt to their changing circumstances in a way that ensured their survival but that also reduced emphasis on teaching in liberal arts fields, whole person formation through residential education, and other hallmarks of this institutional type. More recent research offers some grim confirmation of Breneman's predictions by tracing the decline in degrees that independent colleges have conferred in traditional liberal arts fields.[67]

Further evidence of declines in the articulation of specific missions becomes apparent in analyses of strategic communications. Documents such as viewbooks and mission statements indicate that—with some notable exceptions, such as intentionally religious colleges and HBCUs—independent colleges rarely position themselves as distinct, mission-focused organizations.[68] Those organizations that seek to remain mission-focused, such as evangelical Christian colleges, often find that their decisions reduce their ability to secure financial and human resources. As a result, their faculty and staff remain permanently engaged in a delicate balance between pursuing revenues and fulfilling mission distinctiveness.[69] Adding to the challenge is that the market for faith-focused institutions may be shrinking, as church membership among mainline Christian denominations continues to decline.[70] Consequently, colleges that hold to a strong faith tradition may have a smaller pool of prospective students from which to draw in the future.

This relationship between what Burton Weisbrod and colleagues[71] term "mission and money" is particularly uncomfortable given the stark financial inequalities among independent colleges. In their analysis, independent colleges are among both the most handsomely and the lowest-resourced higher education institutions in the United States.[72] That is, while some independent colleges are fortunate enough to hold large endowments and/or to practice selective admissions, many others feel resource pressures acutely. This variation in levels of resource shapes the extent to which the pressures of "mission and money" intrude on the operations of a particular campus. Recent research indicates that traditional contributions to the public good, such as instruction in the humanities, remain vibrant at well-resourced and highly selective colleges but may be imperiled at less elite institutions.[73] Even explicitly public-facing operations, such as civic engagement offices, may find their missions compromised by resource pressures.[74]

In other words, the challenges facing independent colleges as a whole are not necessarily faced by each college equally. Lucie Lapovsky[75] categorized institutions within this sector as either "medallion" or "non-medallion" colleges. These two categories distinguish institutions by their prestige, selectivity, endowment size, and overall brand strength. Medallion or elite colleges are likely, on the whole, to find it is easier to continue the pursuit of their mission than it is for their less elite, nonmedallion, peers. This occurs because non-medallion institutions need to attract tuition-paying students and may abandon their missions in the pursuit of enrollment gains. By contrast, medallion colleges turn away qualified students to sustain their prestige, and so face no financial incentive to shift their missions.

In this chapter, we understand the work of independent colleges—as a group —is central to the public good. The challenges confronting independent colleges are truly public challenges because these organizations collectively contribute to the general social good. These contributions to the public good are too important to be left solely to those well-resourced institutions that are able to bear them. Both medallion and non-medallion colleges conduct important work, even as that work is imperiled in different ways. As such, it is important to consider how independent colleges can respond to these challenges and so can continue to contribute to the public good.

Opportunities for Independent Colleges

How might campus decision makers respond strategically to these challenges? How might these responses reinvigorate rather than diminish independent colleges' contributions to the public good? These are difficult questions that have vexed scholars for decades.[76] We cannot promise to answer them definitively here, but we do offer three general suggestions. We hope that campus leaders will adapt these broad recommendations to the particular circumstances of their own colleges.

Reinterpreting Mission to Speak to the American Public

As Pusser[77] notes, definitions of the public good have changed over time. One reason for this is that democratic societies are characterized by contest and dissent, especially in the multicultural world resulting from globalization.[78] As the demographics of the public shift to reflect a more inclusive, participatory democracy, so too must understandings of the public good change. Nonprofit organizations play crucial roles in this struggle over the nature of the public good.[79] This is because nonprofit organizations, including independent colleges, constitute a "third space" (i.e., neither government nor market) in which the public good itself is negotiated. In other words, independent colleges not only contribute to the public good; they also help to define it. This is an especially crucial task as the public becomes more diverse and more broadly representative of the country's population. Nonprofit mission-driven organizations possess the flexibility to reflect the changing nature of the public.[80]

Even as college students and faculty have become more diverse over time, colleges and universities have become more limited in type.[81] In contrast to these homogenizing trends, however, ranks of independent colleges include a number of mission-driven organizations that fill particular niches in a diverse, dynamic society. Women's colleges, HBCUs, work colleges, and religiously affiliated institutions are anchored in long-standing traditions, worldviews, and/

or purposes that make distinctive contributions to a pluralistic society. To be sure, the mission of any one of these organizations is unlikely to represent the public. Just as surely, however, the public—particularly as the nation becomes more diverse—cannot be represented without including these multiple missions.

Independent nonprofit organizations can serve as homes of political dissent and voluntarism, and so of participatory democracy.[82] In addition, such colleges contribute to the dialogue in ways not common to public institutions. For example, HBCUs have made both subtle and explicit contributions to the struggle for racial equality in the United States.[83] Faith-based colleges espouse unique perspectives about social purposes of education that connect to human flourishing, redemptive change, and social justice—a concept emanating from Catholic social teaching.[84]

It is important to the public good for independent colleges to remain faithful to their distinct, historical missions. At the same time, however, we acknowledge that resource pressures may make mission faithfulness difficult to maintain. *We therefore suggest that campus officials reinterpret their traditional missions in ways that speak to the changing American public.* Examples might include HBCUs that recruit students from underserved populations (e.g., Latino/a, low-income, LGBTQ, and/or first-generation students). While such actions might appear to shift the mission of HBCUs, such students are also historically underrepresented and so their enrollment is broadly consistent with HBCUs' mission of social uplift.[85] Another example might be religious colleges seeking to enroll students from other faiths or sects so as to engage with those from other worldviews. This could be done in a way that affirms an institution's own faith commitments by insisting on engagement with questions of meaning and purpose.

To be sure, such mission reinterpretation must be undertaken cautiously. Historical missions represent the central rationale for a college's existence. Reimagining the mission can prove controversial, as when Goshen College and Eastern Mennonite University announced their intention to employ openly gay/lesbian faculty members. Campus officials viewed their position as consistent with—if expanding on—their historic religious commitments, as expressed in the most recent conference of the Mennonite Church, USA. However, many other members of the Council of Christian Colleges and Universities (CCCU) disagreed, and the two colleges eventually withdrew from CCCU amid the ensuing controversy.[86] The central challenge of this type of mission reinterpretation, from a market perspective, is that mission-driven colleges leverage their identities to reach a distinct set of students and resource providers (e.g., alumni and donors) that espouse a particular worldview. If an institution is no longer seen as being embedded within the belief system of its primary constituents, it may lose its base of support. Trustees and college leaders must discern whether gains made by these shifts—both in renewed mission and in financial terms—outweigh the costs.

We urge equal measures of creativity and caution when considering changes to a college's historic mission. Such changes certainly can distress important stakeholders and so must be undertaken with great care. At the same time, many of independent colleges' most important contributions to the public good—such as the enrollment of a diverse student body—are relatively recent extensions of historical missions. In aggregate, these transformations embrace changing notions of the public good. In this spirit, we encourage independent colleges to adapt to changing public needs and demands in a way that is broadly consistent with institutional histories. Such an approach is not only mission faithful but also likely to establish the relevance of that mission in a way that may prove more appealing to resource providers than would a simple retreat from historical commitments.

Clearly Articulate the Institution's Contribution to the Public Good

Students, families, policymakers, and other stakeholders increasingly view higher education as a private good. That is, for a growing share of individuals, higher education promises a better life, often measured as higher wages and better social status. The public benefits of higher education, if they are considered at all, are often of secondary importance to the individual benefits.[87]

This conceptualization of higher education is understandable, particularly as students are asked to bear an increasingly high share of the cost of their educations.[88] At the same time, however, this thinking represents a misunderstanding or, at best, a partial understanding of the role of higher education. Independent colleges and universities contribute to the well-being of society in addition to the successes of their students. Because these contributions to the public good are often overlooked, a second step campus officials could take is a fuller articulation of their institutions' contributions to the public good.

We believe that the clear articulation of contributions to the public good can benefit colleges' finances as well as their mission fulfillment. There are many ways that contributions to the public good might be connected to independent colleges' bottom lines. Enrolling students from underrepresented backgrounds certainly is a contribution to the public good. Many of these students, particularly black students and individuals from low-income households, are more likely than other students to overestimate the costs of higher education.[89] Increasing numbers of students from these and other subpopulations make enrollment choices based on tuition price rather than educational preferences and goals.[90] Clear statements reflecting both a commitment to enrolling and graduating these students and transparency on costs are likely to be welcomed broadly and might even increase campus enrollment in the process.

Seek Partners That Can Share Costs

Some of the challenges facing independent higher education—in particular, the inexorable rise of costs—seem almost unavoidable. Many campuses face a difficult trade-off between controlling costs and maintaining quality.[91] *One solution is to seek partner organizations that can share in the costs of expensive but important operations.*

In the face of steeply rising costs, many institutions seek resources "wherever they may be found."[92] We encourage college officials to select their partners carefully. Powerful supporters may have their own goals that can reshape public purposes, while less powerful community-based organizations may face steep challenges that, while worthy of attention, could divert resources from higher education.[93] The ideal partnerships will benefit the pursuit of mission and money rather than make one subordinate to the other.

We suggest that independent colleges would do well to partner with one another on a variety of educational endeavors that serve the public good. For example, global citizenship is an important and emerging lens through which to understand the public good through an international perspective. Yet the establishment and maintenance of international programs can be costly, absorbing both financial resources and the valuable time of faculty and staff members. An independent college could reduce its burden by collaborating with a peer institution in international ventures. Such collaborative efforts offer the dual benefits of reduced expenditures and the placement of global initiatives firmly in the service of the public good (i.e., international efforts would be educational rather than undertaken to identify and recruit tuition payers).[94]

Local independent colleges could more explicitly embed their civic missions within the social and economic needs of their communities. As discussed, independent colleges typically frame their public good contributions through initiatives such as civic learning and leadership that are not necessarily "place-bound."[95] However, independent institutions might be wise to expand their messaging and strategy to contribute more directly to their regions. Doing so has the potential to bolster student recruitment and philanthropic support. A prominent example is Tulane University, which was nearly destroyed by Hurricane Katrina in 2005. The disaster resulted in significant budget cuts, displaced students, and the phasing out of hundreds of faculty members and key programs.[96] Yet, the leadership of Tulane quickly responded, and prioritized "rebuilding New Orleans" as part of its core identity. In doing so, it solidified an image of Tulane as among the most publicly engaged universities in the country. Students flocked to New Orleans to be a part of this agenda. Applications for enrollment soared after Tulane revised its curriculum to focus on rebuilding the city.[97] What followed was a successful capital campaign, "Tulane Empowers," which affirmed this identity and raised significant dollars toward these broader goals. The Tulane example shows how an independent institution expanded its public good identity beyond civic learning to focus on place-bound community revitalization. In doing so it positioned itself to flourish in service to the resurgence of the region.[98] Independent colleges residing in areas with significant community challenges and opportunities might consider a similar strategy to simultaneously bolster the health of the institution and their region.

Conclusion

Independent colleges and universities make crucial, distinct contributions to the public good. Although the scope of these contributions is matched by the challenges that colleges face, we believe that independent colleges are more than capable of surmounting these obstacles. There is a sound historical basis for our confidence. More than 40 years ago the vast majority of independent colleges were already considered "invisible" and likely to disappear.[99] The ongoing contributions of these colleges testify to the resilience of these organizations and the enduring significance of the missions that enervate them. Independent colleges remain an important part of the compact of American higher education[100] and contribute to the overall health of the nation.

NOTES

1. Chambers, "Special Role of Higher Education."
2. Kezar, "Challenges for Higher Education."

3. Pusser, "Reconsidering Higher Education."

4. Chambers, "Special Role of Higher Education."

5. McMahon, *Higher Learning, Greater Good.*

6. Pusser, "Reconsidering Higher Education"; Labaree, "Public Goods, Private Goods."

7. Cohen and Kisker, *Shaping of American Higher Education*; Thelin, *History of American Higher Education.*

8. Vine, "Social Functions."

9. Cremin, *American Education*; Geiger, "Historical Matrix"; Thelin, "Higher Education and Public Trough"; Thelin, *History of American Higher Education.*

10. Dyer, "Retrospect and Prospect"; Furco, "Engaged Campus."

11. Dyer, "Retrospect and Prospect."

12. Bailyn, "Foundations"; Thelin, *History of American Higher Education.*

13. Mettler, *Degrees of Inequality.*

14. Weerts, Sanford, and Reinert, *College Funding in Context.*

15. Ehrenberg and Smith, "Sources and Uses."

16. Vedder, "Princeton Reaps Tax Breaks."

17. On retreat of financial support, see Doyle and Delaney, "Higher Education Funding"; Rizzo, "State Preferences"; on oversight, see Tandberg and Hillman, "State Performance Funding"; Zumeta and Heller, "Public Policy and Accountability."

18. Pusser, "State Theoretical Approach."

19. Kraatz and Zajac, "Exploring the Limits"; Taylor, Cantwell, and Slaughter, "Quasi-Markets."

20. Labaree, "Public Goods, Private Goods."

21. Ibid.

22. Breneman, *Liberal Arts Colleges.*

23. Readings, *University in Ruins.*

24. Hearn and Belasco, "Commitment to the Core."

25. Breneman, *Liberal Arts Colleges.*

26. Astin, "How the Liberal Arts College."

27. Goodman, "Tie That Binds"; Morphew and Hartley, "Mission Statements"; Weerts and Hudson, "Engagement and Institutional Advancement."

28. Brackmann, "Community Engagement"; Weerts and Freed, "Public Engagement."

29. Abbott, *System of Professions*; Freidson, *Professionalism.*

30. Leslie, *Gentlemen and Scholars.*

31. Association of American Colleges and Universities, "Civic Learning."

32. Association of American Colleges and Universities, "Crucible Moment," vi.

33. See http://www.augsburg.edu/news/2011/05/13/augsburg-college-earns-presidential-award-for-service-learning-and-community-service/#more-1174.

34. Pasque, *American Higher Education.*

35. Smith, *To Flourish or Destruct.*

36. Clydesdale, *Purposeful Graduate.*

37. Messiah College, "Agapé Center."

38. Schofer and Meyer, "Worldwide Expansion."

39. Thompson and Zumeta, "Effects of Key State Policies."

40. National Center for Education Statistics, "Status and Trends," tables 24.3, 24.4.

41. Roksa, "Analysis of Learning Outcomes."

42. Astin, "How the Liberal Arts College."

43. Archibald and Feldman, *Why Does College Cost?*

44. Bowen, *Costs of Higher Education.*

45. Archibald and Feldman, *Why Does College Cost?*

46. Marcus, "Why Some Small Colleges."

47. Hunter, "Integrated Framework," 3.

48. Mettler, *Submerged State.*

49. Thompson and Zumeta, "Effects of Key State Policies."

50. Scheck, "DFL Plan."

51. National Science Board, "Science and Engineering Indicators."

52. Austin, "Preparing the Next Generation."

53. On Christian colleges, see Taylor, "Responses to Conflicting Field Imperatives"; on HBCUs, see Renzulli, Grant, and Kathuria, "Race, Gender."

54. College Board, "Trends in College Pricing."

55. Flaherty, "Modest Gains in Faculty Pay."

56. Renzulli, Grant, and Kathuria, "Race, Gender."

57. Flaherty, "Modest Gains in Faculty Pay."

58. Lipka, "Mainline Protestants."

59. Jaschik, "Right to Expel."

60. Berg, "Does This New Bill Threaten."

61. Mooney, "New Study Reaffirms."

62. Routhe, "Reading the Signs of Sustainability."

63. Taylor, "Responses to Conflicting Field Imperatives."

64. Indiana Wesleyan University, "Quick Facts."

65. E.g., Eikenberry and Kluver, "Marketization of the Nonprofit Sector"; Froelich, "Diversification of Revenue Strategies"; Frumkin and Andre-Clark, "When Missions, Markets, and Politics"; Salamon, "Nonprofit Sector at a Crossroads"; Weisbrod, "Nonprofit Mission and Its Financing."

66. Breneman, *Liberal Arts Colleges.*

67. Baker, Baldwin, and Makker, "Where Are They Now?," 48–53; Kraatz and Zajac, "Exploring the Limits"; Taylor, Cantwell, and Slaughter, "Quasi-Markets."

68. Hartley and Morphew, "What's Being Sold"; Morphew and Hartley, "Mission Statements"; Taylor and Morphew, "Analysis of Baccalaureate College."

69. Taylor, "Responses to Conflicting Field Imperatives."

70. Lipka, "Mainline Protestants."

71. Weisbrod, Ballou, and Asch, *Mission and Money.*

72. Ibid., 133.

73. Hearn and Belasco, "Commitment to the Core"; Hearn and Rosinger, "Socioeconomic Diversity"; Taylor, Cantwell, and Slaughter, "Quasi-Markets."

74. Brackmann, "Community Engagement."

75. Lapovsky, "Economic Challenges."

76. E.g., Astin, *Four Critical Years.*

77. Pusser, "Reconsidering Higher Education."

78. Chambers, "Special Role of Higher Education"; Pusser, "State Theoretical Approach"; Pusser, "Reconsidering Higher Education"; Ordorika and Lloyd, "State and Contest."

79. Brilliant, "American Third Sector"; Frumkin, *Strategic Giving*; Munck, "Global Civil Society."

80. Hartley and Saltmarsh, "Creating the Democratically Engaged University"; Moore, "Community-University Engagement"; Pusser, "State Theoretical Approach"; Pusser, "Reconsidering Higher Education."

81. Ehrenberg, "American Higher Education in Transition"; Harris, "Understanding Institutional Diversity"; Morphew, "Conceptualizing Change."

82. Pusser, "State Theoretical Approach"; Hartley and Saltmarsh, "Creating the Democratically Engaged University."

83. Hutcheson, Gasman, and Sanders-McMurtry, "Race and Equality"; Lowe, "Oasis of Freedom."

84. On human flourishing, see Hunter, *To Change the World*; Wolterstorff and Joldersma, *Educating for Shalom*; on redemptive change, see Wilberforce Academy, "Mission and Values"; on Catholic social teaching, see Enke and Winters, "Gender, Spirituality, and Community Engagement."

85. Lee, "Moving beyond Diversity"; Palmer et al., "From Matriculation to Engagement."

86. Jaschik, "To Avoid Split"; Morris, "Eastern Mennonite University"; Weber, "Peace Church Out."

87. Labaree, "Public Goods, Private Goods."

88. Heller, "Changing Nature of Public Support"; Johnstone, "Patterns of Finance"; Johnstone, "Economics and Politics"; McMahon, *Higher Learning, Greater Good*; Taylor and Morphew, "Institutional Contributions"; Taylor and Morphew, "Trends in Cost-Sharing."

89. Grodsky and Jones, "Real and Imagined Barriers."

90. Eagan et al., "American Freshman."

91. Archibald and Feldman, *Why Does College Cost?*

92. Weisbrod, Ballou, and Asch, *Mission and Money.*

93. Brackmann, "Community Engagement."

94. Haigh, "From Internationalisation to Education."

95. Goodman, "Tie That Binds"; Morphew and Hartley, "Mission Statements"; Weerts and Hudson, "Engagement and Institutional Advancement."

96. Selingo, "Tulane Slashes Departments."

97. Pope, "Tulane University Gets Record."

98. Weerts and Freed, "Public Engagement."

99. Astin and Lee, *Invisible Colleges.*

100. Bullock, "Public Good of Private Colleges."

REFERENCES

Abbott, Andrew. *The System of Professions: An Essay on the Division of Expert Labor.* Chicago: University of Chicago Press, 1988.
Archibald, Robert B., and David H. Feldman. *Why Does College Cost So Much?* New York: Oxford University Press, 2011.
Association of American Colleges and Universities. "Civic Learning." 2015. https://www .aacu.org/resources/civic-learning. Accessed March 14, 2017.
———. "A Crucible Moment: College Learning and Democracy's Future." Report of the National Task Force on Civic Learning and Democratic Engagement. Washington, DC: AAC&U, 2012.
Astin, Alexander W. *Four Critical Years.* San Francisco: Jossey-Bass, 1977.
———. "How the Liberal Arts College Affects Students." *Daedalus* 128, no. 1 (1999): 77–100.

Astin, Alexander W., and Calvin B. T. Lee. *The Invisible Colleges: A Profile of Small, Private Colleges with Limited Resources*. New York: McGraw-Hill, 1971.

Austin, Ann E. "Preparing the Next Generation of Faculty: Graduate School as Socialization to the Academic Career." *Journal of Higher Education* 73, no. 1 (January 1, 2002): 94–122. doi:10.1080/00221546.2002.11777132.

Bailyn, Bernard. "Foundations." In *Glimpses of the Harvard Past*, edited by Bernard Bailyn, Donald Fleming, Oscar Handlin, and Stephan Thernstrom, 1–18. Cambridge, MA: Harvard University Press, 1986.

Baker, Vicki L., Roger G. Baldwin, and Sumedha Makker. "Where Are They Now? Revisiting Breneman's Study of Liberal Arts Colleges." *Liberal Education* 98, no. 3 (2012): 48–53.

Berg, Thomas. "Does This New Bill Threaten California Christian Colleges' Religious Freedom?" *Christianity Today*, July 5, 2016. http://www.christianitytoday.com/ct/2016/july-web-only/california-sb1146-religious-freedom.html. Accessed March 15, 2017.

Bowen, Howard R. *The Costs of Higher Education*. San Francisco: Jossey-Bass, 1980.

Brackmann, Sarah M. "Community Engagement in a Neoliberal Paradigm." *Journal of Higher Education Outreach and Engagement* 19, no. 4 (2015): 115–46.

Breneman, David W. *Liberal Arts Colleges: Thriving, Surviving, or Endangered?* Washington, DC: Brookings Institution, 1994.

Brilliant, Eleanor F. "The American Third Sector at the End of the 20th Century." In *Third Sector Policy at the Crossroads: An International Nonprofit Analysis*, edited by Helmut K. Anheier and Jeremy Kendall, 168–82. New York: Routledge, 2001.

Bullock, Mary B. "Public Good of Private Colleges." *University Business*, May 1, 2005. http://www.universitybusiness.com/article/public-good-private-colleges. Accessed March 15, 2017.

Chambers, Anthony C. "The Special Role of Higher Education in Society: As a Public Good for the Public Good." In *Higher Education for the Public Good: Emerging Voices from a National Movement*, edited by Adrianna J. Kezar, Anthony C. Chambers, and John C. Burkhardt. San Francisco: Jossey-Bass, 2006.

Clydesdale, Tim. *The Purposeful Graduate: Why Colleges Must Talk to Students about Vocation*. Chicago: University of Chicago Press, 2015.

Cohen, Arthur M., and Carrie B. Kisker. *The Shaping of American Higher Education: Emergence and Growth of the Contemporary System*. San Francisco: Jossey-Bass, 2010.

College Board. "Trends in College Pricing 2014." Princeton, NJ: College Board, 2015.

Cremin, Lawrence A. *American Education: The Colonial Experience, 1607–1783*. New York: Harper and Row, 1970.

Doyle, William R., and Jennifer A. Delaney. "Higher Education Funding: The New Normal." *Change: The Magazine of Higher Learning* 41, no. 4 (July 1, 2009): 60–62. doi:10.3200/CHNG.41.4.60-62.

Dyer, Thomas G. "Retrospect and Prospect: Understanding the American Outreach University." *Journal of Public Service and Outreach* 4, no. 1 (1999): 52–64.

Eagan, Kevin J., Jennifer B. Lozano, Sylvia Hurtado, and Matthew H. Case. "The American Freshman: National Norms, Fall 2013." Los Angeles: Higher Education Research Institute, UCLA, 2014. http://www.heri.ucla.edu/monographs/theamericanfreshman 2013.pdf. Site discontinued.

Ehrenberg, Ronald G. "American Higher Education in Transition." *Journal of Economic Perspectives* 26, no. 1 (January 1, 2012): 193–216. doi:10.1257/jep.26.1.193.

Ehrenberg, Ronald G., and C. L. Smith. "The Sources and Uses of Annual Giving at

Selective Private Research Universities and Liberal Arts Colleges." *Economics of Education Review* 22, no. 3 (June 2003): 223–35. doi:10.1016/S0272-7757(02)00073-0.

Eikenberry, Angela M., and Jodie Drapal Kluver. "The Marketization of the Nonprofit Sector: Civil Society at Risk?" *Public Administration Review* 64, no. 2 (March 1, 2004): 132–40. doi:10.1111/j.1540-6210.2004.00355.x.

Enke, Kathryn, and Kelly Winters. "Gender, Spirituality, and Community Engagement: Complexities for Students at Catholic Women's Colleges." *Administration Publications*, no. 10 (January 1, 2013): 39–60.

Flaherty, Colleen. "Modest Gains in Faculty Pay." *Inside Higher Ed*, April 13, 2015. https://www.insidehighered.com/news/2015/04/13/aaup-full-time-faculty-salaries-22-percent-year. Accessed March 15, 2017.

Freidson, Elliot. *Professionalism: The Third Logic*. Hoboken, NJ: Wiley, 2010.

Froelich, Karen A. "Diversification of Revenue Strategies: Evolving Resource Dependence in Nonprofit Organizations." *Nonprofit and Voluntary Sector Quarterly* 28, no. 3 (September 1, 1999): 246–68. doi:10.1177/0899764099283002.

Frumkin, Peter. *Strategic Giving*. Chicago: University of Chicago Press, 2006.

Frumkin, Peter, and Alice Andre-Clark. "When Missions, Markets, and Politics Collide: Values and Strategy in the Nonprofit Human Services." *Nonprofit and Voluntary Sector Quarterly* 29, no. 1 (March 1, 2000): 141–63. doi:10.1177/0899764000291S007.

Furco, Andrew. "The Engaged Campus: Toward a Comprehensive Approach to Public Engagement." *British Journal of Educational Studies* 58, no. 4 (December 3, 2010): 375–90. doi:10.1080/00071005.2010.527656.

Geiger, Roger L. "The Historical Matrix of American Higher Education." *History of Higher Education Annual* 1992 (1992): 7–28.

Goodman, Hunter Phillips. "The Tie That Binds: Leadership and Liberal Arts Institutions' Civic Engagement Commitment in Rural Communities." *Journal of Higher Education Outreach and Engagement* 18, no. 3 (2014): 119–24.

Grodsky, Eric, and Melanie T. Jones. "Real and Imagined Barriers to College Entry: Perceptions of Cost." *Social Science Research* 36, no. 2 (June 2007): 745–66. doi:10.1016/j.ssresearch.2006.05.001.

Haigh, Martin. "From Internationalisation to Education for Global Citizenship: A Multi-Layered History." *Higher Education Quarterly* 68, no. 1 (January 1, 2014): 6–27. doi:10.1111/hequ.12032.

Harris, Michael. "Understanding Institutional Diversity in American Higher Education." *ASHE Higher Education Report* 39, no. 3 (August 22, 2013).

Hartley, Matthew, and Christopher C. Morphew. "What's Being Sold and to What End? A Content Analysis of College Viewbooks." *Journal of Higher Education* 79, no. 6 (November 1, 2008): 671–91. doi:10.1080/00221546.2008.11772123.

Hartley, Matthew, and John Saltmarsh. "Creating the Democratically Engaged University: Possibilities for Constructive Action." In *To Serve a Larger Purpose: Engagement for Democracy and the Transformation of Higher Education*, edited by John Saltmarsh and Matthew Hartley, 289–300. Philadelphia: Temple University Press, 2011.

Hearn, James C., and Andrew S. Belasco. "Commitment to the Core: A Longitudinal Analysis of Humanities Degree Production in Four-Year Colleges." *Journal of Higher Education* 86, no. 3 (May 1, 2015): 387–416. doi:10.1080/00221546.2015.11777369.

Hearn, James C., and Kelly Ochs Rosinger. "Socioeconomic Diversity in Selective Private Colleges: An Organizational Analysis." *Review of Higher Education* 38, no. 1 (September 3, 2014): 71–104. doi:10.1353/rhe.2014.0043.

Heller, Don E. "The Changing Nature of Public Support for Higher Education in the

United States." In *Cost-Sharing and Accessibility in Higher Education: A Fairer Deal*, edited by Pedro N. Texeira, D. Bruce Johnstone, Marie Rosa, and Hans Vossensteyn, 133–58. Dordrecht, NL: Springer, 2006.

Hunter, James Davison. *To Change the World: The Irony, Tragedy, and Possibility of Christianity in the Late Modern World*. New York: Oxford University Press, 2010.

Hunter, James M. "An Integrated Framework for Understanding the Financial Health of Small, Private Colleges." PhD diss., 2012.

Hutcheson, Philo, Marybeth Gasman, and Kijua Sanders-McMurtry. "Race and Equality in the Academy: Rethinking Higher Education Actors and the Struggle for Equality in the Post–World War II Period." *Journal of Higher Education* 82, no. 2 (March 1, 2011): 121–53. doi:10.1080/00221546.2011.11779089.

Indiana Wesleyan University. "Quick Facts about Indiana Wesleyan." 2015. https://www.indwes.edu/about/quick-facts. Accessed March 15, 2017.

Jaschik, Scott. "The Right to Expel." *Inside Higher Ed*, July 25, 2014. https://www.insidehighered.com/news/2014/07/25/2-christian-colleges-win-title-ix-exemptions-give-them-right-expel-transgender. Accessed March 15, 2017.

———. "To Avoid Split on Gay Marriage, Two Colleges Quit Christian Group." *Inside Higher Ed*, September 22, 2015. https://www.insidehighered.com/news/2015/09/22/2-colleges-leave-christian-college-group-avoid-split-over-gay-marriage. Accessed March 15, 2017.

Johnstone, D. Bruce. "The Economics and Politics of Cost Sharing in Higher Education: Comparative Perspectives." *Economics of Education Review* 23, no. 4 (August 2004): 403–10. Special issue in honor of Lewis C. Solman. doi:10.1016/j.econedurev.2003.09.004.

———. "Patterns of Finance: Revolution, Evolution, or More of the Same?" *Review of Higher Education* 21, no. 3 (March 1, 1998): 245–55. doi:10.1353/rhe.1998.0004.

Kezar, Adrianna J. "Challenges for Higher Education in Serving the Public Good." In *Higher Education for the Public Good: Emerging Voices from a National Movement*, edited by Adrianna J. Kezar, Anthony C. Chambers, and John C. Burkhardt. San Francisco: Jossey-Bass, 2006.

Kraatz, Matthew S., and Edward J. Zajac. "Exploring the Limits of the New Institutionalism: The Causes and Consequences of Illegitimate Organizational Change." *American Sociological Review* 61, no. 5 (1996): 812–36.

Labaree, David F. "Public Goods, Private Goods: The American Struggle over Educational Goals." *American Educational Research Journal* 34, no. 1 (January 1, 1997): 39–81. doi:10.3102/00028312034001039.

Lapovsky, Lucie. "The Economic Challenges of Liberal Arts Colleges." Liberal Arts Colleges in American Higher Education: Challenges and Opportunities. American Council of Learned Societies Occasional Paper, 2005.

Lee, John Michael. "Moving beyond Racial and Ethnic Diversity at HBCUs." *New Directions for Higher Education* 2015, no. 170 (June 1, 2015): 17–35. doi:10.1002/he.20129.

Leslie, W. Bruce. *Gentlemen and Scholars: College and Community in the "Age of the University, 1865–1917."* University Park: Pennsylvania State University Press, 1992.

Lipka, Michael. "Mainline Protestants Make Up Shrinking Number of Adults." Washington, DC: Pew Research Center, 2015. http://www.pewresearch.org/fact-tank/2015/05/18/mainline-protestants-make-up-shrinking-number-of-u-s-adults. Accessed March 15, 2017.

Lowe, Maria R. "An Oasis of Freedom in a Closed Society: The Significance of Tougaloo College in Mississippi's Civil Rights Struggle, 1954 to 1965." *Journal of Historical Sociology* 20, no. 4 (2007): 486–520.

Marcus, Jon. "Why Some Small Colleges Are in Big Trouble." *Boston Globe*, April 14, 2013. http://www.bostonglobe.com/magazine/2013/04/13/are-small-private-colleges -trouble/ndlYSWVGFAUjYVVWkqnjfK/story.html. Accessed March 15, 2017.

McMahon, Walter W. *Higher Learning, Greater Good*. Baltimore: Johns Hopkins University Press, 2009.

Messiah College. "Agapé Center." 2017. http://www.messiah.edu/agape. Accessed March 15, 2017.

Mettler, Suzanne. *Degrees of Inequality: How the Politics of Higher Education Sabotaged the American Dream*. New York: Basic Books, 2014.

———. *The Submerged State*. Chicago: University of Chicago Press, 2011.

Mooney, Chris. "New Study Reaffirms the Link between Conservative Religious Faith and Climate Change Doubt." *Washington Post*, May 29, 2015. https://www.washington post.com/news/energy-environment/wp/2015/05/29/this-fascinating-chart-on-faith -and-climate-change-denial-has-been-reinforced-by-new-research. Accessed March 15, 2017.

Moore, Tami L. "Community-University Engagement: A Process for Building Democratic Communities." *ASHE Higher Education Report* 40, no. 2 (April 29, 2014).

Morphew, Christopher C. "Conceptualizing Change in the Institutional Diversity of U.S. Colleges and Universities." *Journal of Higher Education* 80, no. 3 (May 1, 2009): 243–69. doi:10.1080/00221546.2009.11779012.

Morphew, Christopher C., and Matthew Hartley. "Mission Statements: A Thematic Analysis of Rhetoric across Institutional Type." *Journal of Higher Education* 77, no. 3 (May 1, 2006): 456–71. doi:10.1080/00221546.2006.11778934.

Morris, Catherine. "Eastern Mennonite University and Goshen College Withdraw from CCCU." *Diverse Education*, September 21, 2015. http://diverseeducation.com/article/ 77856. Accessed March 15, 2017.

Munck, Ronaldo. "Global Civil Society: Myths and Prospects." *Voluntas* 13, no. 4 (2002): 349–61.

National Center for Education Statistics. "Status and Trends in the Education of Racial and Ethnic Minorities." Washington, DC: Department of Education, 2010. https:// nces.ed.gov/pubsearch/pubsinfo.asp?pubid=2010015. Accessed March 15, 2017.

National Science Board. "Science and Engineering Indicators, 2014." Washington, DC: National Science Foundation, 2014.

Ordorika, Imanol, and Marion Lloyd. "The State and Contest in Higher Education in the Globalized Era: Critical Perspectives." In *Critical Approaches to the Study of Higher Education*, edited by Ana M. Martínez-Alemén, Brian Pusser, and Estela M. Bensimon, 130–52. Baltimore: Johns Hopkins University Press, 2015.

Palmer, Robert T., Dina C. Maramba, Taryn Ozuna Allen, and Ramon B. Goings. "From Matriculation to Engagement on Campus: Delineating the Experiences of Latino/a Students at a Public Historically Black University." *New Directions for Higher Education* 2015, no. 170 (June 1, 2015): 67–78. doi:10.1002/he.20132.

Pasque, Penny. *American Higher Education, Leadership, and Policy: Critical Issues and the Public Good*. New York: Palgrave Macmillan, 2010.

Pope, John. "Tulane University Gets Record 44,000 Applications This Year." *New Orleans Times-Picayune*, October 3, 2010. http://www.nola.com/education/index.ssf/2010/10/ tulane_university_gets_record.html. Accessed March 15, 2017.

Pusser, Brian. "Reconsidering Higher Education and the Public Good: The Role of Public Spheres." In *Governance and the Public Good*. Albany: State University of New York Press, 2006.

————. "A State Theoretical Approach to Understanding Contest in Higher Education." In *Higher Education, Stratification, and Workforce Development*, edited by Sheila Slaughter and Barrett J. Taylor, 331–48. Dordrecht, NL: Springer, 2016.

Readings, Bill. *The University in Ruins*. Cambridge, MA: Harvard University Press, 1996.

Renzulli, Linda A., Linda Grant, and Sheetija Kathuria. "Race, Gender, and the Wage Gap: Comparing Faculty Salaries in Predominately White and Historically Black Colleges and Universities." *Gender and Society* 20, no. 4 (August 1, 2006): 491–510. doi:10.1177/0891243206287130.

Rizzo, Michael J. "State Preferences for Higher Education Spending." In *What's Happening to Public Higher Education?*, edited by Ronald G. Ehrenberg, 3–36. Westport, CT: Praeger, 2006.

Roksa, Josipa. "An Analysis of Learning Outcomes of Underrepresented Students at Urban Institutions." Washington, DC: Council of Independent Colleges, 2012.

Routhe, Aaron. "Reading the Signs of Sustainability in Christian Higher Education: Symbolic Value Claims or Substantive Organizational Change?" In *Challenges in Higher Education for Sustainability*, edited by J. Paulo Davim and Walter L. Filho, 35–102. Dordrecht, NL: Springer, 2016.

Salamon, Lester M. "The Nonprofit Sector at a Crossroads: The Case of America." *Voluntas* 10, no. 1 (1999): 5–23.

Schcck, Thomas. "DFL Plan for Free Two Year College Draws Fire." *MPR News*, January 15, 2015. http://www.mprnews.org/story/2015/01/14/tuition-free-proposal. Accessed March 15, 2017.

Schofer, Evan, and John W. Meyer. "The Worldwide Expansion of Higher Education in the Twentieth Century." *American Sociological Review* 70, no. 6 (December 1, 2005): 898–920. doi:10.1177/000312240507000602.

Selingo, Jeffrey J. "Tulane Slashes Departments and Lays Off Professors." *The Chronicle of Higher Education*, December 15, 2005. http://chronicle.com/article/Tulane-Slashes -Departments-and/8437. Accessed March 15, 2017.

Smith, Christian. *To Flourish or Destruct: A Personalist Theory of Human Goods, Motivations, Failure, and Evil*. Chicago: University of Chicago Press, 2015.

Tandberg, David A., and Nicholas W. Hillman. "State Performance Funding for Higher Education: Silver Bullet or Red Herring?" Madison, WI: WISCAPE, 2013. http:// www.wiscape.wisc.edu/wiscape/publications/policy-briefs. Accessed March 15, 2017.

Taylor, Barrett J. "Responses to Conflicting Field Imperatives: Institutions and Agency among Evangelical Christian Colleges." *Sociological Spectrum* 35, no. 2 (March 4, 2015): 207–27. doi:10.1080/02732173.2014.1000556.

Taylor, Barrett J., Brendan Cantwell, and Sheila Slaughter. "Quasi-Markets in U.S. Higher Education: The Humanities and Institutional Revenues." *Journal of Higher Education* 84, no. 5 (September 1, 2013): 675 707. doi:10.1080/00221546.2013.11777305.

Taylor, Barrett J., and Christopher C. Morphew. "An Analysis of Baccalaureate College Mission Statements." *Research in Higher Education* 51, no. 5 (August 1, 2010): 483–503. doi:10.1007/s11162-010-9162-7.

————. "Institutional Contributions to Financing Students in US Higher Education: Trends in General Subsidies, 1987–2007." In *Student Financing of Higher Education: A Comparative Perspective*, edited by Don E. Heller and Claire Callender, 225–51. New York: Routledge, 2013.

————. "Trends in Cost-Sharing among US Public Universities and Their International Implications." *Higher Education Policy* 27, no. 1 (2014): 1–21.

Thelin, John R. "Higher Education and the Public Trough: A Historical Perspective." In

Public Funding for Higher Education: Changing Contexts and New Rationales, edited by Edward P. St. John and Michael D. Parsons, 21–39. Baltimore: Johns Hopkins University Press, 2004.

———. *A History of American Higher Education*. Baltimore: Johns Hopkins University Press, 2011.

Thompson, Fred, and William Zumeta. "Effects of Key State Policies on Private Colleges and Universities: Sustaining Private-Sector Capacity in the Face of the Higher Education Access Challenge." *Economics of Education Review* 20, no. 6 (December 2001): 517–31. doi:10.1016/S0272-7757(00)00031-5.

Vedder, Richard K. "Princeton Reaps Tax Breaks as Public Colleges Beg." *Bloomberg View*, March 18, 2012.

Vine, Phyllis. "The Social Functions of Eighteenth Century Higher Education." In *The History of Higher Education*, 2nd ed., edited by Lester F. Goodchild and Harold S. Wechsler. Needham Heights, MA: Simon and Schuster, 1997.

Weber, Jeremy. "Peace Church Out: Mennonite Schools Leave CCCU to Avoid Same-Sex Marriage Split." *Christianity Today*, September 21, 2015. http://www.christianityto day.com/gleanings/2015/september/cccu-emu-goshen-college-okwu-union-member ship-status.html. Accessed March 15, 2017.

Weerts, David, and Elizabeth Hudson. "Engagement and Institutional Advancement." *New Directions for Higher Education* 2009, no. 147 (September 1, 2009): 65–74. doi:10. 1002/he.359.

Weerts, David, and Gwendolyn Freed. "Public Engagement and Organizational Identity in U.S. Higher Education." *Recherches Sociologiques et Anthropologiques* 47, no. 1 (June 1, 2016): 17–39. doi:10.4000/rsa.1586.

Weerts, David, Thomas Sanford, and Leah Reinert. *College Funding in Context: Understanding the Difference in Higher Education Appropriations across States*. New York: Demos, 2012.

Weisbrod, Burton A. "The Nonprofit Mission and Its Financing." *Journal of Policy Analysis and Management* 17, no. 2 (1998): 165–74.

Weisbrod, Burton A., Jeffrey P. Ballou, and Evelyn D. Asch. *Mission and Money: Understanding the University*. Cambridge: Cambridge University Press, 2008.

Wilberforce Academy. "Mission and Values." 2014. http://www.wilberforceacademy.org. Accessed March 15, 2017.

Wolterstorff, Nicholas, and Clarence Joldersma. *Educating for Shalom: Essays on Christian Higher Education*. Cambridge: Eerdmans, 2004.

Zumeta, William, and Don E. Heller. "Public Policy and Accountability in Higher Education: Lessons from the Past and Present for the New Millennium." In *The States and Public Higher Education Policy: Affordability, Access, and Accountability*, 155–97. Baltimore: Johns Hopkins University Press, 2001.

REACTION

Marc Roy

Barrett Taylor and David Weerts present a compelling overview of some of the challenges facing most independent colleges. The challenges have been well documented in recent years.[1] The authors also offer several suggestions (opportunities) for independent colleges that may help them respond to the challenges they face: reinterpret the mission to speak to the American public, clearly articulate the institution's contribution to the public good, and seek partners that can share costs. In this response, I will focus on small independent colleges, excluding independent research universities and the small percentage of colleges that have endowments approaching a billion dollars or more.

Taylor and Weerts accurately encourage independent colleges to reinterpret their traditional missions in ways that speak to the changing American public. Specifically, they encourage independent colleges to broaden their base of potential students by enrolling more students from underrepresented populations and faith backgrounds that may be different from historic religious connections. Although there are exceptions, many independent faith-based colleges have accepted students of other faiths for decades. For example, the Baylor University website states, "Baylor was founded on Christian values and is affiliated with the Baptist General Convention of Texas. Being a Christian, however, is not required for admission to Baylor. In fact, our undergraduate student body represents about 40 different religious affiliations."[2] Hope College, which has a strong affiliation with the Reformed Church of America has, for decades, welcomed students from all faith traditions. The authors correctly point out that straying from their historic mission can have negative repercussions and college leaders need to carefully consider any changes to their mission.

Recruiting students from underrepresented populations and low-income families is quite common in many independent colleges. Some, such as Albion College, have served underrepresented students since their founding. "Albion College originally met the educational needs of the children of Native Americans and settlers in the area. In 1835, the College was awarded a charter by the Michigan Territorial Legislature, thanks to the efforts of Methodists who were early settlers in the Michigan Territory."[3] To this day, the college also admits students of all faiths as well as students who are agnostic and atheist. Townsley describes several colleges that have turned around difficult financial situations and flourished.[4] Among the strategies that contribute to colleges flourishing is developing relationships with feeder schools that can increase ethnic and racial diversity. Although this is becoming more common, Taylor and Weerts rightly point out that all independent colleges can and should increase their efforts to become more diverse and inclusive communities.

In recent years, calls from political leaders and others have emphasized the need to increase access to college and completion, especially for students from underserved populations, including students from low-income families. A few independent colleges (e.g., Berea College) accept only students with high financial need. Other colleges, to a lesser degree, are enrolling more students who have high financial need and the ability to succeed academically. In doing so, college leaders must seek a balance so that they have sufficient tuition revenue and students do not borrow greater amounts than what they can reasonably repay. Furthermore, as colleges enroll more students with high financial need, leaders need to make sure that they increase and diversify other revenue streams.

Independent colleges need to consider innovations even more broadly than suggested by Taylor and Weerts. A recent report published by the Council of Independent Colleges (CIC) documents adaptations and changes that many colleges have taken.[5] Richard Ekman, president of CIC, states in the preface, "As it turns out, smaller private liberal arts colleges have been far more responsive to environmental shifts than one would expect from what one reads in the popular media. Not only do these institutions intentionally adapt to new challenges, but they do so by embracing—not abandoning—their historic missions. On the whole, the results presented by this report paint a picture of support for institutional change and optimism about the future—a far cry from the bleak portrayal often drawn of liberal arts colleges."[6]

Hearn and Warshaw report that 40 percent of the presidents surveyed stated that their institutions were seeking new revenue sources. In addition, 41.5 percent of the presidents indicated that their colleges shared programs with other institutions.[7] While seeking partnerships can be advantageous because costs are shared, there are many challenges to overcome that can inhibit sharing. These can range from differences in the academic calendars to contracts with different vendors.

There are a number of examples where independent colleges have successfully partnered with other colleges to decrease costs. The Associated Colleges of the South have developed a joint purchasing plan.[8] Academic programs can be shared across colleges as well. This could include less commonly taught languages or courses that typically enroll many students. Goucher College in Maryland offers a joint Russian program with Johns Hopkins University. Faculty members from several colleges in the Associated Colleges of the Midwest (ACM) have offered an online course in applied calculus, titled Calculus: A Modeling Approach, for students enrolled at ACM colleges.

Developing successful partnerships will require many institutions to reconsider operational practices. Switching content management systems or student information systems can be difficult and costly in the short-run. However, it is possible that long-term savings could be realized if colleges can form effective partnerships that also protect confidential information. More realistically, consortia of colleges may be able to collectively provide health insurance for their employees at a reduced cost or share programs that do not typically enroll large numbers of students. Townsley describes other mutually beneficial partnerships between independent colleges, other organizations, and their communities.[9]

In recent years, several organizations have clearly articulated that a liberal education, whether delivered in an independent or public institution, is of significant public good. Beyond the financial gains to individuals and their communities, a liberal education is essential for the development of engaged citizens who will participate in a democratic society at all levels. The Association of American Colleges and Universities has issued a series of statements and publications emphasizing this point.[10] Several years ago, the CIC launched a national initiative to articulate the benefits of a liberal education and the importance of independent colleges.

Reinterpreting their mission, articulating the public good, and developing partnerships are necessary for independent colleges to thrive and to continue as an important sector of American higher education. Independent colleges that flourish also will recognize that multiple approaches are necessary to increase revenue and decrease costs. Thoughtful strategic planning and an ability to adjust strategies and tactics on short notice are also essential for independent colleges to thrive. It is common practice to develop and execute a plan, then to evaluate the degree to which it is successful. College leaders increasingly will need to evaluate plans and make necessary adjustments to changing conditions. As they do so, America's independent colleges will be able to carry out their historic missions while increasing access to education and college completion to underserved populations, serving the public good, and developing viable financial models.

NOTES

1. E.g., Townsley, "Small College Guide."
2. Baylor University, "Spiritual Life."

3. Albion College, "Our History."
4. Townsley, "Small College Guide."
5. Hearn and Warshaw, "Mission-Driven Innovation."
6. Ibid.
7. Ibid.
8. Associated Colleges of the South, "Joint Purchasing Program."
9. Townsley, "Small College Guide."
10. See, e.g., Association of American Colleges and Universities, "Board Statement."

REFERENCES

Albion College. "Our History." 2017. http://www.albion.edu/about-albion/our-history. Accessed March 15, 2017.
Associated Colleges of the South. "Joint Purchasing Program" http://colleges.org/pro grams/joint-purchasing-program. Accessed March 15, 2017.
Association of American Colleges and Universities. "Board Statement on Diversity, Equity, and Inclusive Excellence." June 27, 2013. http://www.aacu.org/about/statements/2013/diversity. Accessed March 15, 2017.
Baylor University. "Spiritual Life." http://www.baylor.edu/admissions/index.php?id=872293. Accessed March 15, 2017.
Council of Independent Colleges. "Securing America's Future: The Power of Liberal Arts Education. https://www.cic.edu/programs/liberal-arts-campaign. Accessed April 19, 2017.
Hearn, James C., and Jarrett B. Warshaw. "Mission-Driven Innovation: An Empirical Study of Adaptation and Change among Independent Colleges." Washington, DC: Council of Independent Colleges, 2015.
Townsley, Michael K. "Small College Guide to Financial Health: Weathering Turbulent Times." National Association of College and University Business Officers, 2009.

2

Access and Affordability

NICHOLAS W. HILLMAN AND VALERIE CRESPÍN-TRUJILLO

Few topics in higher education receive as much public scrutiny as college affordability. Tuition has outpaced inflation since the 1980s, and the sticker price of college has gone up by 250 percent during this time.[1] Outstanding student loan debt has surpassed $1 trillion and is now the largest form of consumer credit, second only to home mortgages.[2] College graduates leave school with an average of $28,400 in debt, far more than past generations.[3] Regardless of what statistic we use, the story leads to the same conclusion: students are carrying an increasingly larger responsibility when paying for college. Consequently, students and their associated tuition dollars are becoming primary sources of revenue for colleges and universities.

This is especially true in the independent sector of higher education—the 3,000 nonprofit and for-profit colleges enrolling approximately 25 percent of the nation's undergraduate students. These colleges have many defining features that distinguish them from one another. They are small liberal arts colleges, elite Ivy League schools, historically black colleges and universities, women's colleges, religiously affiliated schools, and vocational colleges, all serving different corners of the higher education marketplace. Independent colleges are distinctly rooted in American history, where our nation's first (and most prestigious) institutions were established in the colonial period. But independent colleges are also distinctly rooted in American capitalism, where for-profit colleges have grown exponentially since the mid-1970s, while many nonprofits compete for survival. The list of distinguishing features is long, but we will focus on one in particular—the independent sector pricing model and its implications for college access.

Campuses across the country are looking for innovative solutions for recruiting and retaining a diverse student body while also making college more affordable. This chapter reviews the literature on some of the most promising practices that could help colleges achieve these goals. It focuses on the extent to which these efforts can help reverse deeply rooted inequalities that persist within many independent colleges and universities and is written for independent college leaders involved in campus policymaking and planning efforts to navigate and reverse inequality.

Trends in Access and Affordability

College access literature falls into one of these three broad domains—*high school to college, undermatching,* and *geography*—so this essay draws on studies from all three domains to identify promising solutions for reversing inequality. The bulk of literature focuses on how young adults transition from high school to college and consistently finds widening inequalities along lines of socioeconomic class and race/ethnicity.[4] Figure 2.1 displays the college-going rate of recent high school graduates, where we see the gap between wealthy and poor students is as large today as it was in the 1970s.

An increasingly popular line of access research focuses on "undermatch" and the extent to which students enroll in less selective colleges when they could have been admitted to more selective ones.[5] This body of research finds

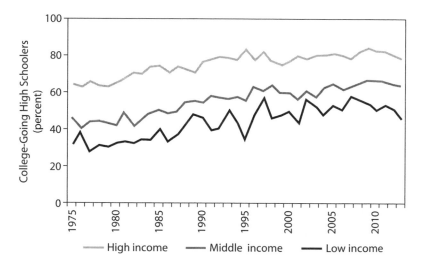

Figure 2.1. High school to college participation rate of graduating seniors, by income group. *Source:* Snyder, de Brey, and Dillow, "Digest of Education Statistics 2014," table 302.30.

Table 2.1.   Undergraduate enrollment by selectivity and control of institution, 2012–13 head count (in millions)

	Public	Nonprofit	For-profit	Total
Highly selective	1.2	0.9	0.0	2.1
Moderately selective	3.2	1.2	0.2	4.6
Nonselective	13.7	1.2	2.2	17.1
Total	18.0	3.3	2.4	23.7

Source: National Center for Education Statistics, Integrated Postsecondary Education Data System.

low-income students and students of color undermatch at higher rates than their peers, and these results could be consequential by slowing time to degree and by increasing debt levels. However, only 2.1 million of the nation's 23.7 million undergraduates (9 percent) attend highly selective colleges (table 1). Another 4.6 million (19 percent) attend moderately selective colleges and the remaining 17.1 million students attend nonselective or open-access institutions. Helping students attend more selective colleges is not a solution to reversing inequality because they enroll few low-income students and students of color in the first place (table 2.2).

Because of these limitations, researchers also focus on geographic access of college to determine whether students even have options nearby.[6] This line of research is more culturally relevant for working-class students who are place-bound and who are unlikely to travel far to attend a selective college. Thinking

Table 2.2.   Undergraduate enrollment by racial/ethnic profile and control, 2012–13 head count (in millions)

	Public	Nonprofit	For-profit	Total
White	9.8	1.9	0.9	12.6
Hispanic	2.9	0.3	0.3	3.5
Black	2.4	0.4	0.6	3.5
Asian	1.0	0.2	0.1	1.2
Native American	0.2	0.0	0.0	0.2
Pacific Islander	0.1	0.0	0.0	0.1
Other	1.7	0.5	0.5	2.6
Total	18.0	3.3	2.4	23.7
Number of institutions	1,632	1,676	1,479	4,787
Average institution size	11,048	1,960	1,632	4,957

Source: National Center for Education Statistics, Integrated Postsecondary Education Data System.

Table 2.3. Distance from student's home to college (in miles),
by Carnegie Classification

	Public		Nonprofit		Total	
	Mean	Median	Mean	Median	Mean	Median
Total	54	11	252	43	106	13
Associate degree	32	8	105	10	37	9
Research and doctoral degree	106	27	352	78	210	36
Master's degree	73	17	197	35	148	24
Baccalaureate degree	60	14	262	56	211	30
Special focus & other	91	22	209	21	185	16

Source: Radwin, Wine, Siegel, and Bryan, "2011–12 National Postsecondary Student Aid Study."
Note: Variables: DISTANCE, ALTONLN, CONTROL, and CC2010C. Excludes students who enrolled exclusively online.

about access from the geographical perspective shows how opportunities are constrained according to one's local community. This literature is particularly relevant for colleges serving nontraditional-aged students who balance work, home, and schooling responsibilities and are likely to enroll part-time. The average distance between undergraduates' home and college, where nonprofit colleges draw from the largest geographic areas relative to other sectors, is shown in table 2.3.[7]

Just as there are many ways to define access, there are also many ways to define the concept of affordability. The *net price* a student pays is a common measure of affordability, which measures the students' cost of attendance minus any grant aid they receive. The average net price for a four-year college is $17,230 (table 2.4); low-income students tend to face the lowest net price, and higher-income students face the highest. However, net price *as a percent of the student's family income* is often a more telling measure of affordability. Despite facing lower net prices, this figure accounts for about 80 percent of low-income students' family income, meaning they must rely on loans or work while enrolled to pay for college.[8]

Consequently, low-income students (including Pell Grant recipients) are more likely to borrow and to borrow more to pay for college.[9] Debt burdens vary according to institutional sector, as displayed in table 2.5, where students attending independent nonprofit colleges carry more debt than those in the

Table 2.4. Average annual net price of four-year colleges and universities, by income groups

	Total	Low income	Middle income	High income
Public	$12,660	$9,230	$14,530	$20,290
Non-profit	$24,510	$18,610	$21,910	$32,520
For-profit	$20,850	$20,000	$24,470	$30,060
Total	$17,230	$13,080	$17,460	$26,190

Source: Snyder, de Brey, and Dillow, "Digest of Education Statistics 2014," table 331.30.

Note: Here, low income is less than $30,000, middle is between $48,000 and $75,000, and high is greater than $110,000.

public sector. Nonprofit graduates carried (in 2012) an average of $24,614 in debt—approximately $2,582 more than a public college graduate. When considering the economic returns to schooling and the students' ability to repay their debt upon graduation, this debt premium for a private education may be a worthwhile investment—particularly if colleges provide supports that help students persist to degree completion.

Table 2.6 extends the prior analysis by focusing on debt levels relative to family income. Quartiles that disaggregate the data by family income quartiles show that the lowest-income students attending public and nonprofit colleges tend to borrow more than their upper-income peers. The average borrower in the lowest-income quartile graduates with $25,016 in debt, whereas their highest-income peers graduate with $22,931. Despite facing lower net prices (due in large part to discounts and other grant aid), low-income students still accumulate larger debt burdens than their upper-income peers, who presumably have less financial need.

Table 2.5. Average student loan debt of graduating seniors (in 2012) by Control and Carnegie Class

	Public	Nonprofit	For-profit	Total
Total	$22,032	$24,614	$34,879	$24,401
Research & doctoral degree	$22,270	$23,239	$37,142	$24,031
Master's degree	$21,873	$26,212	$35,121	$24,835
Baccalaureate degree	$23,014	$24,119	$28,046	$24,198
Special focus & other	$17,880	$21,462	$33,989	$26,253

Source: Radwin, Wine, Siegel, and Bryan, "2011–12 National Postsecondary Student Aid Study."

Note: Variables: FEDCUM1, COLLGRAD, CONTROL, and CC2010C.

Table 2.6.   Average student loan debt of graduating seniors (in 2012)
by income quartile and control

	Public	Nonprofit	For-profit	Total
Total	$22,032	$24,614	$34,879	$24,401
Lowest quartile	$23,626	$25,016	$31,102	$24,719
2nd quartile	$22,368	$25,304	$36,375	$24,787
3rd quartile	$21,676	$25,768	$36,373	$25,256
Highest quartile	$20,457	$22,931	$34,193	$23,030

Source: Radwin, Wine, Siegel, and Bryan, "2011–12 National Postsecondary Student Aid Study."
    Note: Variables: FEDCUM1, COLLGRAD, CONTROL, and PCTAL.

Aligning Problems and Solutions

The statistics provided above set the stage for understanding the problems facing college access and affordability at independent colleges and universities. Many of these challenges are rooted in socioeconomic inequality, where children born into the highest-income families are socialized at a very young age to be "college ready."[10] Other challenges are embedded within the policies and practices of student financial aid administration, enrollment management, and college admissions, where even the "best and brightest" students from low-income families have lower chances of attending college than low-achieving high-income students.[11]

There is no single solution to fix these problems, nor can colleges alone be expected to fully ameliorate these deeply rooted inequalities; nevertheless, there are promising solutions campuses can adopt to help reduce or at least stem them. The following discussion highlights the four main mechanisms through which these inequalities are reproduced: *precollege preparation, college admissions policies, student financial aid,* and *student mobility.* These four mechanisms of inequality are helpful for campus leaders in search of promising solutions; after all, if we misdiagnose the nature of the problem, we will arrive at an ineffective policy solution. Accordingly, the discussion below should help campus leaders diagnose access and affordability problems on their own campus so they can design appropriate policy solutions.

Precollege Preparation
Problems
Before students even apply to college, they are exposed to a number of interventions designed to prepare them for the rigors of college-level coursework.

Advanced Placement (AP), International Baccalaureate (IB), and dual-credit courses are among the most popular "college-readiness" curricular interventions.[12] Beyond these, families also open college savings accounts, purchase test-preparation services (e.g., SAT and ACT prep), and encourage extracurricular activities like volunteering, athletics, and so on to enhance their child's college readiness and competitiveness for admissions. However, these opportunities are highly unequal, where children born into the most advantaged families participate and benefit the most from these efforts.[13] This inequality begins very early in the child's life course, making it difficult for the "best and brightest" student from a working-class family to catch up.[14]

Because of these inequalities, precollege preparation efforts often simply operate as screening/sorting mechanisms that help privileged families maintain their class advantage.[15] For example, English Language Learners, Latinos, and students attending the nation's lowest-income schools have the fewest opportunities to participate in AP or IB courses.[16] Similarly, high school calculus serves as a gatekeeper to college admissions, yet it primarily benefits white students and those from high socioeconomic backgrounds.[17] Beyond these academic inequalities, there are inequalities in social capital where children born into the highest socioeconomic class know how to navigate the application process and engage in activities that are rewarded in college admissions.[18] They also have the financial resources to prepare financially for college by opening savings accounts early in their child's life, knowing how to navigate the student aid system, and leveraging wealth (e.g., home equity) to pay for college.[19]

Solutions

Colleges routinely provide prospective students with information about important deadlines, financial aid options, and steps on how to apply to college. These informational strategies are crucial for recruitment, and behavioral economists consistently find that simple and timely messages are quite effective.[20] This information can be customized to the student's unique circumstances, and they can anticipate just how likely they are to be admitted or how to estimate the "net price" they will likely pay after discounts. However, simply providing "more" or "better" information is not a sufficient strategy since students make choices based on a much wider array of factors.

Some of the most impactful practices are those that couple "better information" with coaching, mentorship, and personalized guidance. For example, summer counseling has been found to help low-income students transition between high school and college.[21] Low-touch and low-cost behavioral nudges like text messages have been successful in reminding students about important deadlines and resources, which in turn increases their matriculation after being admitted.[22] Mentoring and coaching high school students through the college admissions process also has been found to yield positive outcomes.[23] Similarly, working-class students and students of color are more likely to apply to colleges where students from their own high school also attended, regardless of the students' "college knowledge" or information about alternative options.[24] Colleges that provide simple and timely information about the costs of college while also counseling prospective students through the application process will likely make the most progress on reducing access and affordability barriers.[25]

College Admissions
Problems

One of the more popular discussions in college admissions today deals with the phenomenon of "undermatching"—the occurrence of high-achieving, low-income students attending less selective colleges when they could have been admitted to more selective ones.[26] While the methodological and theoretical assumptions built into this line of research have significant limitations, it continues to capture the imagination of elites.[27] The possibility of having a "smart poor kid" aiming low and attending a less selective college means he will be less likely to graduate, have a lower-quality experience, and accumulate more debt.[28] By this logic, the inequalities we see in our admissions systems are due to students making poor choices. To reverse these inequalities, students simply need better information about their "matches" so they can make optimal choices. Unfortunately, this logic is not well situated with culturally relevant theories of college choices, and it does little to change the structural barriers built into the college admissions process that are known to exacerbate inequalities.

We know that application fees and required essays discourage students of color from applying to college. For example, Jonathan Smith, Michael Hurwitz, and Jessica Howell[29] find "Black and Hispanic enrollment is estimated to decrease by over 6% when an essay is required and by 1.1% when the application fee increases by 10%." Students may not know they are eligible for fee waivers or they may be deterred by the paperwork necessary to apply for a waiver,[30] suggesting colleges are not doing enough to reduce these barriers. We also know *early admissions* exacerbates inequalities because students who apply are often from higher socioeconomic backgrounds, making the remaining admission spots even more difficult for lower-income and racial/ethnic minority students to secure.[31] The use of legacy status also exacerbates these inequalities because it provides more advantages in admissions than does racial/ethnic minority status.[32]

Solutions

Colleges have a wide range of strategies for expanding access during the admissions process. One promising solution is to waive application fees for lower-income students or for students from local high schools. Another option is to eliminate using early decision deadlines since it has become an indirect mechanism to screen students by their ability to pay, which reduces access for underrepresented students.[33] Similarly, campuses could also offer a wider array of standardized tests that are accepted for admission, or they could reduce (or even eliminate) the importance standardized tests play in the admissions process.

Another promising admissions practice is to eliminate or significantly reduce the role of essays in the application process. The cost-benefit ratio is likely to be minimal here, particularly in light of studies showing how essays are a screening mechanism that disproportionately discourages low-income students and students of color from applying.[34] Admissions is an obvious and crucial barrier in expanding college access and independent colleges are seeking ways to maintain their reputation while admitting students who are likely to enroll. Rethinking current practices regarding application fees, ending early decision policies, and dropping essays are but a few promising solutions colleges can use to expand access and improve the admissions process. Some colleges may be tempted to go "test optional"[35] or to adopt the Common Application,[36] but neither strategy is supported by evidence and should be not be adopted without careful consideration of its merits.

Financial Aid and Pricing

Problems

The independent college pricing model is perhaps the greatest barrier to entry for low-income students and students of color. Charging sticker prices that are larger than median family income sends a "sticker shock" to students. Tuition discounting—reducing the institution's published tuition through the strategic use of institutional aid—has emerged as a standard enrollment management practice because researchers have consistently found price reductions via grants and scholarships increase students' likelihood to enroll.[37] Even when the average discount rate for nonprofit colleges is 45 percent, the remaining price barrier is still high.[38] On average, a $1,000 reduction in price is associated with approximately 5 percent greater likelihood to enroll, with even greater effects for lower-income students.[39] Students are not just responsive to discounts, they are also responsive to their *expectations* of receiving aid. If an admitted student does not receive the discount he expected, then he is less likely to enroll.[40]

Discounting has also become a revenue and prestige management practice, where colleges can leverage aid in ways that actually bring in more money or higher prestige to the college. Accordingly, colleges do not restrict their discounts to the lowest-income students, and they target a significant amount of aid toward students who have no financial need or are from upper-income families.[41] This only fuels the tuition discounting race, where colleges compete with one another to craft a class of desirable students even if this aid does not expand access or improve affordability for low-income students.[42] As a result, colleges have little incentive to offer a discount to low-income students, which only reinforces stratification and pushes low-income students to either leave without earning a degree or to take out more debt in pursuit of their educational goals.

Yet colleges continue to engage in discounting even when they are aware of the inequality it produces and the negative results the practice has for low-income students. Colleges are the last source of financial aid, so targeting limited campus resources to non-needy students may bring in new revenue but runs the risk of maintaining unequal access and affordability. When low-income students still have unmet need after discounting, loans may become their next option (which we saw in table 6). But not all students are willing to borrow, even if it is in their economic best interest to do so.[43] Leaving money on the table like this is associated with lower access and completion rates, so colleges play a role in reducing low-income students' need to borrow in the first place and then helping students know their aid eligibility options.[44]

Solutions

One of the more common approaches to improving affordability is via loan counseling and financial literacy; however, there is little consensus that these efforts actually change participants' behaviors.[45] Because of this, colleges will likely find it more advantageous to reform what they know will work—tuition discounting practices. By replacing loans with grants in students' aid packages, colleges will likely become more socioeconomically diverse and affordable for low-income students.[46] Of course, most colleges do not have the financial capacity or willingness to target all of their aid in this way, so these efforts should be coupled with innovative strategies to tap into existing campus resources.

Examples of such strategies include aid offices leveraging relationships with campus alumni relations officials, since students who receive institutional aid tend to give back to their alma mater at higher rates.[47] Similarly, when students receive personalized support when navigating the financial aid process, they tend to leave less money on the table and have higher chances of enrolling and persisting in college.[48] Tapping into existing campus networks to support students is likely the most effective and sustainable way to help students manage their finances. However, colleges may be tempted by popular trends such as disbursing aid via a biweekly "paycheck" and other innovations proposed by outside organizations.[49] Popular interventions like these should be implemented judiciously and monitored and evaluated carefully since they are often unproven practices that may not yield large or sustainable impacts.

Student Mobility

Problems

Students respond to prices, and they also respond to the geographic distance and proximity to college. The further away a college is from a student's home, the less likely they are to enroll or even apply.[50] Student mobility is more common today than in past generations due in large part to lower communication and transportation costs.[51] However, this convergence of the higher education marketplace has occurred in uneven ways, where students of color, low-income students, and those whose parents have lower educational attainment levels tend to be more place-bound.[52]

Place also matters because simply having a college nearby increases students' likelihood of attending.[53] Students who live where there are no colleges nearby, or where options are few, will face limited college access. These students may be more inclined to participate in distance learning, which to date has not demonstrated measurable advantages over traditional face-to-face or even hybrid learning. In fact, online learning may produce negative outcomes for working students and students of color.[54] In the absence of equitable, effective, or high-quality distance-learning options, the importance of place remains a salient challenge for colleges. In fact, Caroline Hoxby and Christopher

Avery[55] find that colleges are recruiting "high-achieving, low-income" students from just 15 of the nation's 334 largest metropolitan areas.

It is also possible the amenities competition exacerbates this problem if students perceive their local college to be exclusive, expensive, or otherwise inaccessible. Institutions spend money on facilities, faculty, services, research, and instructional technology in order to have a competitive advantage for the nation's top students.[56] Students and their families may equate these amenities with the "quality" of education, giving institutions an incentive to increase spending that will improve their reputation. Even if these colleges are geographically accessible, students within the local community may perceive them to be off-limits due to the "prestigious" image projected to potential students and their families. Institutional leaders should be aware of these optics and be strategic in their resource allocation decisions so as to not become (or be perceived as) out of reach to members of their local community.

Solutions

Distance learning is often considered as the first solution to the mobility problem—simply provide high-quality content in convenient ways to reduce the geographic barrier for students. Matthew Mayhew and Stephen Vassallo's chapter in this volume describes the challenges that confront independent colleges and universities considering how to use technologies such as distance education. These challenges include those related to equity and mission. Alternatively, independent colleges should consider using existing community networks to reduce access and affordability barriers. Many independent institutions are deeply embedded in their local and regional communities and maintain strong connections with alumni. Alumni can work closely with schools and civic organizations to provide the mentoring necessary to help prospective students prepare for admissions, apply for financial aid, and demystify the net price of college. For place-bound students, this could be a powerful way to increase access for working-class students and students of color, who often make educational decisions based on these important networks. Inviting alumni back to campus and engaging them in the recruitment and retention practices already taking place may be a more sustainable (and less expensive) way to close access gaps. A more systematic reform is related to local "promise programs" in which philanthropists and community partners guarantee accessible and affordable (in some cases free) college opportunities to local high school graduates.[57] But even after engaging alumni and philanthropists, there are still place-based barriers such as transportation cost, child care, and time of course offerings that affect students' choices. A strategic response to student mobility would extend far beyond distance learning and tap into social networks, transportation barriers, and familial commitments. College leaders might look to the Accelerated Study in Associate Programs (ASAP) for examples of how one college responded to these challenges.[58]

Recommendations for Independent College and University Leaders

This overview offers a range of promising evidence-based solutions to help increase college access and improve affordability. College leaders looking to adopt innovative practices can use these results to make the case for adopting new programs, improving the design of existing programs, or considering ways to evaluate their efforts to improve access and affordability. The review focuses on four main barriers to access and affordability: precollege preparation, college admissions policies, student financial aid, and student mobility. There are different interventions available to campus leaders, depending on which barrier they seek to address, and this summary highlights the most promising ones.

Precollege preparation efforts should include targeted outreach to students both before and after applying to college. This outreach can be high-touch by linking peer mentors or other college representatives with incoming students, with mentors helping to ensure students have the information they need to matriculate in the fall term. This information could consist of how to apply for financial aid, updates on when to expect aid awards to be disbursed, and deadlines for housing and/or course registration. This same information can sometimes be provided via low-touch and low-cost avenues such as text message alerts from the college (or a third-party vendor) that remind students of important dates and resources. Whether high-touch or low-touch, these personalized outreach efforts are likely to be the most promising solutions for helping students prepare to transition into college. To the extent colleges can collaborate with local and regional high schools, the likelihood of success will be even greater.

College admissions policies should reflect promising new practices while discontinuing other unproven ones in order to increase access. Starting with the latter, those currently practicing early admissions or requiring essays should consider the merits of such practices since they likely limit access for low-income students and students of color. Instead, colleges could expand access by waiving application fees for lower-income students or even for local high school students. Colleges should resist jumping on the admission policy bandwagon, such as going "test optional" or adopting the Common Application; these efforts (while popular) are not likely to expand access.

Campus financial aid should be redesigned to target resources (both financial and informational) to the neediest students. Replacing loans with grants in financial aid packages, delivering timely information about financial aid deadlines, and offering personalized support for filing aid application material are among the most promising ways to expand access and improve affordability. College leaders may be tempted to adopt politically popular interventions such as financial literacy or aid in the form of a "paycheck," but these are unproven solutions that may yield modest or even no impact on affordability.

Student mobility should play a more central role in access and affordability interventions. Place-based "promise programs" are among the more innovative solutions for improving access and affordability, with early evidence indicating their effectiveness. Of course, developing and sustaining these large-scale reforms may not be feasible, so campus leaders could focus on removing transportation and child-care barriers, which often pose challenges for place-bound students. Similarly, engaging local alumni networks and community-based organizations to provide personalized information to prospective students is a low-cost way to help address access and affordability concerns. Distance education is often seen as a silver bullet to mobility problems, but campus leaders should know these efforts do not have strong research supporting their efficacy. In fact, the best evidence shows distance education has negative impacts on commuter and place-bound students.

Leaders of nonprofit colleges are constantly looking for best practices to help navigate challenging economic times. In our review of the research, we found several well-designed studies that offer promising solutions, but we also found several more (not included in this chapter) that have weak research designs and fail to correct for threats to internal validity. Consequently, we worry many of the best practices college leaders hear about and are encouraged to adopt are grounded in weak evidence. This can create even more problems for college leaders who do not have the time or resources to experiment with ineffective interventions.

It is our hope that some of the research presented here can help campus leaders modify existing programs and policies, make the case for new ones, or seek new strategies that show the greatest promise for improving access and affordability. No single intervention will solve the problems and none in this chapter claim to be a "silver bullet"; nevertheless, the college that adopts a mix of these evidence-based reforms will have a greater chance of success than one that does not. The findings presented throughout this study may also help leaders anticipate unintended consequences of their own ongoing practices, or to weigh the merits of proposed ones.

NOTES

1. Baumol, *Cost Disease.*
2. Federal Reserve Bank of New York, "Quarterly Report."
3. Institute for College Access and Success, "Student Debt."
4. Bailey and Dynarski, "Inequality in Postsecondary Education"; Bastedo and Jaquette, "Running in Place."
5. Hoxby and Avery, "Missing 'One-Offs.'"
6. Turley, "College Proximity."
7. This analysis excludes all students taking distance education courses (*ALTONLN*).
8. Cahalan and Perna, "Indicators of Higher Education Equity."
9. Woo, "Degrees of Debt."
10. Alon, "Evolution of Class Inequality"; Bailey and Dynarski, "Inequality in Post-secondary Education."
11. Black, Cortes, and Lincove, "Apply Yourself"; Kahlenberg, "Rewarding Strivers."
12. Glancy et al., "Blueprint for College Readiness."
13. Alon, "Evolution of Class Inequality."
14. Bastedo and Jaquette, "Running in Place."
15. Lucas, "Effectively Maintained Inequality."
16. Kanno and Kangas, "'I'm Not Going to Be'"; Perna et al., "Unequal Access"; Solórzano and Ornelas, "Critical Race Analysis."
17. Domina and Saldana, "Does Raising the Bar."
18. Engberg, "Pervasive Inequality."
19. George-Jackson and Gast, "Addressing Information Gaps"; Lovenheim, "Effect of Liquid Housing Wealth."
20. Hoxby and Turner, "Informing Students."
21. Castleman, Page, and Schooley, "Forgotten Summer."
22. Castleman and Page, "Summer Nudging."
23. Avery and Kane, "Student Perceptions of College Opportunities."
24. Black, Cortes, and Lincove, "Apply Yourself."
25. For example, see Avery, Howell, and Page, "Review of the Role."
26. Bowen, Chingos, and McPherson, *Crossing the Finish Line.*
27. Bastedo and Flaster, "Conceptual and Methodological Problems."
28. Cohodes and Goodman, "Merit Aid, College Quality"; Goodman, Hurwitz, and Smith, "College Access"; Hoxby and Turner, "Informing Students."
29. Smith, Hurwitz, and Howell, "Screening Mechanisms," 18.
30. Hoxby and Turner, "Informing Students."
31. Kim, "Early Decision and Financial Aid."
32. Espenshade, Chung, and Walling, "Admission Preferences."

33. Kim, "Early Decision and Financial Aid."
34. Smith, Hurwitz, and Howell, "Screening Mechanisms."
35. Belasco, Rosinger, and Hearn, "Test-Optional Movement."
36. Smith, Hurwitz, and Howell, "Screening Mechanisms."
37. Deming and Dynarski, "College Aid."
38. National Association of College and University Business Officers, "2013 Tuition Discounting Study."
39. Deming and Dynarski, "College Aid"; Hossler et al., "Student Aid and Its Role."
40. DesJardins, Ahlburg, and McCall, "Integrated Model."
41. Radwin et al., "National Postsecondary Student Aid Study."
42. McPherson and Schapiro, *Student Aid Game.*
43. Burdman, "Student Debt Dilemma"; Callender and Jackson, "Does the Fear of Debt."
44. Bettinger et al., "Role of Application Assistance"; Cowan, "Testing for Educational Credit."
45. Hastings, Madrian, and Skimmyhorn, "Financial Literacy, Financial Education"; Lusardi and Mitchell, "Economic Importance of Financial Literacy"; Willis, "Evidence and Ideology."
46. DesJardins, Ahlburg, and McCall, "Integrated Model"; Hillman, "Economic Diversity"; Rothstein and Rouse, "Constrained after College."
47. Marr, Mullin, and Siegfried, "Undergraduate Financial Aid"; Meer and Rosen, "Does Generosity Beget Generosity?"
48. Bettinger et al., "Role of Application Assistance."
49. MDRC, "Aid Like a Paycheck."
50. Alm and Winters, "Distance and Intrastate College Student"; Dillon and Smith, "Determinants of Mismatch."
51. Hoxby, "Changing Selectivity of American Colleges."
52. Niu, "Leaving Home State"; Ovink and Kalogrides, "No Place Like Home?"
53. Do, "Effects of Local Colleges"; Griffith and Rothstein, "Can't Get There from Here."
54. Joyce et al., "Does Classroom Time Matter?"; Xu and Jaggars, "Impact of Online Learning"; Xu and Jaggars, "Performance Gaps."
55. Hoxby and Avery, "Missing 'One-Offs.'"
56. Ehrenberg, *Tuition Rising.*
57. Page and Scott-Clayton, "Improving College Access."
58. Scrivener et al., "Doubling Graduation Rates."

REFERENCES

Alm, James, and John V. Winters. "Distance and Intrastate College Student Migration." *Economics of Education Review* 28, no. 6 (December 2009): 728–38. doi:10.1016/j.econe durev.2009.06.008.
Alon, Sigal. "The Evolution of Class Inequality in Higher Education: Competition, Exclusion, and Adaptation." *American Sociological Review* 74, no. 5 (October 1, 2009): 731–55. doi:10.1177/000312240907400503.
Avery, Christopher, Jessica S. Howell, and Lindsay Page. "A Review of the Role of College Counseling, Coaching, and Mentoring on Students' Postsecondary Outcomes." Washington, DC: College Board, 2014.
Avery, Christopher, and Thomas J. Kane. "Student Perceptions of College Opportunities:

The Boston COACH Program." In *College Choices: The Economics of Where to Go, When to Go, and How to Pay for It*, edited by Caroline Hoxby, 355–94. Chicago: University of Chicago Press, 2004.

Bailey, Martha J., and Susan M. Dynarski. "Inequality in Postsecondary Education." In *Whither Opportunity?*, edited by Greg J. Duncan and Richard Murnane, 117–32. New York: Russell Sage, 2011.

Bastedo, Michael N., and Allyson Flaster. "Conceptual and Methodological Problems in Research on College Undermatch." *Educational Researcher* 43, no. 2 (March 1, 2014): 93–99. doi:10.3102/0013189X14523039.

Bastedo, Michael N., and Ozan Jaquette. "Running in Place: Low-Income Students and the Dynamics of Higher Education Stratification." *Educational Evaluation and Policy Analysis* 33, no. 3 (2011): 318–39.

Baumol, William J. *The Cost Disease: Why Computers Get Cheaper and Health Care Doesn't.* New Haven, CT: Yale University Press, 2012.

Belasco, Andrew S., Kelly O. Rosinger, and James C. Hearn. "The Test-Optional Movement at America's Selective Liberal Arts Colleges: A Boon for Equity or Something Else?" *Educational Evaluation and Policy Analysis* 37, no. 2 (June 1, 2015): 206–23. doi: 10.3102/0162373714537350.

Bettinger, Eric P., Bridget Terry Long, Philip Oreopoulos, and Lisa Sanbonmatsu. "The Role of Application Assistance and Information in College Decisions: Results from the H&R Block Fafsa Experiment." *Quarterly Journal of Economics* 127, no. 3 (August 1, 2012): 1205–42. doi:10.1093/qje/qjs017.

Black, Sandra E., Kalena E. Cortes, and Jane A. Lincove. "Apply Yourself: Racial and Ethnic Differences in College Application." Working Paper. Washington, DC: National Bureau of Economic Research, 2015.

Bowen, William G., Matthew M. Chingos, and Michael S. McPherson. *Crossing the Finish Line: Completing College at America's Public Universities.* Princeton, NJ: Princeton University Press, 2009.

Burdman, Pamela. "The Student Debt Dilemma: Debt Aversion as a Barrier to College Access." *Center for Studies in Higher Education*, October 1, 2005. http://escholarship.org/uc/item/6sp9787j. Accessed March 16, 2017.

Cahalan, Margaret, and Laura W. Perna. "Indicators of Higher Education Equity in the United States: 45 Year Trend Report." Pell Institute for the Study of Opportunity in Higher Education, 2015. https://eric.ed.gov/?id=ED555865.

Callender, Claire, and Jonathan Jackson. "Does the Fear of Debt Deter Students from Higher Education?" *Journal of Social Policy* 34, no. 4 (October 2005): 509–40. doi: 10.1017/S004727940500913X.

Castleman, Benjamin L., and Lindsay C. Page. "Summer Nudging: Can Personalized Text Messages and Peer Mentor Outreach Increase College Going among Low-Income High School Graduates?" *Journal of Economic Behavior and Organization* 115 (July 2015): 144–60. doi:10.1016/j.jebo.2014.12.008.

Castleman, Benjamin L., Lindsay C. Page, and Korynn Schooley. "The Forgotten Summer: Does the Offer of College Counseling after High School Mitigate Summer Melt among College-Intending, Low-Income High School Graduates?" *Journal of Policy Analysis and Management* 33, no. 2 (March 1, 2014): 320–44. doi:10.1002/pam.21743.

Cohodes, Sarah R., and Joshua S. Goodman. "Merit Aid, College Quality, and College Completion: Massachusetts' Adams Scholarship as an In-Kind Subsidy." *American Economic Journal: Applied Economics* 6, no. 4 (October 1, 2014): 251–85. doi:10.1257/app.6.4.251.

Cowan, Benjamin W. "Testing for Educational Credit Constraints Using Heterogeneity in Individual Time Preferences." *Journal of Labor Economics* 34, no. 2 (January 19, 2016): 363–402. doi:10.1086/683644.

Deming, David, and Susan M. Dynarski. "College Aid." In *Targeting Investments in Children: Fighting Poverty When Resources Are Limited*, edited by Phillip B. Levine and David Zimmerman, 283–302. Chicago: University of Chicago Press, 2010.

DesJardins, Stephen L., Dennis A. Ahlburg, and Brian P. McCall. "An Integrated Model of Application, Admission, Enrollment, and Financial Aid." *Journal of Higher Education* 77, no. 3 (May 1, 2006): 381–429. doi:10.1080/00221546.2006.11778932.

Dillon, Eleanor Wiske, and Jeffrey Andrew Smith. "The Determinants of Mismatch between Students and Colleges." Working Paper. National Bureau of Economic Research, August 2013. doi:10.3386/w19286.

Do, Chau. "The Effects of Local Colleges on the Quality of College Attended." *Economics of Education Review* 23, no. 3 (June 2004): 249–57. doi:10.1016/j.econedurev.2003.05.001.

Domina, Thurston, and Joshua Saldana. "Does Raising the Bar Level the Playing Field?: Mathematics Curricular Intensification and Inequality in American High Schools, 1982–2004." *American Educational Research Journal* 49, no. 4 (August 1, 2012): 685–708. doi:10.3102/0002831211426347.

Ehrenberg, Ronald G. *Tuition Rising: Why College Costs so Much*. Cambridge, MA: Harvard University Press, 2002.

Engberg, Mark E. "Pervasive Inequality in the Stratification of Four-Year College Destinations." *Equity and Excellence in Education* 45, no. 4 (October 1, 2012): 575–95. doi:10.1080/10665684.2012.717486.

Espenshade, Thomas J., Chang Y. Chung, and Joan L. Walling. "Admission Preferences for Minority Students, Athletes, and Legacies at Elite Universities*." *Social Science Quarterly* 85, no. 5 (December 1, 2004): 1422–46. doi:10.1111/j.0038-4941.2004.00284.x.

Federal Reserve Bank of New York. "Quarterly Report on Household Debt and Credit." New York: Federal Reserve Bank of New York, 2015.

George-Jackson, Casey, and Melanie Gast. "Addressing Information Gaps: Disparities in Financial Awareness and Preparedness on the Road to College." *Journal of Student Financial Aid* 44, no. 3 (January 30, 2015). http://publications.nasfaa.org/jsfa/vol44/iss3/3.

Glancy, Emily, Mary Fulton, Lexi Anderson, Jennifer D. Zinth, Maria Millard, and Brady Delander. "Blueprint for College Readiness." Denver: Education Commission of the States, 2014. http://www.ecs.org/docs/ECSBlueprint.pdf.

Goodman, Joshua, Michael Hurwitz, and Jonathan Smith. "College Access, Initial College Choice and Degree Completion." Working Paper. Cambridge, MA: National Bureau of Economic Research, 2015. http://isites.harvard.edu/fs/docs/icb.topic1457676.files/CollegeTypeQuality_Goodman.pdf.

Griffith, Amanda L., and Donna S. Rothstein. "Can't Get There from Here: The Decision to Apply to a Selective College." *Economics of Education Review* 28, no. 5 (October 2009): 620–28. doi:10.1016/j.econedurev.2009.01.004.

Hastings, Justine S., Brigitte C. Madrian, and William L. Skimmyhorn. "Financial Literacy, Financial Education and Economic Outcomes." Working Paper. Washington, DC: National Bureau of Economic Research, 2012.

Hillman, Nicholas W. "Economic Diversity in Elite Higher Education: Do No-Loan Programs Impact Pell Enrollments?" *Journal of Higher Education* 84, no. 6 (November 1, 2013): 806–33. doi:10.1080/00221546.2013.11777311.

Hossler, Don, Mary Ziskin, Jacob P. K. Gross, Sooyeon Kim, and Osman Cekic. "Student Aid and Its Role in Encouraging Persistence." In *Higher Education: Handbook of The-*

ory and Research, edited by John C. Smart, 389–425. Dordrecht, NL: Springer, 2009. doi:10.1007/978-1-4020-9628-0_10.

Hoxby, Caroline. "The Changing Selectivity of American Colleges." *Journal of Economic Perspectives* 23, no. 4 (November 1, 2009): 95–118. doi:10.1257/089533009789994359.

Hoxby, Caroline, and Christopher Avery. "The Missing 'One-Offs': The Hidden Supply of High-Achieving, Low-Income Students." *Brookings Papers on Economic Activity* 2013, no. 1 (October 31, 2013): 1–65. doi:10.1353/eca.2013.0000.

Hoxby, Caroline, and Sarah Turner. "Informing Students about Their College Options: A Proposal for Broadening the Expanding College Opportunities Project." Washington, DC: Brookings Institution, 2013. https://www.brookings.edu/wp-content/uploads/2016/06/THP_HoxbyTurner_FINAL.pdf.

Institute for College Access and Success. "Student Debt and the Class of 2013." Oakland, CA: Institute for College Access and Success, 2014.

Joyce, Theodore J., Sean Crockett, David A. Jaeger, Onur Altindag, and Stephen D. O'Connell. "Does Classroom Time Matter? A Randomized Field Experiment of Hybrid and Traditional Lecture Formats in Economics." Working Paper. Washington, DC: National Bureau of Economic Research, March 2014. doi:10.3386/w20006.

Kahlenberg, Richard D. "Rewarding Strivers: Helping Low-Income Students Succeed in College." New York: Century Foundation Press, 2010.

Kanno, Yasuko, and Sara E. N. Kangas. "'I'm Not Going to Be, Like, for the AP': English Language Learners' Limited Access to Advanced College-Preparatory Courses in High School." *American Educational Research Journal* 51, no. 5 (October 1, 2014): 848–78. doi:10.3102/0002831214544716.

Kim, Matthew. "Early Decision and Financial Aid Competition among Need-Blind Colleges and Universities." *Journal of Public Economics* 94, no. 5–6 (June 2010): 410–20. doi:10.1016/j.jpubeco.2010.01.003.

Lovenheim, Michael F. "The Effect of Liquid Housing Wealth on College Enrollment." *Journal of Labor Economics* 29, no. 4 (October 1, 2011): 741–71. doi:10.1086/660775.

Lucas, Samuel R. "Effectively Maintained Inequality: Education Transitions, Track Mobility, and Social Background Effects." *American Journal of Sociology* 106, no. 6 (May 1, 2001): 1642–90. doi:10.1086/321300.

Lusardi, Annamaria, and Olivia S. Mitchell. "The Economic Importance of Financial Literacy: Theory and Evidence." *Journal of Economic Literature* 52, no. 1 (March 1, 2014): 5–44. doi:10.1257/jel.52.1.5.

Marr, Kelly A., Charles H. Mullin, and John J. Siegfried. "Undergraduate Financial Aid and Subsequent Alumni Giving Behavior." *Quarterly Review of Economics and Finance* 45, no. 1 (February 2005): 123–43. doi:10.1016/j.qref.2003.08.005.

McPherson, Michael S., and Morton O. Schapiro. *The Student Aid Game: Meeting Need and Rewarding Talent in American Higher Education*. Princeton, NJ: Princeton University Press, 1999.

MDRC. "Aid Like a Paycheck." Washington, DC: MDRC, 2013. http://www.mdrc.org/project/aid-paycheck.

Meer, Jonathan, and Harvey S. Rosen. "Does Generosity Beget Generosity? Alumni Giving and Undergraduate Financial Aid." *Economics of Education Review* 31, no. 6 (December 2012): 890–907. doi:10.1016/j.econedurev.2012.06.009.

National Association of College and University Business Officers. "2013 Tuition Discounting Study." 2014.

National Center for Education Statistics. Integrated Postsecondary Education Data System. https://nces.ed.gov/ipeds.

Niu, Sunny X. "Leaving Home State for College: Differences by Race/Ethnicity and Parental Education." *Research in Higher Education* 56, no. 4 (June 1, 2015): 325–59. doi: 10.1007/s11162-014-9350-y.

Ovink, Sarah M., and Demetra Kalogrides. "No Place like Home? Familism and Latino/a –White Differences in College Pathways." *Social Science Research* 52 (July 2015): 219–35. doi:10.1016/j.ssresearch.2014.12.018.

Page, Lindsay C., and Judith Scott-Clayton. "Improving College Access in the United States: Barriers and Policy Responses." *Economics of Education Review* 51 (April 2016): 4–22. doi:10.1016/j.econedurev.2016.02.009.

Perna, Laura W., Henry May, April Yee, Tafaya Ransom, Awilda Rodriguez, and Rachél Fester. "Unequal Access to Rigorous High School Curricula: An Exploration of the Opportunity to Benefit From the International Baccalaureate Diploma Programme (IBDP)." *Educational Policy* 29, no. 2 (March 1, 2015): 402–25. doi:10.1177/0895904813492383.

Radwin, David, Jennifer Wine, Peter Siegel, and Michael Bryan. "2011–12 National Postsecondary Student Aid Study (NPSAS:12): Student Financial Aid Estimates for 2011–12. First Look. NCES 2013-165." Washington, DC: National Center for Education Statistics, 2013. https://eric.ed.gov/?id=ED544184.

Rothstein, Jesse, and Cecilia Elena Rouse. "Constrained after College: Student Loans and Early-Career Occupational Choices." *Journal of Public Economics* 95, no. 1–2 (February 2011): 149–63. doi:10.1016/j.jpubeco.2010.09.015.

Scrivener, Susan, Michael J. Weiss, Alyssa Ratledge, Timothy Rudd, Colleen Sommo, and Hannah Fresques. "Doubling Graduation Rates: Three-Year Effects of CUNY's Accelerated Study in Associate Programs (ASAP) for Developmental Education Students." New York: MDRC, 2015, https://papers.ssrn.com/abstract=2571456.

Smith, Jonathan, Michael Hurwitz, and Jessica Howell. "Screening Mechanisms and Student Responses in the College Market." *Economics of Education Review* 44 (February 2015): 17–28. doi:10.1016/j.econedurev.2014.10.005.

Snyder, Thomas, Cristobal de Brey, and Sally Dillow. "Digest of Education Statistics 2014." Washington, DC: National Center for Education Statistics, Institute of Education Sciences, US Department of Education, 2016. https://nces.ed.gov/pubs2016/2016006.pdf.

Solórzano, Daniel G., and Armida Ornelas. "A Critical Race Analysis of Advanced Placement Classes: A Case of Educational Inequality." *Journal of Latinos and Education* 1, no. 4 (October 1, 2002): 215–29. doi:10.1207/S1532771XJLE0104_2.

Turley, Ruth N. López. "College Proximity: Mapping Access to Opportunity." *Sociology of Education* 82, no. 2 (April 1, 2009): 126–46. doi:10.1177/003804070908200202.

Willis, Lauren E. "Evidence and Ideology in Assessing the Effectiveness of Financial Literacy Education." *San Diego Law Review* 46 (2009): 415.

Woo, Jennie H. "Degrees of Debt: Student Borrowing and Loan Repayment of Bachelor's Degree Recipients 1 Year after Graduating, 1994, 2001, and 2009. Stats in Brief. NCES 2014-011." Washington, DC: National Center for Education Statistics, 2013. https://eric.ed.gov/?id=ED544217.

Xu, Di, and Shanna S. Jaggars. "Performance Gaps between Online and Face-to-Face Courses: Differences across Types of Students and Academic Subject Areas." *Journal of Higher Education* 85, no. 5 (September 1, 2014): 633–59. doi:10.1080/00221546.2014.11777343.

Xu, Di, and Shanna Smith Jaggars. "The Impact of Online Learning on Students' Course Outcomes: Evidence from a Large Community and Technical College System." *Economics of Education Review* 37 (December 2013): 46–57. doi:10.1016/j.econedurev.2013.08.001.

REACTION
Roger Drake

Nicholas W. Hillman and Valerie Crespín-Trujillo have contributed greatly to the body of research available to independent college and university presidents as we navigate the rapidly changing landscape of higher education. The authors declare that the singular focus of their chapter is the independent sector pricing model and its implications for college access. Their work is timely, as this is the topic that has been keeping independent college presidents awake at night for some time and is likely to continue to do so over the next decade.

While the authors have narrowed their focus to the independent sector, tremendous variations remain between institutions within that grouping. The independent sector is made up of both highly selective and open-admissions institutions, mission-driven and for-profit institutions, religious-affiliated and secular institutions, rural and urban institutions, liberal arts and technical institutions, and institutions with international reputations along with those that are only known within a relatively small radius. Institutions positioned at varying points along each of these continua face somewhat different challenges to accessibility and affordability while possessing vastly different assets that may be leveraged to provide solutions.

The authors took a pragmatic approach to their recommendations. Many colleges have ongoing initiatives to reduce the access gap, although every college could likely do more. Other researchers have suggested far bolder strategies that are targeted at the state and national level, providing fewer actionable items to be undertaken at the campus level. For instance, Stacy Dickert-Conlin and Ross Rubenstein[1] proposed somewhat ambitious recommendations for improving access for this sector. They suggested providing performance-based incentives to institutions that serve disadvantaged groups, capping subsidies for the wealthy institutions, pricing tuition at the "real cost" of instruction, diverting revenue from the affluent toward service for the disadvantaged, and strengthening the states' roles in higher education. While one could build a case that such systemic, dramatic change is necessary to solve the problem of access and affordability, Hillman and Crespín-Trujillo give us actionable direction that we can employ today.

Whether one sees the solution to access and affordability as residing at the national, state, or local level, one must recognize the unfortunate legislative trends in higher education over the past three decades. With our nation's tendency to view higher education as a private good rather than public, and the consequential shift toward the individual bearing a greater share of the cost, the access gap for underrepresented groups has widened.[2] The shift from need-based aid to merit-based aid, both at the state and institutional level, has posed a significant obstacle to access and affordability for lower socioeconomic groups.[3]

William Bowen, Martin Kurzweil, Eugene Tobin, and Susanne Pichler[4] suggest there is an unfortunate tension between access and excellence in higher education. As the accreditation process and other players in the accountability regime demand improvements in retention, completion, and job placement, further strain is placed on the institution's mission-driven need to close the access and affordability gap.

Moody's Global Credit Research[5] forecasts that many nonselective, rural, religious affiliated, enrollment-dependent colleges will fail over the next decade as budget deficits become unsustainable. Again, the unfortunate tension between access for lower socioeconomic groups and many institutions' vital need to enroll students with the ability to pay poses a great challenge.

The authors propose research-based "best practices" that may increase the probability of success in reducing the access and affordability gap. Their recommendations are within the areas of precollege preparation efforts, changes to college admissions policies, campus financial aid, and student mobility.

Precollege preparation best practices such as high-touch messaging, which provides simple and timely information about cost and process, are likely in place at most institutions of higher education. However, the authors prudently suggest that these strategies, when leveraged to their maximum benefit, may make the most progress on reducing barriers to enrollment. At the same time, prior research suggests there are extreme differences in cultural capital that lead to educational stratification and the unintended consequence of social reproduction.[6]

The authors suggest that changes in the admissions process could allow for progress to reduce the accessibility gap. Waiving application fees, discontinuing the requirement of essays, and de-emphasizing early admissions practices could improve access for disadvantaged students. However, each of these strategies may also have an influence on enrollment numbers and the academic preparedness of the entering class.

The recommendations in the area of campus financial aid may provide less practical solutions for the practitioner than the authors' other suggestions. While it would certainly prove to reduce the barrier to access, "replacing loans with grants" is far easier said than done. For cash-strapped, mission-driven institutions, this is not a financially viable option for most. The authors' suggestions to deliver timely information and offer personalized support can and should be optimized on all college campuses.

In the area of student mobility, the authors recommend removing transportation and child-care barriers. To the extent it is economically feasible, it would likely have a positive influence on improving the gap in access. The authors' recommendation of utilizing alumni networks and community-based organizations is insightful, and if successfully executed may have a positive impact on other functions of the organization, such as alumni involvement and advancement as it serves its primary purpose of improving access.

Underrepresented groups and low socioeconomic status students are being educated in greater numbers today than at any time in our history. However, the rate of increase for these disadvantaged groups is less than the rate of increase for more affluent students.[7] As many independent institutions continue to struggle to make their business models work, the unfortunate tension between the mission-driven desire to enroll disadvantaged students and the fiscal need to enroll students with the ability to pay for an education becomes even more tenuous. Hillman and Crispin-Trujillo present some actionable strategies that, when fully deployed, could work in the margins to improve access for underrepresented and disadvantaged students.

NOTES

1. Dickert-Conlin and Rubenstein, eds., *Economic Inequality and Higher Education.*
2. Ross et al., "Higher Education."
3. Griffith, "Keeping Up with the Joneses."
4. Bowen et al., *Equity and Excellence.*
5. Moody's Global Credit Research, "College Consolidations."
6. Bourdieu and Passeron, *Reproduction in Education.*
7. Dickert-Conlin and Rubenstein, *Economic Inequality.*

REFERENCES

Bourdieu, Pierre, and Jean-Claude Passeron. *Reproduction in Education, Society and Culture.* Vol. 4. Newberry Park, CA: Sage, 1990.
Bowen, William G., Martin A. Kurzweil, Eugene M. Tobin, and Susanne C. Prichler. *Equity and Excellence in American Higher Education.* Charlottesville: University of Virginia Press, 2006.
Dickert-Conlin, Stacy, and Ross Rubenstein, eds. *Economic Inequality and Higher Education: Access, Persistence, and Success.* New York: Russell Sage Foundation, 2007.

Griffith, Amanda L. "Keeping Up with the Joneses: Institutional Changes Following the Adoption of a Merit Aid Policy." *Economics of Education Review* 30, no. 5 (October 2011): 1022–33. Special issue on education and health. doi:10.1016/j.econedurev.2011.05.003.

Moody's Global Credit Research. "College Consolidations and Closures Are Credit Positive in an Increasingly Competitive Sector." Alactra Store, March 9, 2015. http://www.alacrastore.com/moodys-credit-research/College-Consolidations-and-Closures-Are-Credit-Positive-in-an-Increasingly-Competitive-Sector-PBM_PBM179715. Accessed April 16, 2017.

Ross, Terris, Grace Kena, Amy Rathbun, Angelina Kewal Ramani, Jijun Zhang, Paul Kristapovich, and Eileen Manning. "Higher Education: Gaps in Access and Persistence Study. Statistical Analysis Report. NCES 2012-046." Washington, DC: National Center for Education Statistics, August 2012. https://eric.ed.gov/?id=ED534691.

3

Assessment of Student Learning Outcomes

JILLIAN KINZIE AND CYNTHIA A. COGSWELL

High-quality learning must be a priority for all undergraduate students. Educators and employers alike agree that the kind of education college students need for success in work, democratic citizenship, and life in the twenty-first century demands greater emphasis on a range of student learning outcomes and competencies.[1] Yet, there remains persistent concern that students are not learning enough, and employers assert that graduates lack preparedness on a wide range of skills and knowledge areas.[2] Even more, assessment experts and higher education scholars who study student learning agree on the importance and the difficulty of measuring student learning.[3] To ensure essential learning outcomes for college graduates, higher education must focus with greater intensity on student learning.

The demands associated with student learning outcomes are significant for all colleges and universities. However, the private, independent college sector faces unique challenges and concerns on this topic. First, the assertion of a high-quality learning experience as the hallmark of the independent sector[4] comes with the expectation to demonstrate evidence of this claim. Second, the press for evidence of student learning is perhaps greatest for institutions most threatened by current concerns about college affordability. In this context, independent colleges and universities are especially challenged to show their value or, to put it bluntly, the return on an investment in a private college education. This chapter presents an overview of student learning outcomes assessment, research on student learning, and assessment practices in the independent college sector, focusing on extant research and practice. The chapter closes with the identification of strengths and challenges for student learning outcomes assessment and recommendations for the independent sector.

Defining Student Learning Outcomes and the Current Context

The past three decades of the assessment movement have placed significant emphasis on student outcomes, including measures of student retention, graduation, grade point average, and cognitive outcomes, or student learning. While all these measures related to student success are important, over the last ten years attention to learning outcomes has particularly increased. For the purposes of this discussion, it is useful to distinguish "student outcomes" from "student learning outcomes." The general category of *student outcomes* refers to aggregate statistics on groups of students, such as retention, graduation rates, and employment data for a graduating class. These outcomes are useful institutional indicators that attempt to measure comparative institutional performance, and sometimes serve as proxies for learning.[5] *Student learning outcomes* (SLOs) represent the broad skills and knowledge that students are expected to attain as a result of engaging in specific educational experiences.[6] They are statements of what students should gain from a specific lesson, course, program, experience, or degree, and reflect growth or change in the students themselves due to their college experience. Learning outcomes dwell at a variety of levels within an institution, including institution, degree, program, and course level—specific to the academic major and sweeping across general education requirements and sometimes the co-curriculum.

Developing statements of expected SLOs is a critical aspect of assessment. Institutional learning outcomes or competencies are typically broad statements about institutionwide learning goals. According to the National Institute for Learning Outcomes Assessment (NILOA) survey of provosts, 84 percent of institutions have stated learning outcomes.[7] Denison University, for example, identified 13 core undergraduate student outcomes, including Civic Life, Global Perspective, and Oral Communications, among others, derived from the institutional mission and general education requirements and developed by a committee of faculty and student affairs staff.[8] The explication of student outcomes and the collection of evidence to demonstrate student attainment was part of Denison's efforts to assess and document these core competencies and prove the "Denison Difference."

Compared to institution-level learning outcomes, course- and program-level learning outcomes are more specific and focus on concise written statements using action verbs, like *identify, solve,* and *evaluate,* to indicate the knowledge, skills, and values students will achieve upon completing a course or degree program.[9] St. Ambrose University's comprehensive assessment plan emphasizes the importance of external benchmarks, curriculum maps, aligning outcomes with curricular requirements, and scheduling so that all SLOs are assessed at least twice every five years.[10] St. Ambrose faculty are advised to state learning outcomes clearly rather than in the language of experts, focus on students instead of what the course or instructor intends to do, and be specific about the level of knowledge expected in the course, for example, "Demonstrate a variety of critical methods of biblical interpretation" and "Identify cultural differences, similarities, and stereotypes." Also noteworthy in the St. Ambrose example is the attention to ensuring alignment between desired outcomes at the institution and department and course levels. The alignment of learning outcomes is key to maximizing student learning and increasing the likelihood that what colleges and universities expect students to learn is what students can actually do upon completion of their course of study.[11] Interestingly, the NILOA survey indicates that more private, baccalaureate institutions reported alignment of institutional and departmental outcomes than institutions that grant doctoral, master, or associate degrees.[12]

Although attention to SLOs has been a persistent theme at most institutions, the work has tended to exist primarily at course-level learning and in evaluating what individual students know after completing a course. That said, more institutions are adopting assessment approaches that represent the accumulation of learning in the major assessed via a culminating experience, including a senior project, portfolio, capstone, or comprehensive exam.[13] However, for the most part, the assurance of student learning is something that is simply certified through the accumulation of a specified number of credit hours, an acceptable GPA, and the conferral of a degree. Most institutions rely on credits accumulated despite the fact that the Carnegie Unit, or the credit hour, "was never intended to function as a measure of what students learned."[14] Yet, the expansion of more explicit demands from accreditors for colleges and universities to demonstrate and assure student learning, and growing out of the national conversation on accountability instigated by the Spellings Commission, the assurance of student learning has become a wider, institution-level concern,[15] and something that all colleges and universities must address.

As attention to SLOs has intensified over the past decade, institutional SLO assessment activities have also increased across all colleges and universities. As the NILOA survey indicates, most higher education institutions now have explicit statements about undergraduate learning outcomes and have implemented at least five forms of institution-level assessments of student learning, with the most popular being national student surveys, rubrics, portfolios, capstones, classroom-based assessments, and general tests of knowledge and skills.[16] Survey results also reveal a couple noteworthy differences in assessment practices between private and public institutions. Private institutions, including many of the Council of Independent Colleges (CIC) member institutions, for instance, are significantly more likely than public institutions to take advantage of portfolios, capstone projects or courses, and information from alumni. In addition, while the impetus for assessing student learning for all colleges and universities was clearly accreditation and institutional improvement, independent colleges and universities reported far less external pressure to assess student learning (i.e., state or federal mandates) than their public counterparts. Generally, private institutions were compelled to assess student learning to show value and for institutional improvement, and to demonstrate learning outcomes through assessment activities close to the academic program and student work.

Research on Student Learning Outcomes in Higher Education Scholarship

Student learning is, of course, a central focus of higher education scholarship. Research documenting the influence of college on student learning is expansive, covering the acquisition of subject matter knowledge and academic skills generally thought to be related to the curriculum or academic program as well as general cognitive development and intellectual skills that are broadly associated with the undergraduate experience, including learning in and out of the classroom.[17] Findings from Pascarella and Terenzini's[18] synthesis of research on learning outcomes is by far the most extensive compendium of research and too comprehensive to summarize here. However, it lays the foundation for SLO assessment work in that it identifies key college learning outcomes as well as the educational practices and experiences that influence them.

Pascarella and Terenzini's[19] syntheses also reveal three conclusions about student learning salient to the discussion of learning outcomes assessment in the independent sector:

- The net effects of college attendance on learning are positive. However, it is difficult to estimate the effect of institutional classifications, including private or independent colleges, from other institutional types. On a related note, because the majority of institutions have important subenvironments with more immediate impacts on individual students, most of the variability in impacts is *within colleges.*

- Much of the evidence about learning in college depends on a combination of what the institution sets up for students in terms of educational experiences and environments, effective instructional practice, and the quality of student effort in making use of the range of learning opportunities provided by the institution.
- Most of the effects of college are related to how specific student characteristics interact with particular college experiences to influence outcomes. In other words, the effects of college on student learning are largely conditional, in that certain student subpopulations are affected to a greater or lesser extent by the program or experience in question.

These three conclusions have implications for the study and assessment of learning outcomes in the independent sector. First, broad institutional classifications tell us little about between-institution effects on student learning, suggesting the challenge of isolating the effects of private, independent institutions on student learning. Second, many of the practices that make a difference for student learning, such as active learning, teaching clarity and organization, and environments that encourage academic engagement and support, among others, can be intentionally designed, manipulated, and even learned. Pascarella and colleagues'[20] longitudinal analyses of the net effects of liberal arts colleges reinforce this point in their central finding that students who attended liberal arts colleges are more likely to encounter good teaching and supportive institutional practices and that this combination of teaching and institutional conditions is associated with greater value-added gains on a variety of desirable outcomes. This suggests the value in studying the influence of particular educational practices and environmental conditions within and among independent colleges on desired learning outcomes and refining interventions based on findings. Third, the conditional effects of college suggest the importance of studying student subpopulations within and among independent colleges to uncover differences in student experiences and outcomes based on race, gender, and socioeconomic status and to examine the extent to which student subpopulations derive different learning benefits from instructional approaches such as collaborative learning, peer learning support, and supplemental instruction.

Overall, research about student learning in the independent college sector supports Astin's[21] conclusion that the undergraduate experience at small, residential, liberal arts colleges promotes cognitive growth, the development of solid values, and a high rate of degree completion. However, a central point of Astin's work is that institutional type and structure are not direct causal factors for student outcomes, including learning. The important lesson is that institutional structures create environmental circumstances, including peer interactions and scholarly orientation, that affect student outcomes.

In a longitudinal study of student learning in college, Arum and Roksa[22] concluded that just less than half of students showed no statistically significant improvement in their critical thinking skills during the first year and a half of college, and even after four years of college, students on average showed limited learning gains.[23] Arum and Roksa also found that only 42 percent of the students in the sample reported reading more than 40 pages per week in their courses and wrote papers of more than 20 pages in the semester, and these two course-related practices contributed to increases in critical thinking. Interestingly, on these two instructional practices, 68 percent of students in more selective colleges and universities reported experiences with both indices in contrast to 37 percent in less selective colleges and universities. Although the sobering conclusion of this study is that postsecondary education has little effect on student learning, the research emphasizes the importance of studying learning growth using longitudinal data, and the need to develop an evidence-based picture of student learning in college to identify fine-grained generalizations about student learning and the instructional practices that could make a difference.

Another aspect of student learning particularly relevant to the independent college sector is research about student-faculty interaction and instructional practices. As Astin[24] asserts and more recent findings from the National Survey of Student Engagement (NSSE) affirm,[25] the quality of interaction between faculty and students and the overall engagement in effective educational practices influence student learning. Instructional practices, including teaching clarity and organization, active learning, cooperative learning, and outside-the-classroom interactions with faculty also matter to student learning.[26] NSSE results, and those of its companion instrument, the Faculty Survey of Student Engagement (FSSE), also associate higher levels of student engagement in learning and students' experiences in deep learning at institutions where faculty report using a wider range of engaging teaching practices.[27] For example, when faculty members emphasize educational practices such as writing, active and collaborative learning, or using diverse perspectives to understand issues, students are more likely to engage in these activities.[28]

Studies of instructional practices and the impact on student learning suggest the positive influence of instruction, with the advantage going to liberal arts colleges versus both research universities and regional institutions Yet, broad surveys of faculty teaching practice suggest there is actually little variety in approaches, with lecture as the primary instructional method, even at small private colleges.[29] This finding is concerning, given the limited effectiveness of lectures in helping students learn and gain and demonstrate skills in applying knowledge to new situations, something employers expect graduates to do.[30] To advance student learning at all institutional types, Fink[31] recommends that instructors create "significant learning experiences," occasions in which students engage deeply in a wider range of learning acts, including experiential, application, and collaborative learning, which connect what is learned in courses to students' lives.

A noteworthy finding from student engagement research that has been elaborated upon in several research publications produced by the Association for American Colleges and Universities (AAC&U), is the positive influence of participating in "high-impact educational practices" (HIEPs) on a range of desirable outcomes, including persistence, GPA, higher-order learning, and overall student engagement and learning.[32] Several HIEPs, including undergraduate research and service learning, have a fairly robust literature base, including studies by control and institutional type and by student population.[33] Brownell and Swaner's[34] summary of peer-reviewed published studies on five high-impact practices—first-year seminar, undergraduate research, learning communities, service-learning, and capstone experiences—lends important foundational research to recent findings of the positive benefits of HIEPs to student learning. Gonyea and Kinzie[35] summarized that private institution students participated in more high-impact practices than did public institution students, particularly at the senior level. Specifically, first-year students attending private institutions were more likely to participate in service learning—and a greater percentage of them participated in at least one HIEP—and senior students were more likely to participate in two or more HIEPs during their college careers.

Student learning outcomes were also the subject of the Wabash National Study of Liberal Arts Education (WNSLAE), a large-scale multi-institutional, multi-method study that involved nearly 20,000 students. Using a pre-test/

post-test design, WNSLAE tested students on six broad outcomes of liberal education—critical thinking and problem solving, inclination to inquire and orientation toward lifelong learning, intercultural effectiveness, leadership, moral reasoning, and personal well-being, and found evidence of positive connections between students' experiences, including measures of engagement from NSSE, and their learning and development.[36] Deep approaches to learning—for example, coursework that emphasizes higher-order cognitive tasks such as synthesis and evaluation, ask students to integrate diverse perspectives and ideas from different courses and encourages reflective learning—positively affected the development of moral reasoning in first-year students.[37] Meaningful discussions with faculty and peers outside of the classroom during the first year of college stimulated a desire to engage in cognitive activities.[38] The WNSLAE studies show how core elements of liberal education connect to outcomes such as intercultural effectiveness, lifelong learning, psychological well-being, and socially responsible leadership.[39] However, the findings also expose areas for improvement in student learning.[40] Some students declined across the same skills, and what causes greater concern is that the majority of seniors actually graduate with less academic motivation and openness to diversity than when they started.

Although learning outcomes assessment activity has increased among colleges and universities, after three decades of assessment work in higher education, it seems that too little productive use has been made of the SLO data.[41] Specifically, while campus improvements have been associated with assessment, it is less common for institutions to assess the impact of the change, or to "close the loop" to determine the extent to which student learning and success has improved, or to fully document findings from the assessment cycle.[42] It is even more unusual for learning outcomes or the impact of an intervention based on assessment results to be studied in a systematic way, or for results to be examined for their contribution to higher education scholarship.

Student Learning Outcomes Assessment: Practice in the Independent College Sector

All institutions in the independent sector have invested in SLO assessments, and some have excelled at the practice. Of special note is the leadership of the Council of Independent Colleges (CIC) to help member institutions assess and improve the quality of education on their campuses.[43]

The Practice of Student Learning Assessment and Improvement

Multiple CIC-sponsored initiatives have helped member colleges respond to calls for evidence of student learning, transparency, and accountability.[44] Notably, CIC campuses were early participants in NSSE to assess educational quality and in the use of a standardized test—the Collegiate Learning Assessment (CLA)—as a means to gauge and improve learning. More recently, about 25 CIC campuses joined together to work with Lumina Foundation's Degree Qualifications Profile (DQP), a learning-centered framework that illustrates how students should be expected to perform across five areas of learning at progressively more challenging degree levels, for use in improving SLOs and assessment and increasing student success. These projects have advanced CIC member efforts to assess, to be transparent, and to document the quality of academic experiences and the resulting improvements in student learning. The strong participation of institutions in various learning outcome projects suggests a keen interest in enhancing assessment practice.

CIC's report on the activities of 40 institutions in the Engaging Evidence Consortium highlights essential lessons for assessment practice in the independent sector.[45] For example, Cedarville University's progress in their project to assess general education learning outcomes was attributed to careful planning regarding the use of standardized tests and embedded assessments and the collection of sufficient data to draw conclusions about learning and implications for changes in the general education curriculum. Two findings about the organization of assessment practice emerged from the work of several institutions. The first lesson specified the importance of identifying "end users"—specifically, who on campus is expected to make use of assessment results—and involving them in the assessment project early, and the need to identify a point person in information technology to work through the technology needs and solutions for collecting data, including digital artifacts. The *Engaging Evidence* report illustrates the value of studying assessment practice and the potential that collective work has for enriching understandings of the effect of assessment and interventions on student learning.

Independent colleges have also been exemplary in the assessment of student learning. St. Olaf College, an independent college in Minnesota, was one of four institutions to receive the national Council for Higher Education Accreditation (CHEA) award for "Outstanding Institutional Practice in Student Learning Outcomes." In 2010, it was the first liberal arts institution to be so recognized. Evidence concerning collegewide SLOs, such as critical thinking, effective writing, quantitative reasoning, and research proficiency is gathered every year at St. Olaf.[46] The college collects a mix of direct evidence concerning students' knowledge, proficiencies, and values, and indirect evidence concerning students' experiences, perceptions, and attitudes by using measuring tools that include an alumni survey, the CLA, NSSE, Research Practices Survey (RPS), and the St. Olaf Learning Goals Questionnaire (LGQ).[47] Evidence of students' knowledge, proficiencies, and learning experiences are examined to sustain what is working and to strengthen what needs to be improved. Most important, St. Olaf worked extensively to make learning outcomes practice meaningful to faculty and staff, and to ensure that everyone understood assessment to be inquiry in support of student learning, not something required for accountability.

California Lutheran University was recognized by NILOA for its centralized repository that provides assessment information in one location, including the presentation of direct and indirect evidence of student learning organized around eight institutional SLOs.[48] Evidence of the impact of program reviews—for example, in sociology, the re-envisioning of program learning outcomes are documented, including greater emphasis on ethical judgment and understanding of identity, and additional assignments related to the consumption and production of research and the identification of signature assignments in key sequences.

Although some general lessons about assessment practice can be drawn across all institutions, the work differs between large and small schools. Large institutions with decentralized structures and unique priorities and values are likely to have departments and programs that disagree on the nature and goals of undergraduate education and approaches to assessment. As a result, these institutions have separate and distinct assessment organizations and little central coordination.[49] In contrast, smaller institutions organize assessment as a centralized function, involving faculty and other units from across the campus that are more likely to agree about undergraduate learning outcomes. The sheer difference in institutional size makes, for example, mapping where learning outcomes are introduced, reinforced, and assessed much more complex at large institutions than at small.[50] In a case study of the conditions that support assessment practice within student affairs divisions at three small col-

leges and universities, Beau Seagraves and Laura Dean[51] found that the size of
an institution influences the organization of assessment efforts because smaller
institutions have limited resources and staffing to conduct assessment. Smaller
size allowed for more informal conversations and greater sharing of assessment
responsibilities because most professionals wore multiple hats, worked collaboratively, and sat on committees together. Their study also identified that assessment was promoted through support from senior student affairs leadership,
informal conversations around assessment, clear expectations, an understanding
of the value of assessment as a means to improve, and a collegial atmosphere
that welcomed both positive and negative results. Collaborative approaches to
assessment are more naturally found in small institutions.

Finally, the central principle of assessment practice is the use of SLO results
to improve educational quality. Evidence of student learning has great potential
to inform improvements to the curriculum; course offerings, content, assignments, and instructional practice; and co-curricular experiences and learning
support programs. For example, Harvey Mudd College faculty members' review of student writing outcome results, including capstone project writing
assessments and NSSE Writing Module results, informed the establishment of
a new required Introduction to Academic Writing (Writ 1) course and faculty
workshops to enhance instructional practices to increase students' application
of writing skills across the disciplines.[52] Prior to teaching Writ 1, faculty members participate in a week-long intensive workshop to focus on current composition theory and pedagogy and to develop strategies for helping students apply
the skills taught in Writ 1 to writing in various disciplines. Early evidence of
the impact of Writ 1 and changes in instructional practice show that first-year
students and seniors experience more writing assignments that ask them to use
evidence and reasoning to argue a position, to explain the meaning of numeri-
cal and statistical data, and to write in the style and format of a specific field—
all outcomes stressed in Writ 1. When learning outcomes results are combined
with indirect evidence—for example, of student engagement in effective educational practice—there is increased capacity for using diagnostic information
to inform improvement.[53] Again, independent colleges have recent experience
working collectively to use evidence to improve and may have an advantage
in this assessment goal because of institutional size and faculty commitment
to teaching. However, the use of evidence for improvement has proven to be
a challenging phase of the assessment process that demands greater attention
from all colleges and universities.

Transparency of Outcomes

The public reporting of institutional activities and evidence related to student academic attainment is now an expectation for colleges and universities.[54] Institutions have been challenged to balance the demands of public interest and institutional autonomy with the applications of transparency efforts and the tricky aspects of making data public. Institutional member organizations have spearheaded some of the efforts. In the independent sector, the National Association of Independent Colleges and Universities (NAICU) initiated the University and College Accountability Network (U-CAN) and another effort in cooperation with the CIC, Building Blocks to 2020, which is a searchable web database of reports on hundreds of programs to expand access and ensure degree completion at private colleges and universities.

Transparency of SLOs is not simply to make information available, or even public. Rather, transparency is meaningfully communicating actionable information to various internal and external audiences to those who can use it. In the case of learning outcomes assessment, these are campus partners and end users: faculty, students, committees, provosts, deans, department chairs, budget officers, president, members of governing boards, and external groups, including prospective students, legislators, and the general public.[55] St. Olaf College has been a leader in transparency, in particular to external audiences, as demonstrated in the presentation of evidence of collegewide SLOs on a website dedicated to outcomes. The clearly titled web page, "Outcomes of a St. Olaf Education," presents evidence of retention and graduation rates, first destination data on recent graduates, visually interesting data displays of SLOs, graduate and professional school outcomes, alumni profiles, and employment outcomes.[56] Being transparent about student outcomes in language that is understandable and visually attractive to external audiences can help demonstrate the value and return on investment of independent institutions.

Enhanced transparency is related to the structure of assessment, including the extent to which collaboration, information exchange, and training are supported. Linda Krzykowski and Kevin Kinser[57] found that campuses were more transparent when they "had one structure that provided oversight for faculty performing assessment (the provost's office or a governance structure that required assessment reports) and a separate one that trained faculty on assessment practices as well as explained and encouraged assessment." For example, Juniata College has a Center for the Scholarship of Teaching and Learning, which supports course-level assessment activities focusing on questions of immediate interest to faculty and supports assessment professional development, while a faculty committee, the Academic Planning and Assessment Committee, reviews and provides feedback on program assessment plans and results.[58]

Student Learning Outcomes Strengths and Challenges at CIC Institutions

The current emphasis on SLOs and educational effectiveness must be addressed by all colleges and universities, but nowhere is this more important than among CIC institutions that claim a strong commitment to undergraduate teaching and learning. This strong commitment, combined with evidence of high-quality learning experiences and outcomes from research and institutional assessment efforts, could well position independent sector institutions to confidently demonstrate their value. Independent sector institutions may also be helped by their practical size to have more educators with firsthand knowledge of students' educational gains and to have assessment approaches in place, including portfolios, capstones, and comprehensive exams that highlight authentic forms of evidence that are not "add-on" or exoskeletal forms of assessment. By demonstrating learning outcomes through assessment activities that are close to the academic program and student work versus in the form of standardized tests, small private institutions have greater chances for engaging faculty in assessment practice and to connect to inquiry into student learning, or more formally in the Scholarship of Teaching (SoTL).

CIC member institutions may also have an advantage due to their reasonable number of disciplinary fields, which enable them to enact the kind of faculty-led, discipline-specific learning outcomes work that Richard Arum, Amanda Cook, and Josipa Roksa[59] advocate. These outcomes aid in the development of appropriate learning outcomes and in facilitating the development of assessment approaches to measure those outcomes. Bringing faculty together in disciplines and departments for consensus-driven discussions about their priorities for student learning, including essential twenty-first-century competencies, conceptual knowledge, and practices that students in their disciplines should develop in college is an important step not only to engage more faculty in assessment but also to establish authentic assessment approaches embedded in programs and courses. In addition, as Richard Shavelson and Arum and colleagues[60] suggest, faculty members' collective discipline-specific insights about learning outcomes are also more likely to lead to granular and diagnostic assessment data that informs improvements to curriculum, learning processes, and, ultimately, student learning. Learning outcomes initiatives at independent sector institutions have already made great strides in terms of collecting and acting on evidence through consortium efforts, including those sponsored by CIC and the Teagle Foundation; discipline-specific outcomes assessment discussions could be the next phase of this kind of consortium work.

At the same time, independent sector institutions face challenges associated with SLO assessments. Time and resources are certainly hurdles to engaging in assessment. More specifically, comprehensive assessment work demands significant administrative leadership, campus coordination, committees, and institutional research support. Institutions with small or no institutional research offices, for example, may struggle to organize data collection efforts, and those without faculty involvement and leadership for assessment may have difficulty getting work started, or acting on results suggesting improvement. This work is even more difficult at small institutions, where faculty have high teaching loads and there is limited leadership for assessment. Even when evidence is assembled, institutions may be challenged to interpret and communicate results to a range of audiences and to tell the story of student learning in ways that are meaningful and transparent.

Strategies to Advance Student Learning Outcomes Assessment in CIC Colleges and Universities

Like all institutions, assessment practices at independent institutions are motivated by external demands, particularly accreditation.[61] Yet, accreditation standards for SLOs are a minimum,[62] and while external demands are motivating, the lack of challenge they provide prompts us to implore the CIC sector to become a leader in this area. Independent colleges and universities have claimed their differentiating capacity to provide high quality education and transferable skills. Given that learning outcomes are a foundational part of the CIC identity, the learning outcomes movement is one that the private institutions should lead, celebrate, embrace, and, most important, use the strong evidence assembled for accreditation and learning outcomes to represent the value of an independent college education.

The practice of assessing SLOs demands greater intentionality and wider involvement of educators on campus, including student affairs staff, students, and higher education scholars. The involvement of a variety of stakeholders in assessing learning outcomes, offering advice on the design of studies, and interpreting findings and decisions about taking action on results is critical to making results more meaningful and useful to improving educational effectiveness and informing higher education scholarship. The involvement of student researchers in assessment proved beneficial to accomplishing assessment at Franklin Pierce University,[63] and at St. Olaf the involvement of more faculty and students in a well-developed faculty governance approach to assessment helped establish a strong culture of assessment.[64] Assessment systems built to satisfy accreditation requirements can be short-lived, but a culture based on faculty involvement and shared values and principles is more likely to be sustained.[65]

As several of the CIC-supported consortium projects (i.e., Engaging Evidence) demonstrate, coordinated inquiry efforts and funding have advanced assessment in the sector and have been successful drivers of change and transparency of outcomes. However, the assessment of SLOs would benefit from greater involvement and collaboration among similar groups and organizations including the CIC, educational leaders, and higher education scholars. Partnering organizations, institutions, funders, and scholars can provide incentives for working on SLOs. Possible strategies include the following:

- Creating a cohort structure where individuals in similar roles or disciplinary fields at different institutions can discuss and study strategies for creating and improving SLOs;
- Funding opportunities for scholars and practitioners to study efforts associated with SLOs;
- Creating a SLO improvement competition to incentivize "closing the loop" or ongoing improvement, and systematically examine what works.

Banding together to build assessment capacity and make the case for independent colleges as institutions that assure student learning is vital. In addition, as external agencies—including the federal government—ruminate on how to measure what students gain from college, along with the imminent update to the Higher Education Opportunity Act, we are likely to see the imposition of mandates and standardization in the reporting of SLOs. Higher education organizations and scholars will need to collaborate to present intrinsic action and study the effect of any mandates.

Transparency requires the articulation of SLOs, measurement, and public disclosure of results. Posting results to a website is a transparent action, but a true commitment to outcomes requires reflection on the information collected. Reflective accountability, as suggested by McCormick,[66] is a strategy for assessing the achievement of the institution's educational mission "with an eye toward improvement. In this sense, the key 'constituent' of reflective accountability is the institution's mission itself, with mission-relevant assessment for improvement as a natural component of the professional responsibility of institutional leadership." For example, while St. Olaf makes its outcomes evidence publicly accessible, its "Assessments of Student Learning" web page includes links to reports that exemplify thoughtful reflection by faculty, staff, and students about fulfilling the institution's mission and assuring that students achieve learning outcomes.[67] Reflective transparency is a conscious institutional process for improvement, and an ongoing effort.

Finally, educators in the independent sector could partner with higher education scholars to address the student learning imperative. Leaders in the independent college sector and higher education scholars could jointly study SLOs by conducting longitudinal analysis of learning gains and review the effectiveness of educational practices that faculty are interested in implementing. Additional explorations on the relationship between organizational theory and assessment practice, and the examination of factors associated with taking action on assessment results, would offer significant advances in the field about using evidence to improve. Finally, the study of the experiences of student subpopulations within and among independent colleges and the impact of specific instructional approaches and educational experiences among different student subpopulations is critical to SLO research and practice. The topic of SLOs needs further scholarly study, and collaboration could help foster concerted action.

Conclusion: Student Learning Outcomes and the Independent Sector

Practitioners and scholars of higher education have too infrequently been on the same page when it comes to student learning. Yet, higher education has entered an era of unprecedented interest in accountability, and accountability is increasingly based on institutional evidence. By making assessment results public, the institution fulfills its obligation to address both the explicit requirements of accreditors and current expectations for transparency. More important, improving quality in undergraduate education in order to foster learning and success for all students is a vital imperative for US higher education. The opportunity this pressure presents to scholars and educators working in the independent sector is vital for improving the work that colleges and universities set out to do—to help students learn.

Evidence of SLOs must be put to more intentional uses to improve student learning and educational effectiveness. However, the assessment of student learning should not just be a campus undertaking. Rather, by connecting learning outcomes assessment more intentionally to higher education scholars and research, and more specifically to questions about student learning in college, efforts to improve our understanding of effective teaching, assessment practice, and constructive responses to the push for accountability, would benefit all of higher education.

NOTES

1. Taylor, *The Next America*; National Task Force, "Crucible Moment."
2. Bok, *Our Underachieving Colleges*; Marcus, "New College Exam"; Selingo, *College (Un)bound*; Hart Research Associates, "Falling Short?"
3. Banta and Palomba, *Assessment Essentials*; Golden, "How to Best Assess?"; Suskie, *Assessing Student Learning*.
4. Thelin, "Crucible Moment."
5. Shavelson, "Assessing Student Learning Responsibly."
6. Ewell, "Accreditation and Student Learning Outcomes."
7. Kuh et al., "Knowing What Students Know."
8. See "Student Outcomes: The Denison Difference."
9. Banta and Palomba, *Assessment Essentials*.
10. St. Ambrose University, "Institutional Research and Assessment."
11. Allen, *Assessing Academic Programs*.
12. Kuh et al., "Knowing What Students Know."
13. Kuh et al., *Using Evidence of Student Learning*.
14. Silva, White, and Toch, "Carnegie Unit," 5.
15. Provezis, "Regional Accreditation"; US Department of Education, "Test of Leadership"; Kuh et al., *Using Evidence of Student Learning*.
16. Kuh et al., "Knowing What Students Know."
17. Pascarella and Terenzini, *Findings and Insights*; Pascarella and Terenzini, *Third Decade of Research*.
18. Pascarella and Terenzini, *Third Decade of Research*.
19. Pascarella and Terenzini, *Findings and Insights*; Pascarella and Terenzini, *Third Decade of Research*.
20. Pascarella et al., "Liberal Arts Colleges."
21. Astin, *What Matters in College*.
22. Arum and Roksa, *Academically Adrift*.
23. Arum, Roksa, and Cho, "Improving Undergraduate Learning."
24. Astin, *What Matters in College*.
25. McCormick, Kinzie, and Gonyea, "Student Engagement."
26. Pascarella et al., "Do Liberal Arts Colleges"; Pascarella et al., "Liberal Arts Colleges."

27. McCormick, Kinzie, and Gonyea, "Student Engagement"; Umbach and Wawrzynski, "Faculty Do Matter."

28. Kuh, Laird, and Umbach, "Aligning Faculty Activities."

29. Fink, *Creating Significant Learning Experiences*; Finkelstein, Seal, and Schuster, *New Academic Generation*.

30. Fink, *Creating Significant Learning Experiences*; Gardiner, "Why We Must Change."

31. Fink, *Creating Significant Learning Experiences*.

32. Kuh, "High-Impact Educational Practices"; Kuh, O'Donnell, and Reed, "Ensuring Quality."

33. See Hunter, Laursen, and Seymour, "Becoming a Scientist"; Lopatto, "Undergraduate Research"; Warren, "Does Service-Learning Increase."

34. Brownell and Swaner, "Five High-Impact Practices."

35. Gonyea and Kinzie, "Independent Colleges and Student Engagement."

36. Blaich and Wise, "Wabash National Study"; Pascarella, Seifert, and Blaich, "How Effective."

37. Mayhew et al., "Going Deep."

38. Padgett et al., "Impact of College Student Socialization."

39. Seifert et al., "Effects of Liberal Arts Experiences."

40. Blaich and Wise, "Wabash National Study."

41. Kuh et al., *Using Evidence of Student Learning*.

42. Banta and Palomba, *Assessment Essentials*.

43. Council of Independent Colleges, "CIC Statement on Assessment."

44. See Coughlin, "Engaging Evidence"; Gonyea and Kinzie, "Independent Colleges and Student Engagement"; Grimes, "Defining Outcomes, Demonstrating Quality"; Paris, "Catalyst for Change"; Roksa, "Analysis of Learning Outcomes."

45. Coughlin, "Engaging Evidence."

46. See St. Olaf College, "Statements of Intended Learning."

47. Ibid.

48. See National Institute for Learning Outcomes Assessment "Making Learning Outcomes Usable."

49. Watt et al., "Building Assessment Programs"; Banta and Palomba, *Assessment Essentials*.

50. Banta and Palomba, *Assessment Essentials*.

51. Seagraves and Dean, "Conditions Supporting a Culture."

52. National Survey of Student Engagement, "Engagement Insights."

53. Shavelson, *Measuring College Learning Responsibly*.

54. Kuh et al., *Using Evidence of Student Learning*.

55. Ibid.

56. See St. Olaf College, "Outcomes."

57. Krzykowski and Kinser, "Transparency in Student Learning Assessment."

58. Jankowski, "Juniata College."

59. Arum, Cook, and Roksa, *Improving Quality*.

60. Shavelson, *Measuring College Learning Responsibly*; Arum, Cook, and Roksa, *Improving Quality*.

61. Kuh et al., "Knowing What Students Know."

62. Provezis, "Regional Accreditation."

63. Brown et al., "Outcomes Assessment at Small Colleges."

64. Jankowski, "St. Olaf College."

65. Ndoye and Parker, "Creating and Sustaining."

66. McCormick, "Toward Reflective Accountability."
67. See St. Olaf College, "Assessment of Student Learning."

REFERENCES

Allen, Mary J. *Assessing Academic Programs in Higher Education.* San Francisco: Jossey-Bass, 2004.
Arum, Richard, Amanda Cook, and Josipa Roksa. *Improving Quality in American Higher Education: Learning Outcomes and Assessments for the 21st Century.* San Francisco: Jossey-Bass, 2016.
Arum, Richard, and Josipa Roksa. *Academically Adrift: Limited Learning on College Campuses.* Chicago: University of Chicago Press, 2011.
Arum, Richard, Josipa Roksa, and Esther Cho. "Improving Undergraduate Learning: Findings and Policy Recommendations from the SSRC-CLA Longitudinal Project." Brooklyn: Social Science Research Council, 2011.
Astin, Alexander W. *What Matters in College: Four Critical Years Revisited.* San Francisco: Jossey-Bass, 1993.
Banta, Trudy W., and Catherine A. Palomba. *Assessment Essentials: Planning, Implementing, and Improving Assessment in Higher Education.* 2nd ed. San Francisco: Jossey-Bass, 2015.
Blaich, Charles, and Kathleen Wise. "The Wabash National Study: The Impact of Teaching Practices and Institutional Conditions on Student Growth." Paper presented at the American Educational Research Annual Meeting, 2011.
Bok, Derek C. *Our Underachieving Colleges: A Candid Look at How Much Students Learn and Why They Should Be Learning More.* Princeton, NJ: Princeton University Press, 2006.
Brown, Jennie, Heather Corday Allard, Dré Goode, and Rachel Rossetti. "Outcomes Assessment at Small Colleges: Achieving Two Goals with One Assessment." *Assessment Update* 27, no. 4 (July 1, 2015): 5–6. doi:10.1002/au.30028.
Brownell, Jayne E., and Lynn E. Swaner. "Five High-Impact Practices: Research on Learning Outcomes, Completion, and Quality." Washington, DC: Association of American Colleges and Universities, 2010.
Council of Independent Colleges. "CIC Statement on Assessment: Leadership for Student Learning Assessment and Accountability." 2012. https://www.cic.edu/r/r/Documents/CIC-Statement-on-Assessment.pdf#search=statement%20on%20assessment. Accessed April 19, 2017.
Coughlin, Mary. "Engaging Evidence: How Independent Colleges and Universities Use Data to Improve Student Learning." Washington, DC: Council of Independent Colleges, 2014.
Ewell, Peter T. "Accreditation and Student Learning Outcomes: A Proposed Point of Departure." CHEA Occasional Paper. Washington, DC: Council for Higher Education, 2001.
Fink, L. Dee. *Creating Significant Learning Experiences: An Integrated Approach to Designing College Courses.* San Francisco: Jossey-Bass, 2013.
Finkelstein, Martin J., Robert K. Seal, and Jack H. Schuster. *The New Academic Generation: A Profession in Transformation.* Baltimore: Johns Hopkins University Press, 1998.
Gardiner, Lion F. "Why We Must Change: The Research Evidence." *Thought and Action* 14, no. 1 (1998): 71–88.
Golden, Serena. "How to Best Assess?" *Inside Higher Ed*, November 18, 2013. https://

www.insidehighered.com/news/2013/11/18/debating-role-student-learning-federal
-ratings-plan. Accessed March 20, 2017.

Gonyea, Robert M., and Jillian Kinzie. "Independent Colleges and Student Engagement: Descriptive Analysis by Institutional Type." Washington, DC: Council of Independent Colleges, 2015.

Grimes, Terry. "Defining Outcomes, Demonstrating Quality: The CIC Degree Qualifications Profile Consortium." Washington, DC: Council of Independent Colleges, 2014.

Hart Research Associates. "Falling Short? College Learning and Career Success. Selected Findings from Online Surveys of Employers and College Students Conducted on Behalf of the Association of American Colleges and Universities." 2015. http://www.aacu.org/sites/default/files/files/LEAP/2015employerstudentsurvey.pdf. Accessed March 20, 2017.

Hunter, Anne-Barrie, Sandra L. Laursen, and Elaine Seymour. "Becoming a Scientist: The Role of Undergraduate Research in Students' Cognitive, Personal, and Professional Development." *Science Education* 91, no. 1 (January 1, 2007): 36–74. doi:10.1002/sce.20173.

Jankowski, Natasha A. "Juniata College: Faculty Led Assessment (NILOA Examples of Good Assessment Practice)." Urbana, IL: University of Illinois and Indiana University, National Institute for Learning Outcomes Assessment, 2011.

———. "St. Olaf College: Utilization-Focused Assessment (NILOA Examples of Good Assessment Practice)." Urbana, IL: University of Illinois and Indiana University, National Institute for Learning Outcomes Assessment, 2012.

Krzykowski, Linda, and Kevin Kinser. "Transparency in Student Learning Assessment: Can Accreditation Standards Make a Difference?" *Change: The Magazine of Higher Learning* 46, no. 3 (May 4, 2014): 67–73. doi:10.1080/00091383.2014.905428.

Kuh, George D. "High-Impact Educational Practices: What They Are, Who Has Access to Them, and Why They Matter." Washington, DC: Association of American Colleges and Universities, 2008.

Kuh, George D., Ken O'Donnell, and Sally Reed. "Ensuring Quality and Taking High-Impact Practices to Scale." Washington, DC: Association of American Colleges and Universities, 2013.

Kuh, George D., Natasha A. Jankowski, Stanley O. Ikenberry, and Jillian Kinzie. "Knowing What Students Know and Can Do: The Current State of Learning Outcomes Assessment at U.S. Colleges and Universities." Urbana, IL: University of Illinois and Indiana University, National Institute for Learning Outcomes Assessment, 2014.

Kuh, George D., Stanley O. Ikenberry, Natasha A. Jankowski, Timothy Reese Cain, Ewell, Pat Hutchings, and Jillian Kinzie. *Using Evidence of Student Learning to Improve Higher Education.* San Francisco: Jossey-Bass, 2015.

Kuh, George D., Thomas F. Laird, and Paul D. Umbach. "Aligning Faculty Activities and Student Behavior: Realizing the Promise of Greater Expectations." *Liberal Education* 90, no. 4 (2004): 24–31.

Lopatto, David. "Undergraduate Research as a Catalyst for Liberal Learning." *Peer Review* 8, no. 1 (2006): 22–25.

Marcus, Jon. "The New College Exam: A Test to Graduate." *Time,* January 25, 2014. http://time.com/2187/the-new-college-exam-a-test-to-graduate. Accessed March 20, 2017.

Mayhew, Matthew J., Tricia A. Seifert, Ernest T. Pascarella, Thomas F. Nelson Laird, and Charles F. Blaich. "Going Deep into Mechanisms for Moral Reasoning Growth: How Deep Learning Approaches Affect Moral Reasoning Development for First-Year Students." *Research in Higher Education* 53, no. 1 (February 1, 2012): 26–46. doi:10.1007/s11162-011-9226-3.

McCormick, Alexander C. "Toward Reflective Accountability." Edited by Robert M.

Gonyea and George D. Kuh. *New Directions for Institutional Research*, no. 141 (2009): 97–106.

McCormick, Alexander C., Jillian Kinzie, and Robert M. Gonyea. "Student Engagement: Bridging Research and Practice to Improve the Quality of Undergraduate Education." In *Higher Education: Handbook of Theory and Research*, edited by Michael B. Paulsen, 47–92. Higher Education: Handbook of Theory and Research 28. Dordrecht, NL: Springer, 2013. doi:10.1007/978-94-007-5836-0_2.

National Institute for Learning Outcomes Assessment. "Making Learning Outcomes Usable and Transparent. Featured Website: California Lutheran University." 2012. http://www.learningoutcomesassessment.org/FeaturedWebsiteCaliforniaLutheran.html. Accessed March 19, 2017.

National Survey of Student Engagement. "Engagement Insights: Survey Findings on the Quality of Undergraduate Education—Annual Results 2015." Bloomington: Indiana University Center for Postsecondary Research, 2015.

National Task Force. "A Crucible Moment: College Learning and Democracy's Future." Washington, DC: Association of American Colleges and Universities, 2012.

Ndoye, Abdou, and Michele A. Parker. "Creating and Sustaining a Culture of Assessment." *Planning for Higher Education* 38, no. 2 (2010): 28–39.

Padgett, Ryan D., Kathleen M. Goodman, Megan P. Johnson, Kem Saichaie, Paul D. Umbach, and Ernest T. Pascarella. "The Impact of College Student Socialization, Social Class, and Race on Need for Cognition." *New Directions for Institutional Research* 2010, no. 145 (March 1, 2010): 99–111. doi:10.1002/ir.324.

Paris, David C. "Catalyst for Change: The CIC/CLA Consortium." Washington, DC: Council of Independent Colleges, 2011.

Pascarella, Ernest T., Gregory C. Wolniak, Tricia A. Seifert, Ty M. Cruce, and Charles F. Blaich. "Liberal Arts Colleges and Liberal Arts Education: New Evidence on Impacts." *ASHE Higher Education Report* 31, no. 3 (2005): 1–148.

Pascarella, Ernest T., and Patrick T. Terenzini. *How College Affects Students: Findings and Insights from Twenty Years of Research*. San Francisco: Jossey-Bass, 1991.

———. *How College Affects Students: A Third Decade of Research*. Vol. 2. San Francisco: Jossey-Bass, 2005.

Pascarella, Ernest T., Tricia A. Seifert, and Charles Blaich. "How Effective Are the NSSE Benchmarks in Predicting Important Educational Outcomes?" *Change: The Magazine of Higher Learning* 42, no. 1 (January 1, 2010): 16–22. doi:10.1080/00091380903449060.

Pascarella, Ernest T., Ty M. Cruce, Gregory C. Wolniak, and Charles F. Blaich. "Do Liberal Arts Colleges Really Foster Good Practices in Undergraduate Education?" *Journal of College Student Development* 45, no. 1 (March 5, 2004): 57–74. doi:10.1353/csd.2004.0013.

Provezis, Staci. "Regional Accreditation and Student Learning Outcomes: Mapping the Territory." NILOA Occasional Paper. Urbana, IL: University of Illinois and Indiana University, National Institute for Learning Outcomes Assessment, 2010.

Roksa, Josipa. "An Analysis of Learning Outcomes of Underrepresented Students at Urban Institutions." Washington, DC: Council of Independent Colleges, 2012.

Seagraves, Beau, and Laura A. Dean. "Conditions Supporting a Culture of Assessment in Student Affairs Divisions at Small Colleges and Universities." *Journal of Student Affairs Research and Practice* 47, no. 3 (July 1, 2010): 307–24. doi:10.2202/1949-6605.6073.

Seifert, Tricia A., Kathleen M. Goodman, Nathan Lindsay, James D. Jorgensen, Gregory C. Wolniak, Ernest T. Pascarella, and Charles Blaich. "The Effects of Liberal Arts Experiences on Liberal Arts Outcomes." *Research in Higher Education* 49, no. 2 (March 1, 2008): 107–25. doi:10.1007/s11162-007-9070-7.

Selingo, Jeffrey J. *College (Un)bound: The Future of Higher Education and What It Means for Students.* Boston: Houghton Mifflin Harcourt, 2013.

Shavelson, Richard J. "Assessing Student Learning Responsibly: From History to an Audacious Proposal." *Change: The Magazine of Higher Learning* 39, no. 1 (January 1, 2007): 26–33. doi:10.3200/CHNG.39.1.26-33.

———. *Measuring College Learning Responsibly: Accountability in a New Era.* Stanford, CA: Stanford University Press, 2010.

Silva, Elena, Taylor White, and Thomas Toch. "The Carnegie Unit: A Century-Old Standard in a Changing Education Landscape." Stanford, CA: Carnegie Foundation for the Advancement of Teaching, 2015.

St. Ambrose University. "Institutional Research and Assessment." www.sau.edu/Assessment/Assessment_Plans.html. Accessed March 18, 2017.

St. Olaf College. "Assessment of Student Learning. http://wp.stolaf.edu/ir-e/assessment-of-student-learning-2. Accessed March 19, 2017.

———. "Outcomes of a St. Olaf Education." http://wp.stolaf.edu/outcomes. Accessed March 19, 2017.

———. "Statements of Intended Learning Outcomes." http://wp.stolaf.edu/ir-e/statements-of-intended-learning-outcomes. Accessed March 18, 2017.

"Student Outcomes: The Denison Difference." http://denison.edu/the-denison-difference. Accessed March 18, 2017.

Suskie, Linda. *Assessing Student Learning: A Common Sense Guide.* 2nd ed. San Francisco: Jossey-Bass, 2009.

Taylor, Paul. *The Next America: Boomers, Millennials, and the Looming Generational Showdown.* New York: Public Affairs, 2014.

Thelin, John R. "Small by Design: Resilience in an Era of Mass Higher Education." In *Meeting the Challenge: America's Independent Colleges and Universities since 1956*, 3–35. Washington, DC: Council of Independent Colleges, 2006.

Umbach, Paul D., and Matthew R. Wawrzynski. "Faculty Do Matter: The Role of College Faculty in Student Learning and Engagement." *Research in Higher Education* 46, no. 2 (March 1, 2005): 153–84. doi:10.1007/s11162-004-1598-1.

US Department of Education. Secretary of Education. Commission on the Future of Higher Education. "A Test of Leadership: Charting the Future of U.S. Higher Education (A Report of the Commission Appointed by Secretary of Education Margaret Spellings)." Washington, DC: US Department of Education, 2006.

Warren, Jami L. "Does Service-Learning Increase Student Learning? A Meta-Analysis." *Michigan Journal of Community Service Learning* 18, no. 2 (2012): 56–61.

Watt, James H., Nancy H. Hungerford Drennen, Raymond J. Rodrigues, Nancy Menelly, and Erica K. Wiegel. "Building Assessment Programs in Large Institutions." In *Making a Difference: Outcomes of a Decade of Assessment in Higher Education*, edited by Trudy W. Banta, 103–20. San Francisco: Jossey-Bass, 1993.

REACTION
Letha B. Zook

Reading Jillian Kinzie and Cynthia Cogswell's chapter enhances my optimism in the future of private higher education. The researchers support the historical claims that, as small liberal arts institutions, we have better outcomes and more often use varied pedagogy. However, they encourage us to be better in our presentation of the evidence that supports our claims. The responsibility for establishing the value proposition for private higher education lies in the hands of the academic leadership at each institution and especially the hands of the faculty as we use assessment to verify our claims. From my perspective, the lessons from this chapter center around three mandates for private higher education: identifying and assessing institutional student learning outcomes is essential, intentionality of curriculum is the path forward, and the scholarship of teaching needs to be the work of our faculty.

Throughout the chapter, the issue of institutional accountability for learning is addressed, and the authors cite political, accreditation, and state and federal mandates. However, the most important reason for any school to focus on student learning outcomes and assessment is the educator's moral imperative to ensure that all students learn the essential skills, attitudes, and knowledge necessary for individual success and for their contribution to a strong, caring, and ethical society. We claim that students receive better instruction and thus learn more, but we must provide the evidence.

Creation, implementation, and assessment of student learning outcomes *is* the work of our faculty, not an add-on activity or the work of administration. At the University of Charleston (UC), the faculty created institutional student learning outcomes in the early 2000s. The Liberal Learning Outcomes (LLOs) are integrated into all programs at three levels of complexity and are assessed at the course, program, and institutional levels. We have been ahead of the curve on this. But we must have authentic evidence that each of our students possess an acceptable level of competency and guarantee employers and graduate faculty that our students can succeed in the next setting. We want to go beyond the basic transparency that just shows data on the website, and we must be able to correlate our learning outcome competency with success of our alumni—not just with the most motivated students, but with every student.

I have come to the conclusion, as do the authors of this chapter, that the only way to get all students to an acceptable level of competency in the learning outcomes is by creating an intentional and integrated curriculum. The process of doing this is iterative in several different ways. First, it includes the intentional mapping of all courses that make up a program curriculum and the assessment of competency of each outcome through to the exit level. The University of Charleston's participation in the Council of Independent Colleges' Lumina

Foundation's Degree Qualifications Profile initiative inspired UC faculty to embark on a different way of assessing the integration of the LLOs within each program. Over the past year, each program has presented an explanation to faculty peer groups (faculty round tables) responsible for each LLO concerning how each course contributes to the accomplishment of the LLOs. The purpose of this process is to ensure that every student, regardless of their major, will progress to higher and higher competencies in the institutional LLOs as they progress through the curriculum.

The intentionality of the above process addresses another challenge stated in the article: "closing the loop" of the learning process. As UC faculty have become more intentional about what is expected at each level, we are able to see what is working and what is not. We can then make changes in the programs to be sure that the best pedagogy is used. The program assessment rubric requires articulation of the impact of specific changes.

A major contribution of this chapter is the synthesis of the research on the impact of pedagogy on learning outcomes with the accompanying call for more collaboration of scholarly activity within and between institutions. The call I hear from this work is that we as small private "teaching" institutions are uniquely equipped to make the scholarship of teaching our primary focus. Just as we make learning the focus of our pedagogy, we can make the investigation of learning accomplished by use of best-practice pedagogy. Our challenges may be resources and significant data points for generalization; however, working collaboratively across disciplines and institutions can help remedy both of these. Employers often say that it is the critical thinking, communication, and other general skills that college graduates lack. I would suggest that we collaborate with our community partners to determine the best assessment data to collect that will allow them to say our students are prepared for the workforce. By aligning our exit measures with the employers' expectations, evidence will be meaningful to the public. As faculty integrate assessment of learning into their daily work, the iterative process of scholarly work can strengthen the evidence of our claims. The flexibility of scholarly expectations and the type of faculty we attract places us in a unique position to focus on the scholarship of teaching.

The pressures crashing in on the small and medium private sector of higher education are real and grand. Kinzie and Cogswell's chapter gives us hope and challenges us to take advantage of our strengths and flexibility. We can strengthen our claims by providing evidence to the public that our student learning outcomes make our graduates better employees and graduate students. Our intentionally designed curriculum can ensure that all students are given the opportunity to attain the required competencies. The tools are in our hands.

4

Leveraging Learning Technologies at Liberal Arts Colleges and Universities

MATTHEW J. MAYHEW AND STEPHEN VASSALLO

In an essay written to celebrate the fiftieth anniversary of the Council of Independent Colleges (CIC), John Thelin[1] wrote that small independent colleges have been remarkably successful at "harmonizing their broad traditional commitments to collegiate education with demographic and economic changes at the national level." While the demographic and economic changes Thelin references continue to impact small independent colleges, the increasing prevalence and importance of digital learning technologies present a fresh set of challenges for CIC members as they seek to deliver a high-quality liberal arts education to a new generation of students.

With 35 percent of all higher education students enrolling in at least one online course, enrollment in digital and online learning environments has grown every year since 2003.[2] Yet CIC members have been slow to adapt to this trend with only 50 percent of all member institutions offering fully online programs and 10 percent not offering a single class versus 80 percent of American Association of State Colleges and Universities members offering at least one fully online program and almost 50 percent offering five or more fully online programs.[3] While this reluctance to offer online programs and classes may be deliberate and perhaps well founded, it is clear that CIC member institutions need to plan and evaluate the extent to which new learning technologies will be integrated into the classroom in the decades ahead. A key challenge for CIC colleges is the extent to which digital learning is congruent with the liberal arts tradition and accompanying cultures.

In this chapter, we develop arguments for leveraging learning technologies among CIC members. The first section of the chapter presents prior research related to each of these three themes. The second provides the areas of strength and challenge for the CIC sector that new digital learning technologies present. The last section frames CIC members' responses to these challenges using empirically based research, along with areas for future exploration.

Prior Research

The rapidly changing technological environment makes relevant and timely research reviews more challenging, as definitions continue to expand, new technologies consistently emerge, and use trends seem to ebb and flow, often unpredictably. Given these limitations, we will present an overview of the literature as it relates to defining key terms associated with learning technologies, addressing the financial implications of their implementation and advancing notions related to best practice. This type of review is particularly relevant for CIC administrators since many are just beginning to think about incorporating digital technology into their academic mission.

Definitions

Elaine Allen and Jeff Seaman[4] define "online courses" as those in which at least 80 percent of the content is delivered online as opposed to face-to-face. Of the courses and environments meeting this standard, the primary attribute that separates them is whether content delivery is asynchronous or synchronous. In the context of online learning, Anthony Picciano defines asynchronous as learning delivered online that can be accessed "anytime or in anyplace";[5] by contrast, synchronous learning is delivered to students at a specific set time but still can be accessed at different locations.[6] While for-profit and larger nonprofit schools have generally focused on creating asynchronous classes that allow students to download course content, engage with fellow students via discussion boards, and submit assignments electronically to instructors, smaller institutions have concentrated efforts on synchronous learning, with the hope that appealing to time-set sensibilities will be pedagogically appealing for both students and faculty.

Massive Open Online Classes (MOOCs) represent one of the most recent online learning platforms and can be either synchronous or asynchronous. Although most MOOCs are offered within the context of a semester, others (e.g., Udacity) allow students to take and finish the course at their pace. MOOCs are created by companies such as Udacity, Coursera, and edX and have gained popularity as universities leverage their industry networks to partner with the companies that create the platforms. For example, the Georgia Institute of Technology partnered with Udacity in 2013 and now offers an online Master's

Program in Computer Science for less than $7,000, or about the price of an associate's degree at a community college.[7] At less than $7,000 for a master's degree program through a university that generally charges six to ten times that amount, there are clearly economic implications for offering online classes.

Research has focused primarily on the question of the costs of the various inputs to build, offer, and sustain an online learning program and platform that matches the quality of education offered in a face-to-face classroom. We turn now to a brief discussion of costs.

Costs

William Bowen and William Baumol were first to coin the phrase "the cost disease" in the mid-1960s when they observed that institutional costs per student in higher education (among other industries) tended to rise faster than costs in the broader economy in the long term.[8] They argued that since higher education is primarily a service-oriented industry whereby increasing the production of unit outputs (e.g., enrollment and research) requires a similar increase of labor unit inputs (e.g., faculty teaching loads), productivity gains are elusive both over time and when production is increased.[9] Some have argued, however, that new digital learning technologies and the prevalence of broadband and high-speed Internet access may finally be the cure to the "cost disease."[10]

As early as 1998, a report issued through the University of Illinois concluded that online instruction was likely to cost more than traditional instruction.[11] Bowen[12] presented a lecture on the topic in 2012 and noted that there continues to be a lack of hard evidence as to the cost savings (or increase) inherent in building online programs and leveraging learning technologies at institutions. Though he did not provide empirical evidence, Bowen argued that campuses leveraging MOOCs have the greatest potential to be cost-effective, since once they are developed, the marginal cost of adding an extra thousand students is close to zero. The problem with this line of thinking, however, is that it assumes a one-size-fits-all approach without the need for course customizations. For CIC schools, this is of particular importance since liberal arts classes are often taught differently depending on the individual instructor and culture of the institution.

Once a particular MOOC or any online class requires customization, the potential student population starts to shrink toward a normal class size and instructor costs may simply be replaced by consulting fees or an increase in other information technology expenditures.

One question for CIC members seeking to leverage learning technologies is how much will marginal costs truly be reduced, and is the increase in fixed costs pervasive over time? In a similar way, can learning technologies be used to reduce marginal costs while maintaining the academic mission focus?

David Deming, Claudia Goldin, Lawrence Katz, and Noam Yuchtman[13] borrowed a phrase from the health care industry, posing the question another way by asking, "Can online learning bend the higher education cost curve?" Tyler Cowen and Alex Tabarrok[14] noted that online courses reduced the marginal cost of teaching and increased the fixed costs of producing the classes. As a result, the marginal cost of faculty salaries decreased with the production of a new class, but the permanent cost of infrastructure required to support these classes, both technical and administrative, increased.

Deming and colleagues[15] used IPEDS data to examine degree-seeking undergraduates who attended open access and less-selective postsecondary institutions; the authors found some evidence that colleges are charging lower prices for online coursework after controlling for detailed institutional characteristics and for geographic market and institution fixed effects. From a cost perspective, the literature is both incomplete and inconclusive, though economic theory substantiated by some empirical evidence suggests that it is at least possible to deliver online classes in a cost-effective manner relative to face-to-face classes. This implies that CIC members seeking to produce new online classes and programs to reduce institutional costs should not accept that expenditures will automatically be reduced. In the challenges and response section, we elaborate on how to evaluate the potential impact of producing new digital technologies on the bottom line.

Turning to MOOCs, Caroline Hoxby[16] was one of the first researchers to specifically examine MOOCs and ask whether they could be incorporated into an economically sustainable model of postsecondary education. She contrasted nonselective postsecondary education (institutions that require only a high school diploma or GED for admission) with highly selective postsecondary education (institutions as defined by Barron's magazine as "most competitive," where median student SAT or ACT scores are at or above the ninety-fifth percentile) and found that MOOCs could be financially sustainable substitutes for nonselective postsecondary education but not for highly selective postsecondary education unless these institutions "deal with two problems: (i) the selectivity necessary for offering advanced education and (ii) the experiences that build the beliefs and adherence that sustain the venture capital-like financial model."[17] The first problem relates to the inherent open nature of MOOCs, where anyone, anywhere can essentially enroll. The lack of selectivity, rightly or wrongly, is too easily interpreted as lower quality.

Trying to replace courses at a liberal arts college with MOOCs generally cannot solve the first problem as many view MOOCs as a poor substitute for the traditional classroom experience, regardless of evidence to the contrary.[18] The second problem would require a major cultural shift among liberal arts educators and, most important, in the faculty who choose to work at the selective liberal arts institutions; faculty would have to engage in a paradigmatic shift from one that embraces higher education as a public good to one that embraces the idea of higher education as a commodity. Given these parameters, it is unlikely that MOOCs would be a viable option for most CIC member institutions as a strategy for enhancing the liberal arts classroom experience.

Learning Efficacy of Online Classes

Given the economic possibility of offering online courses to students at smaller institutions, a first step toward implementation involves reviewing the research on the efficacy of taking classes in an online learning environment. Of course, the target continues to move with regard to the research designed to examine learning gain differences between online and face-to-face courses. Methodological flaws continue to plague these studies, as scholars struggle with issues of randomization, treatment validity (e.g., same instructor for online versus face-to-face courses), and confounding variables.[19] Despite these limitations, there are a few studies that offer insights into the differences in learning gains reported or achieved by students in face-to-face versus online environments.

One of the most widely cited studies is the 2009 meta-analysis published by the US Department of Education (DOE) entitled, "Evaluation of Evidence-Based Practices in Online Learning: A Meta-Analysis and Review of Online Learning Studies." This meta-analysis reviewed the literature from 1996–2008 and screened over a thousand studies of online learning to find those that (1) contrasted an online to a face-to-face condition; (2) measured student learning outcomes; (3) used a rigorous research design; and (4) provided adequate information to calculate an effect size. The meta-analysis found that, on average, learning outcomes of students enrolled in online courses were similar to those receiving face-to-face instruction.[20]

This finding from the DOE oversimplifies the literature base, however, and specifically the way in which the authors narrowly defined outcomes. For example, many of the studies essentially compared grades from an online class against those from a similar face-to-face class and used this as a proxy for learning. In more recent studies, researchers have begun to approach studying outcomes with greater sophistication, possibly nuanced to inform small liberal arts institutions. Gouri Banerjee[21] surveyed students from a small liberal arts institution and concluded that "student satisfaction with blended learning environments depends largely on the challenges presented by the subject matter, the degree to which self-directed learning and problem solving are required, and the effectiveness of the chosen pedagogies by which face-to-face and online methods are combined."[22]

As more and more students replace or augment face-to-face classes with online programs, researchers have begun employing more robust experimental designs. Theodore Joyce and colleagues[23] randomized 725 college students into twice-per-week fully face-to-face lectures and once-per-week hybrid classes where students supplemented the lecture with online materials such as pre-recorded video lectures. Nominal effects were noted for students in the two face-to-face classes, as these students scored approximately 2.5 out of 100 points better on test scores and grades. The authors also found that there was no difference in the probability of withdrawing from the class regardless of format.

Potential Implications for CIC Member Institutions

These results may have potential implications for CIC members considering and comparing fully online programs against the hybrid format. One of the primary concerns with online courses and MOOCs in particular is student motivation since they have much lower retention rates even when controlling for factors such as cost and other variables.[24] Based upon Joyce and colleagues'[25] and William Bowen, Matthew Chingos, Kelly Lack, and Thomas Nygren's[26] findings, we offer the conclusion that hybrid classes appear to retain the same level of student engagement and motivation as face-to-face classes, and there are zero to nominal differences in educational outcomes for students in online versus face-to-face environments.

From the advent of distance education, theories were developed to describe the nature of these interactions in various environments. In 1997, Michael Moore presented a theory of transactional distance applying to all distance education forms and noted that transactional distance first appeared in the literature in 1972. All distance education forms are defined by a teacher-learner relationship separated by space and/or time.[27] The concept of transaction "connotes the interplay among the environment, the individuals and the patterns of behaviors in a situation."[28] In online learning environments the teachers and learners are separated; therefore, one immediate need is for "psychological and communications space to be crossed."[29] The greater the transactional distance, the bigger the challenges for creating an environment conducive to learning and development. In short, the success of moving a culture toward embracing an online environment is dependent on how well an institution builds bridges to cross these spaces. This is a major challenge for CIC member institutions given that most have rich cultural histories that developed over long periods of time. To overcome this challenge, CIC member institutions need to first find a connection between their already established academic cultures and digital technologies. This connection may come in the form of a department championing digital technologies or a group of students that works with faculty members to produce an online class.

From a qualitative perspective, researchers have examined what interactions take place in the online space and also how individuals make meaning of these interactions. Like the face-to-face classroom, online classes represent a community where members acquire a sense of shared history, purpose, norms, hierarchy, ritual, belonging, and continuity.[30] In this community, interactions are at least partially governed by each individual's sense of identity, and without physical proximity, this sense of identity is often built on the relational dialogue of textual interaction where words represent actions.[31] The reliance on text without the nonverbal cues that help build social presence—cues such as gestures, body-lean, and facial expressions—creates potential barriers to positive and meaningful interactions.[32]

Importantly, the specifics of each learning technology—whether the class is synchronous or asynchronous—and the design of the user experience facilitating dialogue from chat rooms and message boards to group video environments can impact the processes dictating interactions. Given the rapid changes in technology over the past 15 years, Philip Abrami, Robert Bernard, Eva Bures, Eugene Borokhovski, and Rana Tamim[33] observed a clear demarcation between simple and more advanced means for facilitating interactions in digital learning environments. The authors refer to most studies on online interactions before 2009 as first generation interactive distance education (IDE1), where interactions were limited and "learners were able to interact but may not have done so optimally given the quality and quantity of interactions that occurred."[34] Since 2011, a second generation of digital learning environments is now available whereby designers have employed cognitive research and have taken advantage of more computing power, faster Internet speeds, and large quantities of data that help them understand how interactions take place online. Given these trends, the reluctance of CIC members to implement online classes and programs in the past decade may be an advantage as more evidence-based approaches to building online platforms are designed to maximize interactions online despite the lack of physical proximity. If CIC members are to adopt online classes, now is the time.

Areas of Strength and Challenge for the CIC Sector

Although CIC members have been slower to implement digital learning platforms relative to larger public and private colleges and universities, they are now poised to take advantage of the lessons learned from the first movers. The learning technologies themselves have also improved as new software designs incorporate educational pedagogy grounded in the cognitive and social sciences. For those CIC members that are only just beginning to explore implementing online programs, they may be in a position of strength, having the opportunity to increase student access, enrollment, revenue, and even make pedagogic improvements.

However, the CIC sector also faces many challenges with regard to implementing online education. These include the following: the administration and service offerings for online programs, the balance between tenure and tenure-track and contingent faculty teaching classes, faculty compensation, lower completion rates in online classes, and, finally, the key issue for CIC member institutions—replicating the liberal arts classroom experience online.[35]

One of the primary goals for many institutions is to generate additional resources from online courses and programs, and this means constraining marginal costs associated with building and supporting them. The CIC members that have established larger online programs generally set up a dedicated central administrative unit along with a senior administrator responsible for online operations.[36] This added expense means that CIC members must generate revenue in excess of the new costs that also does not cannibalize tuition generated from face-to-face classes. The challenge for CIC members that implement large programs is to either increase enrollment through online classes or to reduce administrative costs elsewhere in the institution. The latter is likely difficult to attain since most CIC members have reported that they have added responsibilities to their traditional administrative units such as enrollment management, academic advising, student retention and overall support for the online programs. At this time, it is still unclear whether institutions can generate sufficient new enrollment and tuition dollars to cover the increase in costs.

Enlisting the right mix of faculty is also an important and difficult challenge to address for CIC members since there is generally a wide range of technical skill sets. Interestingly, over 80 percent of CIC members report that full-time faculty are teaching online courses as part of their regular course load and in combination with face-to-face classes. This contrasts with AASCU universities, where 32 percent report having full-time faculty members who only teach online.[37] One of the challenges for any school is determining which faculty are best equipped to teach online and what type of incentive structure should be set up to encourage faculty to leverage learning technologies. Faculty compensation is thus another challenge for CIC members when setting up online programs since schools will likely need to provide additional compensation to incentivize both online curriculum development and teaching classes online. To produce positive outcomes for both faculty and student while increasing or maintaining the bottom line is a challenge.

Similarly to MOOCs and other online programs, CIC members also report lower course completion rates than face-to-face classes.[38] Over 70 percent of CIC members with online programs report students' lack of discipline to succeed, and the lower completion rates associated with this lack of discipline, as a major concern. This challenge clearly represents an issue from a number of perspectives. First, traditional forms of engagement in the classroom that faculty are familiar with may not be available in an online environment. Second, if this challenge persists at the institution, both faculty and students will never view online classes on an equal footing with face-to-face classes since completion rates, and thus positive outcomes, would be so much lower. Last, replicating the liberal arts and small campus feel that accompanies the classroom experience for faculty and students among CIC institutions represents a difficult challenge to overcome. Regardless of software, bandwidth, and other technological advances that occur in the future, online classes are inherently different environments from the face-to-face, in-person experience. The liberal arts classroom represents a place for a relatively small number of students and faculty to question and debate ideas and produce meaningful dialogue that includes nonverbal and immediate physical cues. All CIC members must grapple with that inherent tension that exists between the two environments.

Response to Challenges

Given the evolving nature of and early stages of online programs at most colleges and universities, the literature base for directly responding to these challenges is relatively sparse. Nevertheless, there are useful lessons that can at least be contextualized into a CIC member's specific circumstances when determining how best to leverage learning technologies. In this section, prior research is drawn upon to recommend how CIC members can address each of the primary challenges noted above.

Most university leaders will not implement and sustain online learning programs unless they are economically feasible and, more likely, unless the program generates additional resources for the institution. It is important that university administrators produce financial models that account for the underlying economic differences of online learning programs. Online teaching can reduce the marginal cost of teaching since there may be some classes that can scale to thousands of students, but it also raises the fixed cost since course development is more resource intensive.[39] To address this issue, CIC members should focus on employing a standardized technology platform where possible to spread fixed costs more broadly throughout the institution.

Clinefelter and Magda[40] also recommend that universities invest in hiring a dedicated online leader and appropriate staff and centralize the administration of online programs. To help measure the economics of the programs, schools can set up a budget process whereby all revenue and expenses associated with creating and supporting the online programs are tracked in a centralized location. By centralizing the finances, the institution has the ability to determine whether the program is providing additional resources or at least breaking even.

Potentially the most important challenge to overcome for CIC members is finding the right mix of faculty to develop curriculum and deliver classes for online programs. Though all of the challenges are connected in some way, the faculty that ultimately participate in a school's online program are interconnected with the economics of the program and have a large impact on both completion rates and student outcomes. *Compensation incentives* should be set up to enlist top faculty members, including full professors who may initially be wary of online pedagogy. If a central administrative body is set up as recommended above, one of the online learning office's primary strengths should be training faculty members on how best to utilize the software platforms in place, with a particular focus on how best to replicate important elements of the face-to-face classroom environment.[41]

Since it is unlikely any school will be able to fully staff an online program with only full-time faculty, part-time faculty or adjunct professors should be utilized with specific criteria in mind. Colleges should focus on *hiring part-time faculty with prior experience teaching online classes* and preferably the same classes they are being hired to teach face-to-face. If no part-time faculty members with prior experience are available, colleges should *contractually require part-time faculty* to complete a robust training program so that they are essentially experts in delivering courses with whatever online platform the college sets up. As opposed to full-time faculty, who should have the option to leverage support from administration, part-time faculty as experts in online teaching could then be relied upon for enhancing online classes in the future.[42]

Given the variety of different teaching models available for implementing an online learning strategy, CIC members should also consider developing a new approach for measuring course delivery activities, outputs, and costs. Massy[43] argues that universities embrace an Activity-Based Costing (ABC) model with a focus on quantifying both costs and associated course-based teaching activities, such as curriculum planning, creating student resources, and out-of-class interactions. Institutions that adopt course-based ABC should introduce the model for all courses to help track and measure how online classes compare to the face-to-face environment in terms of both outcomes and cost. Massy provides an ABC design structure for assembling courses into categories that reflect various teaching methods called "mezzanine-level design." This level of analysis classifies courses by unit or program, primary and secondary class size, and delivery method to provide stakeholders with a comparative picture of the different types of teaching approaches and mediums.[44] Though course-based ABC is not the only method for measuring teaching costs, CIC members will need some system for determining whether online courses are achieving the expected cost savings.

A similar support system should also be available to students to ensure that completion rates of classes are maintained regardless of class delivery type. As noted above, online classes generally suffer from lower completion rates for a variety of reasons. The online administrative body should provide information to students before they enroll in an online or blended class.[45] This could include *videos and other tutorials* showing students what to expect from the class. Technology can also play a role in improving completion rates of online courses by taking advantage of the natural advantages of digital environments. For example, system-generated reminder e-mails that are based upon student actions can help students stay on track with assignments. Course designers can also build in support mechanisms that are common in the classroom environment by providing students with positive feedback as they complete tasks and learning benchmarks throughout the course.

CIC members should work to create an online classroom environment that exhibits as many of the positive attributes of the face-to-face liberal arts environment as possible. Since the primary difference is the lack of physical proximity and presence, course designers should focus much of their attention on promoting positive interactions. Abrami and colleagues[46] recommend four features and principles that designers should focus on to encourage positive and more advanced interactions in the online classroom: (1) instructional designers should pay more attention to ease of use as an overall design objective; (2) students need more guidance about when, under what circumstances, and for what purposes to use the tool; (3) users need practice to use the tool well and wisely; and (4) cognitive tools and learning strategies may work best when they are an integral feature of a course.

To create the small-college feel within the online context, CIC members need to implement the good teaching practices known for influencing subject content mastery in undergraduate students. Face-time is important, so design a video sequence of the instructor, either lecturing or explaining challenging themes emerging from class discussions. Also, instructors must provide in-depth and critical feedback to students if they are to make any demonstrable learning gains; the amount of feedback is not as important as the quality of feedback.[47] Finally, the course must be challenging, not perceived by students as a credit-bearing necessity, but as an environment that spurs innovation. Educators can assess how students use theories, frameworks, and narratives to create case studies rather than respond to them; to develop an informed opinion rather than merely articulating competing hypotheses; and to argue for a position as opposed to just taking one.

NOTES

1. Thelin, "Crucible Moment," 35.
2. Allen and Seaman, "Grade Level."
3. Clinefelter and Magda, "Online Learning."
4. Allen and Seaman, "Grade Level."

5. Picciano, "Developing an Asynchronous Course Model," 4.
6. Midkiff and DaSilva, "Leveraging the Web."
7. Young, "Georgia Tech to Offer."
8. Bowen, "'Cost Disease' in Higher Education."
9. Archibald and Feldman, "Explaining Increases."
10. Christensen and Eyring, *Innovative University.*
11. Regalbuto, "Teaching at an Internet Distance."
12. Bowen, "'Cost Disease' in Higher Education."
13. Deming et al., "Can Online Learning Bend?," 1.
14. Cowen and Tabarrok, "Industrial Organization of Online Education."
15. Deming et al., "Can Online Learning Bend?"
16. Hoxby, "Economics of Online Postsecondary Education."
17. Ibid., 18.
18. Allen and Seaman, "Grade Level."
19. Mayhew et al., *How College Affects Students.*
20. Means et al., "Evaluation of Evidence-Based Practices."
21. Banerjee, "Blended Environments."
22. Ibid., 8.
23. Joyce et al., "Does Classroom Time Matter?"
24. Scholz, "MOOCs and Liberal Arts College."
25. Joyce et al., "Does Classroom Time Matter?"
26. Bowen et al., "Interactive Learning Online."
27. Moore, "Editorial."
28. Boyd and Apps, *Redefining the Discipline*, 165.
29. Ibid.
30. Lapadat, "Discourse Devices"; Rovai, "Building Sense of Community."
31. Koole, "Web of Identity."
32. Hron et al., "Implicit and Explicit Dialogue."
33. Abrami et al., "Interaction in Distance Education."
34. Ibid., 87.
35. Clinefelter and Magda, "Online Learning."
36. Ibid.
37. Ibid.
38. Adamopoulos, "What Makes a Great MOOC?"
39. Cowen and Tabarrok, "Industrial Organization of Online Education."
40. Clinefelter and Magda, "Online Learning."
41. Ibid.
42. McNaught, "Effectiveness."
43. Massy, *Reengineering the University.*
44. Ibid.
45. Owston, York, and Finkel, "Evaluation."
46. Abrami et al., "Interaction in Distance Education," 99.
47. Mayhew et al., *How College Affects Students.*

REFERENCES

Abrami, Philip C., Robert M. Bernard, Eva M. Bures, Eugene Borokhovski, and Rana M. Tamim. "Interaction in Distance Education and Online Learning: Using Evidence and Theory to Improve Practice." *Journal of Computing in Higher Education* 23, nos. 2–3 (December 1, 2011): 82–103. doi:10.1007/s12528-011-9043-x.

Adamopoulos, Panagiotis. "What Makes a Great MOOC? An Interdisciplinary Analysis of Student Retention in Online Courses." *ICIS 2013 Proceedings*, December 17, 2013. http://aisel.aisnet.org/icis2013/proceedings/BreakthroughIdeas/13. Accessed March 21, 2017.

Allen, I. Elaine, and Jeff Seaman. "Grade Level: Tracking Online Education in the United States." Babson Survey Research Group, 2015. https://www.onlinelearningsurvey.com/reports/gradelevel.pdf. Accessed April 28, 2017.

Archibald, Robert B., and David H. Feldman. "Explaining Increases in Higher Education Costs." *Journal of Higher Education* 79, no. 3 (May 1, 2008): 268–95. doi:10.1080/0022 1546.2008.11772099.

Banerjee, Gouri. "Blended Environments: Learning Effectiveness and Student Satisfaction at a Small College in Transition." *Journal of Asynchronous Learning Networks* 15, no. 1 (February 2011): 8–19.

Bowen, William G. "The 'Cost Disease' in Higher Education: Is Technology the Answer?" The Tanner Lectures. Stanford University, 2012.

Bowen, William G., Matthew M. Chingos, Kelly A. Lack, and Thomas I. Nygren. "Interactive Learning Online at Public Universities: Evidence from a Six-Campus Randomized Trial." *Journal of Policy Analysis and Management* 33, no. 1 (January 1, 2014): 94–111. doi:10.1002/pam.21728.

Boyd, Robert D., and Jerold W. Apps. *Redefining the Discipline of Adult Education*. San Francisco: Jossey-Bass, 1980.

Christensen, Clayton M., and Henry J. Eyring. *The Innovative University: Changing the DNA of Higher Education from the Inside Out*. San Francisco: Jossey-Bass, 2011.

Clinefelter, David L., and Andrew J. Magda. "Online Learning at Private Colleges and Universities: A Survey of Chief Academic Officers." Louisville, KY: The Learning House, 2013.

Cowen, Tyler, and Alex Tabarrok. "The Industrial Organization of Online Education." *American Economic Review* 104, no. 5 (May 1, 2014): 519–22. doi:10.1257/aer.104.5.519.

Deming, David J., Claudia Goldin, Lawrence F. Katz, and Noam Yuchtman. "Can Online Learning Bend the Higher Education Cost Curve?" Working Paper. National Bureau of Economic Research, January 2015. doi:10.3386/w20890.

Hoxby, Caroline M. "The Economics of Online Postsecondary Education: MOOCs, Nonselective Education, and Highly Selective Education." Working Paper. National Bureau of Economic Research, January 2014. doi:10.3386/w19816.

Hron, Aemilian, Friedrich W. Hesse, Ulrike Cress, and Christos Giovis. "Implicit and Explicit Dialogue Structuring in Virtual Learning Groups." *British Journal of Educational Psychology* 70, no. 1 (March 1, 2000): 53–64. doi:10.1348/000709900157967.

Joyce, Theodore J., Sean Crockett, David A. Jaeger, Onur Altindag, and Stephen D. O'Connell. "Does Classroom Time Matter? A Randomized Field Experiment of Hybrid and Traditional Lecture Formats in Economics." Working Paper. National Bureau of Economic Research, March 2014. doi:10.3386/w20006.

Koole, Marguerite. "The Web of Identity: Selfhood and Belonging in Online Learning Networks." In *Seventh International Conference on Networked Learning*, 2010.

Lapadat, Judith. "Discourse Devices Used to Establish Community, Increase Coherence, and Negotiate Agreement in an Online University Course." *International Journal of E-Learning and Distance Education* 21, no. 3 (January 4, 2007): 59–92.

Massy, William F. *Reengineering the University: How to Be Mission Centered, Market Smart, and Margin Conscious*. Baltimore: Johns Hopkins University Press, 2016.

Mayhew, Matthew J., Alyssa N. Rockenbach, Tricia A. Seifert, Nicholas A. Bowman, and Gregory C. Wolniak. *How College Affects Students: 21st Century Evidence That Higher Education Works.* San Francisco: Jossey-Bass, 2016.

McNaught, Carmel. "The Effectiveness of an Institution-Wide Mentoring Program for Improving Online Teaching and Learning." *Journal of Computing in Higher Education* 15, no. 1 (September 1, 2003): 27–45. doi:10.1007/BF02940851.

Means, Barbara, Yukie Toyama, Marianne Bakia, and Karla Jones. "Evaluation of Evidence-Based Practices in Online Learning: A Meta-Analysis and Review of Online Learning Studies." US Department of Education, May 2009. https://eric.ed.gov/?id=eD505824. Accessed March 21, 2017.

Midkiff, Scott F., and Luiz A. DaSilva. "Leveraging the Web for Synchronous versus Asynchronous Distance Learning." Paper presented at International Conference on Engineering Education. August 14–18, 2000, Taipei, Taiwan.

Moore, Michael G. "Editorial: Three Types of Interaction." *American Journal of Distance Education* 3, no. 2 (January 1, 1989): 1–7. doi:10.1080/08923648909526659.

Owston, Ron, Dennis York, and Janna Finkel. "Evaluation of Blended and Online Learning Courses in the Faculty of Liberal Arts and Professional Studies and the Faculty of Health." Technical Report. Toronto: York University, 2013.

Picciano, Anthony G. "Developing an Asynchronous Course Model for a Large, Urban University." *Journal of Asynchronous Learning Networks* 2, no. 1 (1998): 3–19.

Regalbuto, John. "Teaching at an Internet Distance: The Pedagogy of Online Teaching and Learning." Report of a 1998–99 University of Illinois Faculty Seminar, 1998. https://www.sfu.ca/~andrewf/TIDreport.pdf. Accessed April 28, 2017.

Rovai, Alfred P. "Building Sense of Community at a Distance." *International Review in Open and Distance Learning* 3, no. 1 (2002): 1–16.

Scholz, Claudia W. "MOOCs and the Liberal Arts College." *Journal of Online Learning and Teaching* 9, no. 2 (2013): 249–60.

Thelin, John R. "A Crucible Moment: College Learning and Democracy's Future." In *Meeting the Challenge: America's Independent Colleges and Universities since 1956*, 3–35. Washington, DC: Council of Independent Colleges, 2006.

Young, Jeffrey R. "Georgia Tech to Offer a MOOC-like Online Master's Degree, at Low Cost." *Chronicle of Higher Education*, May 14, 2013. http://www.chronicle.com/article/Ga-Tech-to-Offer-a-MOOC-Like/139245. Accessed March 21, 2017.

REACTION
Kevin M. Ross

"The increasing prevalence and importance of digital learning technologies present a fresh set of challenges for CIC members as they seek to deliver a high-quality liberal arts education to a new generation of students."

—Matthew J. Mayhew and Stephen Vassallo

Independent colleges and universities, particularly members of the Council of Independent Colleges (CIC), historically have played—and continue to play—unique roles in the higher education landscape. Each of these institutions was founded at a moment in time to serve a specific population and for a compelling reason. They are not land-grant, government-created or -owned entities, and they are, for the most part, free from the pressures and challenges that accompany being part a state university system. Despite the various and distinct reasons how they came to be, many independent colleges have evolved over time to serve a broader mission and audience. They have done so for a multitude of reasons, though opportunity and survival are most often cited as the motivation for change. Independent colleges through their histories have proven themselves time and again to be adaptable, agile, and prepared to meet new challenges. The above quote highlights another significant opportunity for independent institutions as they consider how to leverage learning technologies.

Though the comparative metrics cited on the number of CIC institutions offering fully online programs (50 percent) versus AASCU institutions (80 percent) are cause for alarm, the authors of this chapter rightly point out that perhaps independent institutions "poised to take advantage of the lessons learned from the first movers" could learn from these previous institutions. They further state that independent colleges "that are only beginning to explore implementing online programs . . . may be in a position of strength, having the opportunity to increase student access, enrollment, revenue, and even make pedagogic improvements."

Each independent institution has a distinct nature. Therefore, detailed prescriptions on how to create and administer a new online program may or may not be effective across independent institutions. Faculty development strategies and incentives may be effective at one institution but not work well at another due to institutional culture, history, and leadership.

Though half of the independent colleges considered in this study have been slow to adopt online degrees, some of the most successful online programs in not-for-profit higher education are associated with CIC member institutions. Institutions such as Chapman University (doing business as Brandman University), St. Leo University, Southern New Hampshire University, Webster University, and other non-CIC member private, not-for-profit institutions were early adopters of online learning and have successfully scaled their programs to tens of thousands of students. In many cases, the populations these institutions sought out were new markets of nontraditional adults whom they had never served before (or at least not at scale), leading to new revenues that were never contemplated before. These pioneering institutions now successfully compete online for students with state university programs.

It is worthwhile to learn from those independent institutions by studying their administrative structure and modes of delivery. Some of these institutions have formed more centralized organizational and administrative structures that are separate from their traditional units, while others remain part of traditional independent university operations.

Students in on-ground classes at large state universities often have the opposite of an independent college student's experience and, in some ways, are truly learning by distance even as they attend class. Large lecture hall format classes taught by teaching assistants or faculty they will never meet stand in stark contrast to faculty-led discussion or seminar-style classes characteristic of most CIC member independent colleges. So, how can an independent institution replicate the best of what happens in their classrooms online?

The second-generation learning environments that have emerged since 2011 provide a robust opportunity for independent colleges to engage current and new populations of students through online and hybrid courses. With the tools available today, true collaboration is possible, and independent colleges' online offerings more closely resemble their on-ground classes, which can be far more engaging than solely asynchronous courses.

Analytics now provide metrics on student learning outcomes and engagement with course material. This data provides opportunities for targeted human interactions by faculty and staff to ensure students remain on track. These experiences more closely resemble what occurs in on-ground independent college teaching environments, but with more regularity and precision. Academic coaches and guides are often assigned to students online in addition to their faculty, which allows for the connections that are missing from solely asynchronous courses.

The new generation learning tools are not just reserved for online classes. On-ground classes are now utilizing content capturing and collaboration tools to engage students after the face-to-face class meetings have ended. As Mayhew and Vassallo state, by utilizing a standard technology platform across traditional undergraduate and online programs, independent institutions may realize cost savings and avoid lack of adoption due to requiring faculty and staff to understand multiple platforms. In this scenario, both current full-time and new part-time faculty are a viable pool of instructors for online programs at independent colleges and universities.

The authors elucidate the remarkable opportunity available to independent colleges and universities to leverage new learning technologies for students they have historically served while also expanding to new markets not previously considered. While these institutions hold not-for-profit status, they are not for loss either. New and expanded programs on ground and online will likely result in additional revenue to support traditional and expanded mission-based activities, ensuring continued institutional health. Whether motivated by competition, survival, or relevancy, independent colleges and universities find themselves in a unique position to once again display their adaptability as they leverage new learning technologies.

5

Ensuring Student Success

LAURIE A. SCHREINER

Scholarly literature on student success in postsecondary education spans over five decades of research that has developed extensive frameworks for defining and understanding the complex nature of such success, as well as strategies for creating campus environments to cultivate it. Despite this attention and the concerted effort of many campuses to foster success for a greater percentage of their students, retention and graduation rates have changed little over the past 30 years, with 41 percent of all students who enter four-year institutions failing to graduate within six years.[1] Of greater concern, however, is the lack of progress in closing the more than 15 percentage point achievement gap that continues to exist between the graduation rates of historically underrepresented students and their Asian and Caucasian counterparts.[2]

The current US legislative and political environment focuses on student success primarily in terms of graduation rates and gainful employment after college; however, focusing solely on retention and graduation rates leads to the inevitable conclusion that admissions selectivity is the best student success strategy,[3] a conclusion that is not helpful for most small independent colleges. Although persistence in the first year is an important index of success and is the gateway to further success in college,[4] a richer and more expansive definition of student success provides greater opportunity to enable students entering private independent colleges to meet their educational goals and make the most of their college experience. A holistic view of student success is congruent with the missions of these institutions, many of which seek to foster character development, civic and moral engagement, service, and leadership, in addition to intellectual development.[5] Such expanded definitions of student success have emerged in the past decade and have encompassed a broad array of attitudes, behaviors, and cognitive outcomes. Perhaps the most comprehensive definition is that of George Kuh, Jillian Kinzie, Jennifer Buckley, Brian Bridges, and John Hayek: "academic achievement; engagement in educationally purposeful activities; satisfaction; acquisition of desired knowledge, skills, and competencies; persistence; and attainment of educational objectives."[6] A recent emphasis on psychosocial elements predictive of student success has led to a holistic conceptualization of student success that focuses not only on cognitive and behavioral aspects of success but also on psychological well-being. Research on *thriving*[7] views student success as optimal functioning in these three domains and has connected students' intellectual, social, and psychological engagement to a wide variety of student success outcomes. Thriving students are engaged in their learning, investing effort and applying their strengths to the challenges they face. They are connected to others in healthy and supportive ways, are open to differences in others, and have a desire to make a difference in the world around them. They have a positive perspective on life that is growth-oriented and that enables them to reframe negative events as learning experiences. Each of these aspects of thriving is malleable, as well as predictive of student persistence,[8] meaning that intentional interventions can enhance levels of thriving and that students' precollege experiences and characteristics are not as likely to influence their success when programs and services are carefully and intentionally designed to promote student thriving.[9]

Background Research

Student success is best viewed as a longitudinal process that begins with college readiness and enrollment, moves through achievement and personal development during college, and culminates in postcollege attainment of rewarding work, relationships, and civic engagement.[10] Each aspect of the process is shaped by multiple factors, with both the institution and the student contributing to the outcome; as a result, there are rarely single solutions for addressing student success challenges. Although John Braxton asserts that "faculty members bear the primary responsibility for most forms of college student success,"[11] in smaller private colleges faculty play an even more important role, as they have made professional choices to join institutions with strong teaching cultures where their actions in and out of the classroom can significantly enhance student success. Thus, the interventions and institutional actions likely to have the greatest effect on student success on these campuses are those that involve the faculty.

Research on student success has focused on student characteristics that predict success in college, the behaviors in which students engage that lead to their learning and persistence, the campus experiences and programming that can enhance student success, and the campus climate that nurtures student success. Awareness of the major findings in each of these areas can enable a campus leader to maintain a two-pronged focus on student success: (a) individual students, and (b) the institutional actions and campus experiences that support student success.

Focus on the Individual Student
Student Characteristics that Predict Success in College

Demographic characteristics that are predictive of student success include household income, generation status, race/ethnicity, and gender, as well as indicators of academic preparation, such as high school GPA or rank in class, admission test scores, number of advanced placement courses, and taking college preparatory courses in high school. Research indicates that low-income, first-generation students from historically underserved populations enter college underprepared and at risk for lower academic performance, dropping out or taking longer to complete their degrees, with men being at greater risk than women.[12] Students' household income, race, gender, generation status, and academic preparation account for about 35 percent of the variation in college students' first-year GPA, with academic preparedness accounting for the largest amount of the variation.[13]

However, recent research indicates that psychosocial factors add significantly to the prediction of college student success. For example, Stephen Robbins and colleagues[14] have found that levels of *academic discipline* are highly predictive of success; that is, students who work hard, invest effort in their academic pursuits, and are motivated to achieve are more likely to succeed. This concept is similar to Angela Duckworth, Christopher Peterson, Michael Matthews, and Dennis Kelly's concept of "grit," defined as "perseverance and passion for long-term goals."[15] William Sedlacek[16] refers to characteristics such as positive self-concept, realistic self-appraisal, strong leadership skills, and having long-range goals as "noncognitive variables" and encourages their use in the admissions process, particularly with students from disadvantaged backgrounds. Citing evidence from universities using noncognitive variables in their admissions processes, Sedlacek[17] indicates that inclusion of these variables increased retention an average of 10 percent for each point increase on the noncognitive assessment instrument, which was significantly greater than using GPA as the predictor.

Rather than "noncognitive factors," Robbins and colleagues[18] prefer the term "psychosocial factors," which incorporate motivation and academic skills, social skills and connection, and self-management. The *thriving* construct incorporates five such psychosocial factors that explain an additional 11–18 percent of the variation in student success outcomes after taking demographic characteristics and campus experiences into consideration: (a) engaged learning, (b) academic determination, (c) diverse citizenship, (d) social connectedness, and (e) positive perspective.[19] Most of the research indicates that many of the psychosocial factors are strongly correlated with personality,[20] but that intentional interventions can teach students these qualities and coping skills. Michelle Louis[21] suggests that students' beliefs about themselves, about learning, and about the academic environment are all characteristics that can be changed within the early weeks of the first semester so that a greater percentage of students succeed. For example, when students have a growth mindset and a mastery goal orientation, they approach the learning process with greater confidence because they view effort as a necessary part of the learning process that they value. Likewise, students with high levels of curiosity, those who believe they are capable of succeeding, and those who are goal-directed tend to experience higher levels of success because they see the academic experience as under their control in the long run. These beliefs and perspectives toward learning can be taught and can directly influence students' likelihood of success.

Student Behaviors Predictive of Success: The Role of Engagement

Much of the current emphasis in the student success literature is on the *educationally purposeful* behaviors in which students engage; for example, the National Survey of Student Engagement (NSSE)[22] is built on the assumption that behavioral engagement leads to student success outcomes. Based on C. Robert Pace's research on quality of effort, as well as Alexander Astin's model of student involvement,[23] the premise is that the amount of time and effort students invest in the academic experience leads to significant success outcomes, including the "skills and dispositions people need to live a productive, satisfying life after college."[24] Each of the behaviors measured is empirically linked to student learning, as well as to persistence to degree. For example, the more students engage in active and collaborative learning behaviors, the greater their academic success and persistence to graduation.[25] Among the ten engagement indicators measured by NSSE, other behaviors include learning strategies, interaction with faculty and other students, and discussions with diverse others.

Notably, NSSE not only assesses student engagement in educationally purposeful behaviors but also aspects of the campus environment that support and encourage greater engagement.[26] However, the motivational factors that lead students to engage in educationally purposeful behaviors are not measured by this instrument; thus, a comprehensive approach to student success would include measures of both psychosocial factors and behavioral predictors of success, along with an assessment of institutional practices.

Focus on Institutional Support for Student Success
Campus Experiences and Programs That Enhance Student Success

The student success literature is replete with evidence that student-faculty interaction, cooperation among students, active learning, prompt feedback, time on task, high expectations, and a respect for diverse talents and learning styles is associated with student success.[27] In addition, the Association of American Colleges and Universities[28] has emphasized the adoption of *high-impact practices*[29] that are strongly connected to student learning and success. These include:

- First-year experiences
- Common intellectual experiences
- Learning communities
- Writing-intensive courses
- Collaborative assignments and projects
- Undergraduate research
- Diversity/global learning
- Service learning, community-based learning
- Internships
- Capstone courses and projects

Research indicates that college students who engage in these high-impact practices each year report higher levels of deep learning and greater gains in learning and personal development.[30] Notably, these high-impact practices benefit underserved students even more than cultural majority students, yet underserved students are also least likely to access these practices.[31] Colleges that are less selective are just as able to incorporate these practices into their students' experiences as institutions that are more selective, providing myriad opportunities to impact the success of a diverse student body. Particularly as the faculty of liberal arts colleges tend to engage to a greater degree with their students and express greater commitment to a learning ethos on campus,[32] there is a powerful resource available to impact student success through the practices of faculty. Such practices as active learning, higher order questions, meaningful assignments, use of clear and relevant examples, timely and instructive feedback, and frequent rewarding interaction are empirically supported strategies by which faculty can enhance student success.[33]

In addition to high-impact practices, there is strong evidence that particular campus programs and services are connected to higher rates of student success. These include one-stop student services; access to learning technologies that are mobile, flexible, and encourage student involvement in the learning experience; academic advising that is goal-oriented, relational and instructive, and functions "as the hub of support services for students;" and career planning and advising services that connect students to a sense of meaning and purpose in life.[34] Although "the impact of college is largely determined by individual effort and involvement in the academic, interpersonal, and extra-curricular offerings on campus,"[35] the institution plays a powerful role in shaping its programs and services to encourage student engagement.

A Campus Climate That Nurtures Student Success

Perhaps more important than the programs and services that institutions offer is the campus ethos that communicates expectations to students and sends signals regarding the value the institution places on students' learning and personal development. Braxton and colleagues[36] refer to this institutional stance as "institutional integrity" and a "commitment to student welfare." Institutional integrity reflects the degree to which an institution is accurately portrayed during admissions, faculty and staff embody the mission of the institution, and students' expectations are met or exceeded. Institutional commitment to student welfare is expressed in policies and practices that convey "an abiding concern for the growth and development of its students."[37] Research indicates that both of these institutional features are strongly connected to students' social integration on campus, which then influences their persistence to degree in residential colleges and universities such as those in the Council of Independent Colleges.[38]

The most thoroughly researched components of campus climate that matter to student success, however, include the following elements that are characteristic of institutions studied by Kuh and associates,[39] those whose student success rates were significantly above what would be predicted by their entering student profile:

- A clear, coherent mission and philosophy
- An unshakeable focus on student learning
- High performance expectations for all students
- The widespread use of effective educational practices
- Human-scale settings
- A collaborative, improvement-oriented ethic
- Language and traditions supporting student success.[40]

Institutions whose members see student learning and success as a high priority and shared responsibility of all and work together to create and communicate clearly identified pathways for students to succeed are likely to have higher graduation rates, more satisfied alumni, and a higher percentage of students who have the "habits of the mind and heart that enlarge their capacity for continuous learning and personal development."[41] The fundamental belief underlying this positive campus climate is the talent development philosophy;[42] those who subscribe to this perspective believe that "every student can learn under the right conditions,"[43] and they structure the learning environment accordingly.

For students of color, sense of belonging and validation[44] are critical ingredients of the campus climate. Sense of belonging refers to social support and feeling valued, while validation confirms to students that they deserve to be in college and can succeed. In addition, perceptions of institutional integrity and commitment to student welfare contribute significantly to variations in the sense of belonging experienced by students of color.[45] Faculty are in a particularly powerful position to validate students; Ash and Schreiner's[46] research on students of color in independent colleges found that students' perceptions of institutional integrity and commitment to student welfare as well as their ability to thrive in college were directly influenced by faculty's inclusive pedagogy. Faculty who choose to teach in Council of Independent Colleges (CIC) institutions often have done so because of their commitment to students and the learning process, finding enjoyment in teaching and mentoring;[47] CIC institutions thus have a powerful lever for impacting the success of students of color.

Strengths and Challenges for CIC Institutions

Research conducted on behalf of the CIC has noted a considerable number of strengths of private independent colleges, as well as common challenges faced by such institutions. This research tends to compare private, nonprofit, nondoctoral four-year institutions to their public counterparts; at times, the comparison is between the four-year private and public sectors of higher education.[48]

Strengths of Private, Nonprofit, Nondoctoral Four-Year Institutions

The strengths of this sector of higher education are evident in both their practices and their outcomes. Students attending private colleges and universities are more likely to be engaged in educationally effective experiences than those attending public institutions. In addition, students attending private nondoctoral four-year institutions are more likely to engage in multiple high-impact practices, to be academically challenged, and to encounter effective teaching practices.[49] Gonyea and Kinzie conclude that "a more academically challenging education, better relations with faculty members, more substantial interactions with others on campus, and the consistent perception that students have learned and grown more"[50] characterize the experiences of students in private colleges and universities. As a result, students in this sector of higher education tend to have more favorable outcomes, such as higher overall satisfaction, greater learning gains (except in quantitative reasoning), higher likelihood of choosing the institution again, higher graduation rates (52.7 percent in four years, compared to 27.1 percent at public nondoctoral institutions), and less time to degree completion, all of which are notable student success outcomes. Added to these outcomes is the success these institutions have with low-income and first-generation students, as well as historically underrepresented students. Rine[51] noted that although fewer of these students enroll in this sector of higher education, they tend to be more successful within it: 42.3 percent of first-generation students and 36.1 percent of low-income students graduate in four years, compared to four-year graduation rates of 18.4 percent for first-generation students and 12.7 percent for low-income students in the public nondoctoral sector. Students of color are also more likely to graduate at independent colleges and universities: 45 percent of black students and 62 percent of Hispanic students graduate within six years, compared to 40 percent and 50 percent, respectively, at public institutions.[52]

Contributing to these success outcomes is an environment that tends to be characterized by higher levels of meaningful and rewarding student-faculty interaction outside of class and active learning within the classroom. Classes tend to be smaller, students are more likely to meet with their advisor, and mentoring experiences are more common. There is greater involvement in campus life, including leadership opportunities, athletics, and service-learning experiences.[53] Thus, CIC institutions are well positioned to positively influence student success.

Challenges of the CIC Sector of Higher Education

The significant strengths of this sector of higher education are evident despite the challenges these institutions face. Most are tuition-driven institutions, about one-third are located in parts of the United States where the college-going population is in significant decline,[54] and the lack of diversity within the institutions creates a challenging environment for recruiting and retaining historically underserved students.

Given the demographic shifts in the United States, the future of higher education rests squarely with institutions that are best equipped to serve students of color, as well as students who are first generation or from low-income homes. Although CIC institutions have done relatively well in enabling these students to succeed, most low-income and first generation students and students of color do not choose to enroll in private, nonprofit, nondoctoral colleges and universities.[55] Latino students, in particular, are among the least likely to choose this sector of higher education, yet this ethnic group is the fastest-growing in higher education.[56]

The relative lack of compositional diversity within the student body of many CIC institutions, coupled with challenging locations, is compounded by a lack of diverse faculty, staff, and administrators. Even when the student body becomes more diverse, if campus leadership and role models are mostly white there remains a cultural dominance that affects the campus ethos and may hinder the success of students of color. In addition to less racial and ethnic diversity on campus, students attending small independent colleges report fewer discussions with others who hold different political and religious views,[57] which may be partially a function of the number of religiously affiliated colleges within this sector of higher education.

Strategies to Foster Student Success at Independent Colleges and Universities

Any strategies to enable students to succeed in small and mid-sized independent colleges must take into consideration the mission, strengths, and challenges of the institution, as well as the characteristics of the students whom campus leaders desire to enroll. There is no single prescription for student success; what works for one campus may not work as well for another. But foundational to all student success efforts is a shared mission and vision within the institution, along with specific knowledge about the institution and the students it admits. What a campus leader chooses to measure is a reflection of what matters; thus, carefully selecting and assessing student success outcomes is the first step to creating an environment for success. Many instruments exist to help institutional leaders gather data connected to student success; more important is how that data is used to make decisions that affect student success.

Before beginning any student success initiatives, the following questions should be asked by campus leaders to drive the decision-making process:

- How do we define student success—and why has that definition been chosen over others?
- Who thrives on this campus? Are there differences in subpopulations of students' intellectual, social, and psychological engagement with this institution? Does this matter to us?
- Are there certain types of students who are more likely to graduate from this place than other types of students? How do we know?
- What outcomes do we desire in our students, and how are those in alignment with our mission and our recruiting practices? Are we helping students achieve these outcomes?
- Who are we serving well? What types of students are most satisfied with their experiences here? Are there subpopulations of students who are significantly less satisfied or successful than others?

When an institution selects outcomes in advance of any new initiative and assesses the effect of all programs and services on campus, including the campus climate, it initiates a continuous feedback loop of goal setting, data gathering, and analysis of the data that leads to better programs and services to foster student success. Disaggregating the data by race, socioeconomic status, gender, class level, commuter status, generation status, and other variables important to the institution allows for greater precision in targeting students most in need of particular services. Having all voices at the table when analyzing and interpreting the results and determining a course of action ensures that the needs of underrepresented students are not overlooked.[58] Being willing to stop doing what does not work takes courage, but it is also a necessary aspect of ensuring student success.

Once campus leaders have conducted a thorough assessment of the current state of success among all students on campus, a simultaneous two-pronged approach targeting individual students as well as institutional actions is most likely to foster student success and thriving. The recommendations below are framed in terms of these two strategies.

Equip Students for Success

Strategies focused on helping each individual student succeed on campus begin with recruitment, continue through admissions and orientation, and are most evident at each transition a student experiences within the college environment. The more unfamiliar students are with the college experience or the institution itself, the more important it is to communicate these strategies and provide individual support.

1. Identify the Talents, Needs, and Expectations of Each Student at Entrance

Because students' level of academic preparation is highly predictive of their academic success in college, most institutions welcome students to campus with a battery of placement tests aimed at assessing deficits and areas of underpreparedness. Although this process may be necessary, coupling it with assessments of students' talents sends a message of validation that emphasizes the contribution each student is expected to make to the learning environment and begins the college journey by addressing the single most powerful element in student success: motivation.[59] Talent assessments such as the Clifton StrengthsFinder[60] or the Values in Action Inventory of Strengths (VIA-IS);[61] identify assets that students already possess; reminding students of these areas of potential strength within them has been shown to increase their motivation, bolster their self-confidence, and equip them with pathways for reaching their goals.[62]

Smaller independent colleges are ideally positioned not only to identify their students' talents and needs at entrance but also to respond more quickly with personal attention. For example, a strengths identification process during orientation can seamlessly move into small group discussions with peer leaders, a focus on calling and vocation with their advisor or career coach, and a strengths development curriculum undergirding the faculty-led first-year seminar. In addition, assessing first-year students' expectations of college in a conversation with a peer mentor or an academic advisor can help set the student on a positive trajectory, as areas of unfamiliarity are highlighted and adjustments are made. Providing this data to the institution equips leaders with actionable information for addressing students' needs and raising campus awareness of the hopes and goals of the incoming class.

2. Communicate Expectations for Success

Because first-generation students or those from low-income neighborhoods and schools may be unfamiliar with the college environment and not know what to expect, communicating expectations for success begins during recruitment and continues through graduation, and should engage the entire campus. Messages that convey high standards, as well as a belief in students' ability to meet those standards, and that articulate appropriate success strategies are needed from the moment a student steps on campus, as these messages serve to validate students and provide a road map for their success, strategies that are an important foundation.[63] These messages can be from institutional representatives during orientation, faculty in each class, advisors, peer leaders, and student life professionals. Examining the frequency, timing, and content of institutional messages to students; ensuring that there are multiple "touch points" for students, particularly during transitions; and providing ongoing navigational systems for students who may not have the cultural capital to know what strategies will help them be successful can enable a broader variety of students to succeed on campus.

3. Create Individualized Pathways to Success for Each Student That Connect Them to Campus Resources and Relationships

Advising is often a strength of smaller independent colleges. Good advising is not simply course selection; it is an intentional, student-centered, and learning-oriented process of helping students make meaning within their college experience.[64] Ensuring that every student designs a clear pathway to success in consultation with their advisor is one of the most effective ways to help students thrive.[65] Particularly when the pathways to thriving differ across cultural contexts and student backgrounds,[66] advisors who are culturally competent, knowledgeable about student development and the institution, and who see their mission as helping students find meaning and purpose in their college experience can make a significant difference in these students' lives. Partnering advising with career services, so that students encounter a seamless experience of choosing a major and exploring career options within a context of meaning and purpose, exponentially increases the impact of advising.

As advisors work with students to create an individualized success plan that includes accessing specific campus resources, they normalize the help-seeking process, which can enable a greater proportion of students to experience success. When peer leaders, resident assistants, tutors, and other student leaders can direct students to campus resources as well as explicitly relate how they personally have accessed those resources, it sends a powerful message to students that they are expected to utilize campus resources and connect with people in order to be successful.

4. Teach Students Coping Skills from the Beginning of Their First Year

College students inevitably face challenges and experience negative events, despite individualized plans for success. Because students with proactive coping skills and an ability to reframe negative events as learning opportunities have a higher likelihood of success in college and report higher levels of thriving,[67] teaching students these skills early in their college experience sets them on a trajectory for success. Specific coping skills that can undergird student success include what Carol Dweck[68] calls a "growth mindset"—a belief that change is possible and that it is the quality of the effort that determines the level of one's success. Research has demonstrated that faculty can teach students a growth mindset using readings, brief videos, and tips from successful students.[69] Studies on thriving indicate that students with a positive perspective, defined as realistic optimism, are more resilient in the face of challenges because they believe they will succeed eventually if they invest quality effort and use the appropriate strategies.[70] Michelle Louis[71] suggests that these coping skills can be introduced at orientation and taught by peer leaders, advisors, and faculty early in the term, then reinforced as students seek help from academic support services, career counselors, and counseling center professionals.

Often overlooked as a coping resource, acknowledging and cultivating students' spirituality can also be a pathway to success, particularly for students of color.[72] An environment that allows students' spirituality to flourish is a strength of independent colleges, particularly those that are faith-based. Large national studies of student spirituality, as well as studies of thriving in college have indicated that spirituality is a pathway to success for many students, and particularly for students of color.[73] Building on this strength means expanding campus awareness of different cultural expressions of faith and spirituality and providing welcoming space for students to explore meaning and purpose in life and to struggle with existential questions.

5. Ensure That All Students Experience Appropriate High-Impact Practices Each Year

Because high-impact practices are empirically connected to student success[74] and are typically a strength of independent colleges, ensuring that these practices are accessible to all students and are intentionally placed at appropriate times in a student's experience increases the likelihood of students' success. For example, placing all entering students—including commuters—into a learning community of linked courses that includes their required first-year seminar and incorporates significant service learning, is one of the most successful approaches that impacts deep learning.[75] Continuing the intentional design of high-impact practices into the sophomore year, with study abroad and student-faculty research partnerships, for example, can address the "invisibility" and lack of meaning and purpose that can contribute to sophomore disengagement.[76]

Create a Thriving Campus Culture

Focusing on individual students is only part of a comprehensive strategy for student success; the corollary focus is on institutional actions that can enhance students' likelihood of succeeding. Effective institutions are proactive and responsive, a stance that necessitates an organizational climate in which collaboration and trust characterize daily work, feedback is valued, and there is a commitment to keeping the promises made at admission and implicit within the mission of the institution. The recommendations below are aimed at creating and sustaining a thriving culture on campus.

1. Cultivate a Sense of Community

Research on student thriving in college indicates that a sense of community on campus is the key predictor of whether students thrive.[77] Students, faculty, and staff who report a strong sense of community on campus feel they are part of and can contribute to a dependable network of people who value them, are committed to their welfare, and are able to meet their needs.[78] A sense of community thus encompasses not only a sense of belonging but also a feeling of ownership, emotional connections, and support, as well as a commitment to common goals and the ability to collaborate effectively to accomplish those goals. Cheng[79] has found that a campus ethos centered on engagement in learning, where students feel accepted and valued and are encouraged to express their own beliefs, is the strongest contributor to a campus sense of community.

Faculty, staff, and administrators who are not only committed to the mission of the institution but also exhibit "an unshakeable focus on student learning"[80] as their primary purpose, create a climate in which students are likely to feel valued and supported in their educational goals.

2. Capitalize on the Strength of the Faculty

Faculty are one of the greatest assets for student success and are a strength of independent colleges. In this sector of higher education, faculty are likely to be committed to effective teaching and to rewarding interactions with students.[81] Building on a strong faculty means ensuring that faculty are expected and equipped to use the most effective teaching practices, are supported in their efforts to interact with students and to partner in research with undergraduate students, and are rewarded in the tenure and promotion process for engaging in these strategies. These actions are characteristic of college and university leaders who create an "institutional culture of teaching"[82] that is one of the surest ways to support student success on a campus.

Ken Bain[83] notes in his study of the best college teachers that they were those who "look for and appreciate the individual value of each student" and "had great faith in students' ability to achieve." Institutional hiring, professional development, and promotion practices should clearly indicate that this type of faculty member is highly valued by the institution. Including faculty in institutional plans for enhancing student success is vital in smaller independent colleges.

3. Develop Partnerships between Academic and Student Affairs Professionals

Collaborative engagement is one of the hallmarks of campuses whose student success rates are higher than predicted.[84] When student success is perceived as a shared responsibility, partnerships between academic and student affairs professionals create "seamless learning environments"[85] that can impact students' lives. Examples of partnerships include care teams of faculty, academic support staff, and student life staff who respond to students in need; team approaches to learning communities; and regular cross-department collaboration on the design, implementation, and assessment of student success programs.

4. Deliver on Institutional Promises

An integral element of whether students experience a strong sense of community on campus is their perception of *institutional integrity,* the degree to which the institution is delivering on its promises.[86] Such promises are implicit as well as explicit and begin during the admissions process, as they are conveyed through admissions materials, websites, campus tours, and conversations with admissions counselors. When the post-enrollment campus experience is not what was portrayed during the admissions process, students feel a sense of betrayal—and this perception is more keenly felt by students of color.[87] Examining policies and practices through the eyes of students, and particularly through the eyes of students who are not in the majority on campus, can pinpoint ways in which the institution may not be portraying itself accurately or may not be meeting students' expectations.

A critical aspect of delivering on institutional promises is that inclusivity becomes imperative. Colleges and universities must prepare students to navigate an increasingly diverse and complex world; equipping them with multicultural competence and communication skills for this world is an integral part of the educational process. As Daryl Smith[88] notes, diversity therefore must be one of the core indicators of institutional effectiveness. She likens diversity to technology, which is no longer an optional part of teaching, learning, research, or any other function on campus. All campus members are expected to be skilled and use technology; in the same way, effectively teaching and working with students who represent multiple and intersecting identities on campus is a skill we all must develop in ourselves so that our students are well equipped for success in life. Our future sustainability demands that we create inclusive learning environments where all students can thrive.

Institutions that ensure student success are those that keep the focus on each individual student while addressing the systems that help or hinder success for all students. A key question leaders committed to student success ask before making any decision is "How will this action help our students learn and thrive here?" When campus leaders are aware of the wide variety of students on campus and the needs and expectations of these students, they can begin to create responsive systems to address those needs. Keeping student success at the forefront of the institution as a shared responsibility of all campus members is the ongoing leadership task; when each faculty, staff, and administrator sees himself or herself as a contributor to student learning and success, then all students can thrive.

Suggested Areas for Future Exploration

I suggest three areas for future exploration by scholars and practitioners in smaller private colleges. First is to gather data more specific to CIC institutions and their needs. Most of the current reports on the CIC website compare private nondoctoral to public nondoctoral, or all private institutions to all public institutions. Particularly when all private nonprofit universities are a proxy for the CIC, the results may mask some of the realities in the smaller, less selective CIC members. Studies in which data is gathered directly for the CIC could illuminate additional strengths and challenges for this sector of higher education. Institutional leaders could agree to gather and report data as part of a CIC consortium in order to better describe their students and their needs.

The second recommendation for future exploration is to determine the predictors of student success on CIC campuses. At this point, it is not possible to ascertain how much of the variation in success rates is institutional and how much is at the student level. Scholars within the CIC or in the broader arena of higher education could use hierarchical linear modeling of data gathered from CIC institutions to begin to address this question of what student characteristics, campus experiences, and institutional qualities are most predictive of student thriving and success on CIC campuses.

The final recommendation is to study success, both within the students themselves and within CIC institutions. For example, alumni directors and career counselors on individual campuses can interview successful graduates in order to paint a picture for incoming students of what it takes to succeed on their campus. Faculty in each classroom can highlight the strategies that successful students have used in their courses and can share their own journey with students as an example of how to engage in the learning process. Student life professionals can assess the thriving levels of students in their residence halls and can use thriving as an additional indicator of program effectiveness. By studying the experiences of thriving students, the pathways employed by successful and satisfied alumni, the campuses with high percentages of diverse students who are thriving, and the programs and services that are effective, a picture can begin to emerge of the elements that are most conducive to student success in CIC institutions.

NOTES

1. US Department of Education, "Condition of Education 2015."
2. Ross et al., "Higher Education."
3. Kinzie, "New View of Student Success."
4. Braxton et al., *Rethinking College Student Retention*.
5. Braskamp, Trautvetter, and Ward, *Putting Students First*.

6. Kuh et al., *Piecing Together*, 10.

7. Schreiner, "From Surviving to Thriving"; Schreiner, "'Thriving Quotient.'"

8. Schreiner et al., "Measuring the Malleable"; Schreiner et al., "College Student Thriving."

9. Schreiner, "Positive Psychology and Higher Education."

10. Perna and Jones, *State of College Access*.

11. Braxton, "Theory of Faculty Professional Choices," 181.

12. Adelman, "Toolbox Revisited."

13. Robbins et al., "Unraveling the Differential Effects."

14. Ibid.

15. Duckworth et al., "Grit," 1087.

16. Sedlacek, *Beyond the Big Test*.

17. Ibid.; Sedlacek, "Case for Noncognitive Measures."

18. Robbins et al., "Unraveling the Differential Effects."

19. Schreiner, "Positive Psychology and Higher Education."

20. Robertson-Kraft and Duckworth, "True Grit."

21. Louis, "Enhancing Intellectual Development."

22. NSSE, "NSSE Engagement Indicators."

23. Pace, "Measuring the Quality"; Astin, "Student Involvement."

24. Kuh, " Student Engagement: Conceptual and Empirical," 5.

25. NSSE Psychometric Portfolio, "Validity."

26. Kuh, "Student Engagement: Conceptual Framework."

27. Chickering and Gamson, "Seven Principles for Good Practice."

28. Association of American Colleges and Universities, "LEAP Vision for Learning."

29. Kuh, "High-Impact Educational Practices."

30. Brownell and Swaner, "Five High-Impact Practices."

31. Kuh, "High-Impact Educational Practices."

32. Braxton, "Theory of Faculty Professional Choices."

33. Ibid.

34. Respectively, Lonabocker and Wager, "Connecting One-Stop Student Services"; DeBlois and Oblinger, "Learning Technologies Habley and Bloom"; "Advice that Makes a Difference," 174; Bullock, Reardon, and Lenz, "Academic and Career Decisions."

35. Pascarella and Terenzini, *How College Affects Students*, 602.

36. Braxton et al., *Rethinking College Student Retention*.

37. Ibid., 86.

38. Ibid.

39. Kuh et al., *Student Success in College*.

40. Kinzie and Kuh, "Creating a Student-Centered Culture," 21.

41. Kuh, "Student Engagement: Conceptual and Empirical," 5.

42. Astin, *Achieving Educational Excellence*.

43. Kuh et al., *Student Success in College*, 77.

44. For sense of belonging, see Hurtado and Carter, "Effects of College Transition"; Strayhorn, *College Students' Sense of Belonging*. For validation, see Rendon, "Validating Culturally Diverse Students."

45. Ash and Schreiner, "Pathways to Success."

46. Ibid.

47. Gonyea and Kinzie, "Independent Colleges and Student Engagement."

48. Ibid.; Rine, "Expanding Access and Opportunity"; Strand, "Making Sure They Make It."

49. Gonyea and Kinzie, "Independent Colleges and Student Engagement."
50. Ibid., 4.
51. Rine, "Expanding Access and Opportunity."
52. Council of Independent Colleges, "Students of Color Graduation Rates."
53. Rine, "Expanding Access and Opportunity."
54. Council of Independent Colleges, "Making the Case."
55. US Department of Education, "Condition of Education 2013."
56. Ibid.
57. Gonyea and Kinzie, "Independent Colleges and Student Engagement."
58. Smith, *Diversity's Promise.*
59. Pintrich, "Motivational Science Perspective."
60. Gallup Organization, "Clifton StrengthsFinder."
61. Seligman, Park, and Peterson, "Values in Action."
62. Schreiner, "From Surviving to Thriving."
63. Rendon, "Validating Culturally Diverse Students."
64. Kimball and Campbell, "Advising Strategies."
65. Bloom, Hutson, and He, "Appreciative Advising."
66. Schreiner, "Different Pathways to Thriving."
67. On likelihood of success, see Bean and Eaton, "Psychological Model"; on thriving, see Schreiner, "Positive Psychology and Higher Education."
68. Dweck, *Mindset.*
69. As cited in Louis, "Enhancing Intellectual Development."
70. Schreiner, "Positive Psychology and Higher Education."
71. Louis, "Enhancing Intellectual Development."
72. McIntosh, "Thriving and Spirituality."
73. On spirituality, see Astin, Astin, and Lindholm, *Cultivating the Spirit*; on thriving, see Schreiner et al., "Measuring the Malleable"; on students of color, see McIntosh, "Thriving and Spirituality."
74. Kuh, "High-Impact Educational Practices."
75. Kuh, O'Donnell, and Reed, "Ensuring Quality."
76. Kennedy and Upcraft, "Keys to Student Success."
77. Schreiner et al., "Measuring the Malleable."
78. Lounsbury and DeNeui, "Psychological Sense of Community."
79. Cheng, "Students' Sense of Campus Community."
80. Kinzie and Kuh, "Creating a Student-Centered Culture," 21.
81. Gonyea and Kinzie, "Independent Colleges and Student Engagement."
82. Braxton, "Theory of Faculty Professional Choices," 194.
83. Bain, *Best College Teachers*, 72.
84. Kuh et al., *Student Success in College.*
85. Kuh, "Guiding Principles," 135.
86. Braxton et al., *Rethinking College Student Retention.*
87. Schreiner, "Different Pathways to Thriving."
88. Smith, *Diversity's Promise.*

REFERENCES

Adelman, Clifford. "The Toolbox Revisited: Paths to Degree Completion from High School through College." Washington, DC: US Department of Education, 2006.

Ash, Allison N., and Laurie A. Schreiner. "Pathways to Success for Students of Color in Christian Colleges: The Role of Institutional Integrity and Sense of Community." *Christian Higher Education* 15, no. 1–2 (January 1, 2016): 38–61. doi:10.1080/1536375 9.2015.1106356.

Association of American Colleges and Universities. "The LEAP Vision for Learning: Outcomes, Practices, Impact, and Employers' Views." Washington, DC: Association of American Colleges and Universities, 2011.

Astin, Alexander W. *Achieving Educational Excellence.* San Francisco: Jossey-Bass, 1985.

———. "Student Involvement: A Development Theory for Higher Education." *Journal of College Student Personnel* 25 (1984): 297–308.

Astin, Alexander W., Helen S. Astin, and Jennifer A. Lindholm. *Cultivating the Spirit: How College Can Enhance Students' Inner Lives.* San Francisco: Jossey-Bass, 2010.

Bain, Ken. *What the Best College Teachers Do.* Cambridge, MA: Harvard University Press, 2004.

Bean, John P., and S. Bogdan Eaton. "A Psychological Model of College Student Retention." In *Reworking the Student Departure Puzzle*, edited by John M. Braxton, 48–61. Nashville: Vanderbilt University Press, 2000.

Bloom, Jennifer L., Bryant L. Hutson, and Ye He. "Appreciative Advising." In *Academic Advising Approaches: Strategies that Teach Students to Make the Most of College*, edited by Jayne K. Drake, Peggy Jordan, and Marsha A. Miller, 83–100. San Francisco: Jossey-Bass, 2013.

Braskamp, Larry A., Lois Calian Trautvetter, and Kelly Ward. *Putting Students First: How Colleges Develop Students Purposefully.* Bolton, MA: Anker, 2006.

Braxton, John M. "Toward a Theory of Faculty Professional Choices in Teaching that Foster College Student Success." In *Higher Education*, edited by John C. Smart, 181–207. Handbook of Theory and Research 23. Dordrecht, NL: Springer, 2008. doi:10.1007/978-1-4020-6959-8_6.

Braxton, John M., William R. Doyle, Harold V. Hartley III, Amy S. Hirschy, Willis A. Jones, and Michael K. McLendon. *Rethinking College Student Retention.* San Francisco: Jossey-Bass, 2014.

Brownell, Jayne E., and Lynn E. Swaner. "Five High-Impact Practices: Research on Learning Outcomes, Completion, and Quality." Washington, DC: Association of American Colleges and Universities, 2010.

Bullock, Emily E., Robert C. Reardon, and Janet G. Lenz. "Planning Good Academic and Career Decisions." In *Fostering Student Success in the Campus Community*, edited by Gary L. Kramer, 193–213. San Francisco: Jossey-Bass, 2007.

Cheng, David X. "Students' Sense of Campus Community: What It Means, and What to Do About It." *NASPA Journal* 41, no. 2 (January 1, 2004): 216–34. doi:10. 2202/1949-6605.1331.

Chickering, Arthur W., and Zelda F. Gamson. "Seven Principles for Good Practice in Undergraduate Education." *AAHE Bulletin* (March 1987): 3–7.

Council of Independent Colleges. "Students of Color Graduation Rates." 2014. https://www.cic.edu/resources-research/charts-data?&keyMessage=2&topic=24. Accessed April 11, 2017.

DeBlois, Peter B., and Diana G. Oblinger. "Learning Technologies that Serve Students." In *Fostering Student Success in the Campus Community*, edited by Gary L. Kramer, 145–70. San Francisco: Jossey-Bass, 2007.

Duckworth, Angela L., Christopher Peterson, Michael D. Matthews, and Dennis R. Kelly. "Grit: Perseverance and Passion for Long-Term Goals." *Journal of Personality and Social Psychology* 92, no. 6 (2007): 1087–1101. doi:10.1037/0022-3514.92.6.1087.

Dweck, Carol S. *Mindset: The New Psychology of Success.* New York: Random House, 2006.

Gallup Organization. "Clifton StrengthsFinder." Princeton, NJ: Gallup Press, 1999.

Gonyea, Robert M., and Jillian Kinzie. "Independent Colleges and Student Engagement: Descriptive Analysis by Institutional Type." Washington, DC: Council of Independent Colleges, 2015.

Habley, Wesley R., and Jennifer L. Bloom. "Giving Advice that Makes a Difference." In *Fostering Student Success in the Campus Community*, edited by Gary L. Kramer, 171–92. San Francisco: Jossey-Bass, 2007.

Hurtado, Sylvia, and Deborah Faye Carter. "Effects of College Transition and Perceptions of the Campus Racial Climate on Latino College Students' Sense of Belonging." *Sociology of Education* 70, no. 4 (1997): 324–45. doi:10.2307/2673270.

Kennedy, Kristen, and M. Lee Upcraft. "Keys to Student Success: A Look at the Literature." In *Helping Sophomores Succeed: Understanding and Improving the Second-Year Experience*, edited by Mary S. Hunter, Barbara F. Tobolowsky, John N. Gardner, Scott E. Evenbeck, Jerry A. Pattengale, Molly A. Schaller, and Laurie A. Schreiner, 30–42. San Francisco: Jossey-Bass, 2010.

Kimball, Ezekiel, and Susan M. Campbell. "Advising Strategies to Support Student Learning Success: Linking Theory and Philosophy with Intentional Practice." In *Academic Advising Approaches: Strategies that Teach Students to Make the Most of College*, edited by Jayne K. Drake, Peggy Jordan, and Marsha A. Miller, 3–16. San Francisco: Jossey-Bass, 2013.

Kinzie, Jillian. "A New View of Student Success." In *Thriving in Transitions: A Research-Based Approach to College Student Success*, edited by Laurie A. Schreiner, Michelle C. Louis, and Denise D. Nelson, xi–xxx. Columbia: University of South Carolina, National Resource Center for the First-Year Experience and Students in Transition, 2012.

Kinzie, Jillian, and George D. Kuh. "Creating a Student-Centered Culture." In *Fostering Student Success in the Campus Community*, edited by Gary L. Kramer, 17–43. San Francisco: Jossey-Bass, 2007.

Kuh, George D. "Guiding Principles for Creating Seamless Learning Environments for Undergraduates." *Journal of College Student Development* 37, no. 2 (1996): 135–48.

———. "High-Impact Educational Practices: What They Are, Who Has Access to Them, and Why They Matter." Washington, DC: Association of American Colleges and Universities, 2008.

———. "The National Survey of Student Engagement: Conceptual and Empirical Foundations." *New Directions for Institutional Research* 2009, no. 141 (March 1, 2009): 5–20. doi:10.1002/ir.283.

———. "The National Survey of Student Engagement: Conceptual Framework and Overview of Psychometric Properties." Bloomington: Indiana University, Center for Postsecondary Research, 2001.

Kuh, George D., Jillian Kinzie, Jennifer A. Buckley, Brian K. Bridges, and John C. Hayek. *Piecing Together the Student Success Puzzle: Research, Propositions, and Recommendations: ASHE Higher Education Report.* San Francisco: Jossey-Bass, 2011.

Kuh, George D., Jillian Kinzie, John H. Schuh, and Elizabeth J. Whitt. *Student Success in College: Creating Conditions that Matter.* San Francisco: Jossey-Bass, 2005.

Kuh, George D., Ken O'Donnell, and Sally Reed. "Ensuring Quality and Taking High-Impact Practices to Scale." Washington, DC: Association of American Colleges and Universities, 2013.

Lonabocker, Louise, and J. James Wagner. "Connecting One-Stop Student Services." In

Fostering Student Success in the Campus Community, edited by Gary L. Kramer, 120–44. San Francisco: Jossey-Bass, 2007.

Louis, Michelle C. "Enhancing Intellectual Development and Academic Success in College: Insights and Strategies from Positive Psychology." In *Positive Psychology on the College Campus*, edited by John C. Wade, Lawrence I. Marks, and Roderick D. Hetzel, 99–132. Oxford: Oxford University Press, 2015.

Lounsbury, John W., and Daniel DeNeui. "Psychological Sense of Community on Campus." *College Student Journal* 29, no. 3 (1995): 270–77.

McIntosh, Eric James. "Thriving and Spirituality: Making Meaning of Meaning Making for Students of Color." *About Campus* 19, no. 6 (January 1, 2015): 16–23. doi:10.1002/abc.21175.

NSSE. "NSSE Engagement Indicators." 2014. http://nsse.indiana.edu/html/engagement_indicators.cfm. Accessed March 24, 2017.

NSSE Psychometric Portfolio. "Validity—Predicting Retention and Degree Progress." Bloomington: Indiana University, Center for Postsecondary Research, 2010.

Pace, C. Robert. "Measuring the Quality of Student Effort." *Current Issues in Higher Education* 2 (1980): 10–16.

Pascarella, Ernest T., and Patrick T. Terenzini. *How College Affects Students: A Third Decade of Research*. Vol. 2. San Francisco: Jossey-Bass, 2005.

Perna, Laura W., and Anthony P. Jones, eds. *The State of College Access and Completion: Improving College Success for Students from Underrepresented Groups*. New York: Routledge, 2013.

Pintrich, Paul R. "A Motivational Science Perspective on the Role of Student Motivation in Learning and Teaching Contexts." *Journal of Educational Psychology* 95, no. 4 (2003): 667–86. doi:10.1037/0022-0663.95.4.667.

Rendon, Laura I. "Validating Culturally Diverse Students: Toward a New Model of Learning and Student Development." *Innovative Higher Education* 19, no. 1 (September 1, 1994): 33–51. doi:10.1007/BF01191156.

Rine, Jesse P. "Expanding Access and Opportunity: How Small and Mid-Sized Independent Colleges Serve First-Generation and Low-Income Students." Washington, DC: Council of Independent Colleges, 2015.

Robbins, Steven B., Jeff Allen, Alex Casillas, Christina Hamme Peterson, and Huy Le. "Unraveling the Differential Effects of Motivational and Skills, Social, and Self-Management Measures from Traditional Predictors of College Outcomes." *Journal of Educational Psychology* 98, no. 3 (2006): 598–616. doi:10.1037/0022-0663.98.3.598.

Robertson-Kraft, Claire, and Angela Lee Duckworth. "True Grit: Trait-Level Perseverance and Passion for Long-Term Goals Predicts Effectiveness and Retention among Novice Teachers." *Teachers College Record* 116, no. 3 (2014). http://www.ncbi.nlm.nih.gov/pmc/articles/PMC4211426. Accessed March 24, 2017.

Ross, Terris, Grace Kena, Amy Rathbun, Angelina Kewal Ramani, Jijun Zhang, Paul Kristapovich, and Eileen Manning. "Higher Education: Gaps in Access and Persistence." Washington, DC: National Center for Education Statistics, 2012. http://nces.ed.gov/pubsearch/pubsinfo.asp?pubid=2012046. Accessed March 24, 2017.

Schreiner, Laurie A. "Different Pathways to Thriving among Students of Color: An Untapped Opportunity for Success." *About Campus* 19, no. 5 (November 1, 2014): 10–19. doi:10.1002/abc.21169.

———. "From Surviving to Thriving during Transitions." In *Thriving in Transitions: A Research-Based Approach to College Student Success*, edited by Laurie A. Schreiner, Michelle C. Louis, and Denise D. Nelson, 1–18. Columbia: University of South Carolina, National Resource Center for the First-Year Experience and Students in Transition, 2012.

———. "Positive Psychology and Higher Education: The Contribution of Positive Psychology to Student Success and Institutional Effectiveness." In *Positive Psychology on the College Campus*, edited by John C. Wade, Lawrence I. Marks, and Roderick D. Hetzel, 1–26. Oxford: Oxford University Press, 2015.

———. "The 'Thriving Quotient': A New Vision for Student Success." *About Campus* 15, no. 2 (May 1, 2010): 2–10. doi:10.1002/abc.20016.

Schreiner, Laurie A., L. Kalinkewicz, A. P. Cuevas, and Eric James McIntosh. "Measuring the Malleable: Expanding the Assessment of Student Success." Paper presented at the annual meeting of the Association for the Study of Higher Education, St. Louis, 2013.

Schreiner, Laurie A., S. Pothoven, Denise D. Nelson, and Eric James McIntosh. "College Student Thriving: Predictors of Success and Retention." Paper presented at the annual meeting of the Association for the Study of Higher Education. Vancouver, 2009.

Sedlacek, William E. *Beyond the Big Test: Noncognitive Assessment in Higher Education*. San Francisco: Jossey-Bass, 2004.

———. "The Case for Noncognitive Measures." In *Choosing Students: Higher Education Admission Tools for the 21st Century*, edited by Wayne Camara and Ernest W. Kimmel, 177–93. Mahwah, NJ: Lawrence Erlbaum, 2005.

Seligman, M. E. P., N. Park, and C. Peterson. "The Values in Action (VIA) Classification of Character Strengths." *Research in Psychology* 27, no. 1 (2004): 63–78.

Smith, Daryl G. *Diversity's Promise for Higher Education: Making It Work*. Baltimore: Johns Hopkins University Press, 2009.

Strand, Kerry J. "Making Sure They Make It: Best Practices for Ensuring the Academic Success of First-Generation College Students." Washington, DC: Council of Independent Colleges, 2013.

Strayhorn, Terrell L. *College Students' Sense of Belonging: A Key to Educational Success for All Students*. New York: Routledge, 2012.

US Department of Education. "The Condition of Education 2013, Total Fall Enrollment in Degree-Granting Institutions, by Control and Level of Institution, Level of Enrollment, and Race/Ethnicity of Student: 2011." National Center for Education Statistics, 2013. https://nces.ed.gov/programs/digest/d12/tables/dt12_268.asp. Accessed March 24, 2017.

———. "The Condition of Education 2015 (NCES 2015-144), Institutional Retention and Graduation Rates for Undergraduate Students." 2015. http://nces.ed.gov/fastfacts/display.asp?id=40. Accessed March 24, 2017.

REACTION
Charlie McCormick

Laurie Schreiner has prepared an excellent primer in the research-based strategies and initiatives that make a difference in student success for higher education. Her succinct article is entirely comprehensive and covers several decades of findings. Leaders at small independent colleges will use this chapter as a framework for implementing a student success strategic plan on their own campuses to improve retention and graduation rates, as well as student satisfaction, development, and preparedness for life after college. As Schreiner notes, though, her catalog of strategies would need to be adapted for the institution's specific history and context. Her "thriving" framework is particularly useful as it encourages institutional leaders to think about student success across a variety of domains (cognitive, behavioral, and psychological), while drawing attention to the possibility that these domains can be shaped by intentional interventions. In arguing this point throughout her article, Schreiner reminds the leadership at small independent colleges that, while we may be seduced by the notion of creating student success by being selective in the recruitment of students, our future success lies in a deliberate creation of excellence by design. There are, then, things that institutional leaders can do and strategies that can be implemented that make students' characteristics upon entering not irrelevant but subject to transformations that could not be predicted based on those characteristics. Schreiner detours from this message only once in her article when she discusses recent trends in selecting (recruiting) students who exhibit characteristics such as grit and resilience. While this is an appropriate admission strategy for an institution to pursue if it wants to create student success by selection (and it is more likely to be an indicator of success than many other current recruitment metrics), it is not the strategy that the article overall encourages: creating student success by intentional design.

The challenge for many—if not most—small independent colleges is to know where to begin implementing the student success strategies Schreiner has identified. Given the limited resources at most of our institutions, leaders must be very strategic in where and when they will stretch their time, personnel, and budgets. Schreiner does not suggest a priority order—and no doubt researchers differ on which of her identified strategies are the most important and therefore the best place to begin—though her organization of the "strategies for equipping students" for success reads as though the priority order follows the experience of the individual student from recruitment to orientation and from the first semester to later semesters. The logic here is to start at the beginning. The sequence of strategies in the "create a thriving campus culture" section does not seem to suggest a priority order. Deciding which strategies to implement first—rather than adopting an approach that assumes they can all be accomplished at once—requires institutional leaders to be diligent in the assessment effort that Schreiner identifies as being preliminary to any student success efforts.

Implicit in Schreiner's documentation of student success strategies is the importance of a campus that is integrated and aligned around the goal of student success. The size of the small independent college suggests that integration and alignment is more likely at this type of institution than others but, as those of us who work at small colleges well know, too often we are not as fully integrated and aligned as would like to be. For example, the strategy of developing a "clear pathway for success" seems like it should be easy enough to implement—and it certainly would be in a single course such as a first-year seminar. A fully integrated and aligned "pathway," though, would be tied into registration processes, incentivizing or restricting students from enrolling in particular courses; inform students' participation in co-curricular and extra-curricular activities; be able to be updated and recalculated to lead to the outcome of success in real time; and be continually consulted by students, families, advisors, coaches, faculty, and others to make certain the pathway was being followed. Though technology is getting us closer to achieving this level of integration and alignment, there does not appear to be an existing solution that enables small independent colleges to operate in a fully integrated and aligned environment. Until that happens, it will be difficult to fully experience all of the benefits of the strategies Schreiner identifies.

Several times in the chapter, Schreiner suggests that faculty at small independent colleges have intentionally selected this type of educational environment in which to work. In my experience, that is rarely the case except—perhaps—in a select few disciplines in which the faculty need is so great that individuals can, in fact, choose the type of institution at which they want to work. This is not to suggest that faculty at small independent colleges lack commitment to their students. I would argue—and Schreiner makes this point, too—that the faculty commitment to students is greater in this type of institution since the learning environment is fundamentally relational. Faculty who do not adapt to this relational dynamic typically will not remain at a small independent college. Nonetheless, their lack of intentionally in selecting the type of institution in which they work makes it incumbent upon institutional leaders to establish and incentivize professional development experiences for the faculty who are being asked to interact with their students for student success in ways in which they have not been trained.

Schreiner's chapter provides the leadership of small independent colleges a strategic template for designing environments that help students be successful in a variety of domains. Of course, every college and university has to compete with numerous other designers of environments that lead students away from success. These designers can be institutional agents, but they are more often peers, families, and the individual students themselves. The design of these environments that lead students away from our institutional definitions of success makes our work unceasing and any single strategy or collection of strategies insufficient. Be that as it may, the institutional work is still necessary, and Schreiner provides the framework through which we can all do the work to help students succeed.

6

Student Demographics and Equity

JULIE J. PARK

Many of today's college campuses are host to unparalleled levels of diversity. America's youth continue to diversify, and high school graduation rates are relatively high in comparison to previous decades, meaning that the college-going population is more diverse than ever.[1] At the same time, barriers to access and equity are pervasive, and institutions still struggle to support a positive campus racial climate. In this chapter, I will review key trends in student demography as related to race, diversity, and gender and will comment on some of the particularly salient challenges to equity and diversity prevalent within higher education. In particular, I will identify areas of strength and challenge for Council of Independent Colleges (CIC) institutions and make suggestions for how institutions can effectively respond to these challenges. Challenges and responses to supporting racial/ethnic diversity in the student body and supporting positive race relations are listed, as well as recommendations around supporting low-income students, women and lesbian, gay, bisexual, transgender, and questioning (LGBTQ) students, and religious pluralism. I conclude by highlighting the need for institutions to adopt an equity-minded approach to addressing these issues and understanding the roots and continuing presence of inequality in higher education.

Demographic Trends

The American college-going population continues to diversify, more and more reflecting the demographics of the overall country. However, significant inequities and barriers to college access still exist, with low-income students and underrepresented minority (URM) students, a group that consists of black or African American, Latino/a, Southeast Asian American, Pacific Islander,

Native American, and indigenous students, being more likely than white and more affluent peers to not attend college. Low-income and URM students are also more likely to attend community college or for-profit institutions instead of traditional four-year institutions.[2] These trends are troubling due to the generally low transfer rates between community colleges and four-year institutions, as well as the high cost, low graduation rates, and on occasion, suspect practices of for-profit institutions.

One continuing trend is the increasing enrollment of women at many institutions,[3] as well as the increase in international students. Recognizing enrollment breakdowns by both race and gender unveil troubling inequities. Enrollment, persistence, and graduation rates are particularly low for URM males, in addition to challenges that males in general may be experiencing in the college pipeline.[4] Approximately one-third of students at private, four-year institutions are students of color, meaning that support for these students is critical for the sustainability of CIC institutions.[5] Encouragingly, black and Latino/a students have higher graduation rates at four-year independent colleges overall, versus four-year public and for-profit institutions.[6]

With increasing diversity comes the continual need to attend to a student body that is highly complex in its needs. Although the foundations of supporting the campus climate for diversity that emerged during the 1990s and 2000s are still relevant and needed, campuses need to evolve in how they are tailoring and implementing these policies to fit the needs of today's campuses. US high schools still maintain a high level of racial homogeneity,[7] and more and more students are coming to college with a greater knowledge around diversity issues due to exposure through the media, classmates, or other sources. At the same time, prior to college they are developmentally unprepared and unequipped to handle complex issues of diversity and difference in ways that go beyond superficial platitudes toward colorblindness or "can't everybody just get along?"[8]

Colleges need to be prepared to make significant investments to make sure their students are ready to deal with the complexities of citizenship in a diverse democracy. Such actions are both in line with the mission of many CIC institutions and are critical to ensuring the survival and relevance of institutions in a diverse and complex society. With their small size, focus on student learning, and close-knit student communities, CIC institutions are in a prime position to support the flourishing of diverse student bodies. Indeed, CIC institutions have an important role to play in supporting the overall educational pipeline and promoting equity and social mobility for diverse populations.

Challenges to Supporting a Racially Diverse Student Body

CIC institutions must continue to work hard to recruit and retain racially and socioeconomically diverse student bodies. The challenges are clear: Most institutions do not reflect the diversity of the country, which is rapidly diversifying at an unprecedented rate. Most institutions, particularly private four-year institutions, also lag significantly in socioeconomic diversity.[9] At private, non-doctoral four-year institutions in 2012, 33 percent of students came from families making less than $40,000 a year, a rate that slightly exceeds the proportion of low-income students at private doctoral four-year institutions and public institutions.[10] However, there is still considerable work that needs to be done for higher education to narrow the gap between the rich and the poor.[11] Further, the events of Ferguson, the Black Lives Matter movement, and beyond have highlighted the systemic inequities that contribute to continued racial inequality in our country. Black or African American, Latino/a, Native American, Southeast Asian American, and Pacific Islander students are more likely to start their college journey in community colleges, where they face significant hurdles to transferring and completing a four-year degree.

The ability of institutions to consider race as one of numerous factors in the holistic admissions process has been affirmed and reaffirmed in the two *Fisher v. Texas* Supreme Court cases. While most high-profile affirmative action cases have addressed public institutions such as the University of Michigan and the University of Texas, Austin, CIC institutions that receive federal funds (i.e., basically all institutions) are affected by Supreme Court rulings. The continuously precarious legal landscape for race-conscious admissions may discourage institutions from investing significant resources in recruiting students of color. This trend presents a significant threat to the lack of racial/ethnic diversity in student bodies. A tempting option for some institutions may be to eliminate or diminish any emphasis on race, either due to the uncertain sustainability of race-conscious admissions or because of a genuine conviction that inequality is defined solely by social class in this country.

However, consideration of both race/ethnicity and social class during the admissions process is still greatly needed.[12] Research indicates that admissions policies that strongly consider *both* race/ethnicity and social class in the admissions process are more effective in boosting both racial *and* economic diversity than policies that only consider social class.[13] Further, it is critical to note that recognizing the race/ethnicity of applicants is relevant in assessing the context in which SAT scores come from, given that the rate of participation in SAT preparation classes varies between racial/ethnic groups.[14] Further, disparities exist in terms of which groups benefit from taking SAT prep, even when key background characteristics are controlled for.[15]

Recommendations: Opportunities for CIC Institutions

While higher education and CIC institutions face numerous challenges to recruiting a diverse student body, they have numerous tools available to take a proactive stance toward boosting diversity. A report from the American Council on Education affirms that colleges use a variety of methods, both race-neutral and race-conscious, in seeking to bolster diversity in enrollment.[16] There is no reason that institutions need to abandon race-conscious approaches, and they can be combined with other approaches to cast the broadest net possible to recruit talented students of all races and economic backgrounds.[17] It is imperative that universities are intentional and unfaltering in their commitment to recruiting and enrolling racially and socioeconomically diverse student bodies, including the use of targeted financial aid in order to encourage enrollment and retention for diverse student populations. Some options viewed as effective by admissions practitioners in the ACE report include making the SAT/ACT optional and building articulation agreements or transfer partnerships with local community colleges.[18]

Responding to these options, given that many CIC institutions are smaller and private, they may be in an optimal position to become SAT-optional as a means of promoting equity and opening the door to a more diverse applicant pool. Jonathan Lash, the president of CIC institution Hampshire College, wrote a highly positive review in the *Washington Post* of the college's decision to go SAT-optional.[19] He noted that the overemphasis on rankings and test scores ran counter to his institution's mission and values around diversity, and shortly after enacting the policy, the percentage of students of color rose a noteworthy ten percentage points. The percentage of first-generation college students also rose from 10 percent to 18 percent as well. Lash noted other advantages to the policy shift, stating that the overall quality of the applicant pool increased. Being able to have a more focused applicant pool streamlined the admissions process and allowed reviewers to more clearly discern interest among applicants. Tellingly, the yield of applicants rose from 18 percent to 26 percent. Lash's narrative shows how intentional measures to boost diversity need not be at odds with ensuring quality; indeed, diversity enhances quality and helps an institution better live out its mission and goals. Further, going SAT-optional is another way to combat the widespread disparities around the SAT prep methods that were mentioned earlier in this article.

Specifically seeking a mix of students from different economic backgrounds *within* each racial/ethnic group can help encourage cross-racial interaction, spurring the educational benefits of diversity.[20] Healthy interaction across race is linked to retention,[21] and thus universities should be aware of the need to recruit and retain students from different economic backgrounds from each racial/ethnic group. Retaining low-income students in particular will likely require proactive intentionality and will be further addressed in this chapter.

One population within a diverse student body that requires special attention is undocumented students. An increasing presence on college campuses, private colleges have the special opportunity to offer need-based financial aid to these students. Supporting these students requires special attention and leadership, as well as investments in making sure that there is ample support for students whose status may affect their ability to participate in campus life. With their close-knit communities that can respond more flexibly to unique student needs, CIC institutions have the special chance to play a leadership role in this area. Institutions should have visible designated staff able to address the myriad of concerns that come from immigration status, making them accessible resources for this population of students. Financial aid offices also need to be attuned to the sensitivity of undocumented students' situations.

Challenges to Race Relations at Smaller Private and Liberal Arts Colleges

Most CIC institutions are either smaller private and/or liberal arts colleges, and these types of institutions have great promise for nurturing a close-knit community of students and nurturing a positive campus racial climate. However, they also present certain challenges. While diversity is certainly more than numbers, the campus racial climate is interlinked with demographic features of the student body.[22] Due to their relatively small enrollments, even if an institution is 10 percent to 20 percent students of color, the actual numbers of racial/ethnic minority students may still be relatively small. For example, if an institution of 4,000 students has a 5 percent black or African American student population, that would be 200 black students. In contrast, a large state institution of 20,000 may have only 5 percent black or African American students, but that would result in 1,000 black students—enough to form multiple niche communities. Thus, the small size of the racial/ethnic student populations at smaller institutions may feel stifling or challenging to students of color.[23] Many CIC institutions are also located in places that are somewhat limited in racial/ethnic diversity, offering fewer off-campus options for students to find support and community. Thus, institutions must work hard to foster an intentional sense of community on campus, creating programs and initiatives that are attractive to students of diverse backgrounds.

However, recent years have seen a growing number of racialized and racist incidents on college campuses, along with the rise of social media technology, which enables a rapid-fire dissemination of such incidents across campuses and even nationwide. Beyond overt instances of racism, institutions need to learn how to diagnose more subtle manifestations of racism on college campuses. Some CIC institutions are religiously affiliated, and researchers have documented that the dominant form of discourse among white Christians is color-blindness—a tendency to downplay or even refuse to recognize the continuing significance of race.[24] Such an approach is highly limited in its ability to diagnose and address inequities related to race.[25]

Recommendations for Supporting Positive Race Relations

Response to Hate Crimes

In the case of overtly racist incidents, colleges should implement protocols for both reporting and responding to harmful hate crimes and race-related incidents. These incidents not only have a detrimental effect on those who are immediately targeted, they can also have a broader chilling effect on the campus, sending the message that diverse populations are not welcome. Unfortunately these incidents continue on college campuses across the nation, and colleges must be ready to send a strong message that they are unacceptable.

Response to Subtle Racism, Supporting Student Activism, and Dialoging Openly on Race

Changing a culture around how individuals talk about race and identity on a campus is challenging but possible. Creating and supporting both curricular and co-curricular opportunities to have a dialogue about race in an open fashion is important. One type of program with an impressive track record is the intergroup dialogue program, where students are brought together over the course of a semester to hold a dialogue on a component of identity.[26] Groups are typically split between majority and minority status members (e.g., whites and students of color, low-income and upper-income students, men and women). Throughout the semester, facilitators help students to discuss openly issues that are typically swept under the rug, while accompanying their efforts with relevant academic readings and coursework.

Colleges can also model discourse around more subtle manifestations of racism by holding campuswide dialogues, forums, and—in the case of religiously affiliated colleges—chapel or other worship service programming. Provocative texts such as *The New Jim Crow* by Michelle Alexander (on the mass incarceration of black men) or *American Apartheid* by Douglas Massey (on housing segregation) could be adopted as campuswide readings or first-year book projects. Getting students to understand how systemic inequality over the years has led to current-day manifestations of inequality such as the prison industrial complex, the underrepresentation of faculty of color, and K-12 educational inequality is critical to helping them understand the world around them. All of these activities can help foster more complex ways of thinking and analyzing the world, a goal vital to CIC institutions.

Recent years have seen a renaissance of student activism in response to persisting racial inequities. Student activism and administrators have historically had a complex relationship, but educators should recognize that activism represents a critical opportunity for learning and development, as students grapple with how to respond to campus and societal injustices. Indeed, college campuses are a crucial training ground as students deliberate on how to participate in a diverse democracy.

Support for Ethnic Student Organizations

Supporting student organizations that cater to particular racial/ethnic groups (e.g., Black Student Alliance, Asian American Student Association) is an important part of fostering a healthy campus racial climate. Contrary to popular belief, these groups do not foster "self-segregation"; instead, they are either statistically unrelated to students' interactions across race and have even been linked to significantly higher levels of cross-racial interaction overall, and higher rates of interracial friendship for Latino/a students.[27] Students of color have by far the highest rates of cross-racial interaction and interracial friendship on college campuses,[28] and they need time among peers of a similar racial/ethnic background as a way of refueling and having some same-race community, which can be a source of strength as they seek to navigate interacting with students of other races. It seems counterintuitive, but supporting ethnic student organizations is needed to *avoid* campus balkanization; they are rarely the source. These organizations often work together, creating other opportunities for interracial cooperation and coalition building. Having senior-level campus administrators show support for such groups by attending their programs and events on occasion can send a strong signal to students of color that their presence is both welcomed and valued.

Administrative Support

Creating and supporting an administrative structure to support campus diversity and equity efforts is essential. Due to budget constraints, it may be tempting for institutions to consider consolidating administrative roles related to diversity; for instance, reassigning the responsibilities of a chief diversity officer to another position. Another critique of administrative positions related to diversity is that they relegate the responsibilities related to diversity to a single person (or small group of people) when in fact diversity is the responsibility of everyone. Cultivating a healthy campus climate for diversity cannot be, and should never be, the job of just one person or even a small group of people. That said, supporting campus diversity requires so much intentionality and leadership that it is essential that there are people throughout campus whose sole role is to provide leadership and centralization for diversity-related efforts, and these same individuals can also work throughout campus to make sure that other units on campus have support for diversity-related programming and initiatives. A chief diversity officer (CDO) position is particularly critical to ensure that advancing diversity is an integral part of institutional culture and top-level priorities.[29] Such a position can provide valuable coordination across campus and advance and support faculty diversity. Having a high-visibility, senior-level (ideally cabinet-level) position sends a strong message to the campus community about institutional priorities and investments.

In addition to a CDO position, institutions need multiple individuals and programmatic units running and coordinating support for diversity efforts across campus. It is essential to maintain positions for diversity-related co-curricular engagement. We encourage institutions to think beyond just one position to meaningfully address the unique needs that exist on their campus. We encourage CIC institutions to realize that supporting diversity at the co-curricular level cannot just be a one-person job, even on a small campus. Institutions should create infrastructure for ensuring that staff across campus receive training and continuing education around diversity-related issues because diversity affects the fabric and day-to-day operations of every facet of campus life.[30]

Diversity and Academic Affairs

At the vast majority of institutions, the diversity of the professoriate needs constant monitoring and proactive outreach to support the recruitment, development, and retention of faculty of color and women. CIC institutions are known for their commitment to students and intimate learning environments. Faculty of color in particular are known for greatly enriching academic environments with not just traditional forms of scholarship (i.e., publishing in academic outlets), but using scholarship to give back to students, communities, and society—all forms of creativity that can contribute to the academic climate that many CIC institutions seek to foster.[31] Retaining faculty of color and women needs to be a special priority in fields in which they tend to be underrepresented, such as science, technology, engineering, and mathematics departments. Leadership from the CDO, provost's office, and academic departments is critical to making this happen. The provost's office in particular should incentivize the hiring of diverse faculty in order to send a clear message that faculty diversity is a key priority. Clear and supportive parental leave policies and on-campus daycare facilities are also essential to retaining talent and supporting faculty diversity, and too many institutions have lagged behind in proactively supporting the needs of diverse families.[32]

In addition to diversifying the faculty, it is critical to provide academic infrastructure for diversity-related curriculum. At many institutions, course requirements related to the critical and nuanced study of diverse populations are a beginning step to making sure that all students have the opportunity to study these issues in the classroom. Strengthening women's or gender studies and ethnic studies (African American, Latino/a, Native and indigenous peoples, and Asian American studies) courses is critical in ensuring that students have opportunities to participate in courses that reflect their own history and heritage, as well as to learn about populations that are different from their own. Such courses also have a strong tradition of incorporating service learning and civic engagement components, reflecting unique partnerships between academic and student affairs that can spur deep and meaningful learning among students. These types of courses are a natural fit for CIC institutions, given their historic commitment to the liberal arts and student learning.

Recommendations on Supporting Low-Income Students

Earlier in the chapter, challenges to recruiting and retaining low-income students were listed as the key need in supporting a diverse student body. Small private colleges need to be proactive about supporting low-income students. It is critical that colleges build partnerships with high-need high schools to build a pipeline of students who would not otherwise consider their institution.[33] Because CIC institutions are private, the initial high cost of tuition will likely cause "sticker shock" among families. Education and awareness around financial aid and scholarship opportunities are crucial in order to encourage applicants from a diverse pool of students. Research indicates that low-income and first-generation students are more likely to be familiar with "name brand" institutions (e.g., Harvard, MIT), but less familiar with institutions like small private colleges such as those found in the CIC.[34] Further, low-income students are less likely to have access to adequate college counseling.[35] The combination of these forces means that CIC institutions must be proactive about reaching out to lower-income populations through partnerships with high schools and communities.

Once low-income students are enrolled, institutions must be proactive about the ways they may be more vulnerable due to the cumulative costs of day-to-day college life. Colleges may consider hosting food pantries and taking other measures to address food insecurity among students.[36] Special funds to assist with purchases such as textbooks or even winter coats send a message to students that colleges care about their holistic needs and recognize that many students cannot take it for granted that their financial needs will be met by their families. Making social class part of everyday conversations on campus can help break the norms set by the dominant culture of privilege. Addressing low-income students' sense of belonging is also vital. In one social psychology-based intervention, an institution had more advanced students address new first-year college students about some of the fears and insecurities they had when starting college as first-generation students.[37] Critically, the older students discussed how they were able to persevere and overcome challenges incrementally, finding their place in college. The intervention was linked with participating first-generation students being more likely to seek out campus resources and having higher grade point averages. They also had higher levels of psychological well-being, perceived social fit, and appreciation for diversity, showing the impact on the psychological transition to college.[38] Overall, the experiment demonstrates the relevance of addressing the more subjective but still highly relevant emotions around belonging in the collegiate setting that affect success for traditionally disenfranchised populations. As we have noted, such interventions can play a pivotal role in closing the social-class achievement gap.

Recommendations on Supporting a Positive Climate for Sexual Orientation, Gender Identity, and Women

In addition to racial and economic diversity, college campuses across the country have been constantly challenged to become welcoming places for LGBTQ students. More recent years have also raised questions about how colleges are equipped to support the unique needs of transgender students, and it is important to have university staff tasked to keep abreast of the constantly changing national conversation and movement around how to best support these students. As noted for race-related incidents, it is essential for universities to clarify both their reporting and response protocols for responding to hate crimes or incidents that target these communities.

Related to transgender students, institutional reforms can include, but are not limited to, the allocation of gender-neutral bathrooms or ensuring that no single-usage bathroom is gender-specific and gender-neutral or mixed-gender housing in residence life. Normalizing the use of preferred pronouns is another step institutions can take toward cultivating a culture where conversations around gender identity are common. Employee benefits for faculty and staff must seek to equitably address benefits for same-sex households and make sure that human resources units are equipped to support both individuals and families. Student affairs educators can support robust programming and creative dialogues that can help bring awareness, understanding, and critical thinking to LGBTQ students. Colleges should also be aware of the intersectional identities of their students; that is, the differences in the experiences between LGBTQ students of color and white students, or how the experiences of LGBTQ students may differ markedly depending on social class.

CIC institutions include a number of religiously affiliated colleges who are just beginning to address the existence of LGBTQ students on their campuses, and it is important to provide safe spaces for student development. LGBTQ alumni groups are springing up at religiously affiliated institutions, and student organizations are seeking the right to gather and recognize their existence. There are unique challenges to supporting LGBTQ students at these institutions given the evolving conversations around sexual orientation and identity. Instead of denying the existence of this issue, which could lead to a seriously negative climate for mental health for these students, religiously affiliated CIC institutions might consider how to support LGBTQ students in their particular contexts and have a dialogue with students to better understand their needs. At the end of the day, all institutions exist, in theory, to support the holistic development of their students—mind, body, and spirit. It behooves religiously affiliated institutions to not deny the existence of a crucial aspect of students' identities and instead begin to ask critical questions about what it means to care for one another in a community as students prepare to serve others in a diverse democracy.

Additionally, sexual assault prevention is a top and unavoidable priority for campuses, and Title IX regulations require that universities address this tremendous need. For too long colleges have failed to lead proactively in this area, but recent years have brought national media attention on the continuing barriers to promoting a safe environment for women. It is essential for CIC institutions to take ownership of this issue, demonstrating leadership and clear support that a climate detrimental to women will not be tolerated. Once again, intersectionality is relevant in that unique challenges may affect the safety and well-being of women of color, and institutions should ensure that sexual assault prevention is not simply delivered through a one-size-fits-all model. Women continue to make strides on college campuses, and at many campuses they have been outpacing male students in enrollment and graduation. However, a more nuanced look unveils that female students still face unique challenges and barriers in the college arena. Colleges should be proactive about supporting and encouraging female enrollment and success in science, technology, engineering, and mathematics majors, areas that still tend to be male-dominated.

Recommendations for Fostering Religious Pluralism

The last section of focus under the umbrella of diversity and equity may be surprising to some, but recent years have seen a rise in high-profile incidents of anti-Semitism on campus, and just as colleges have struggled for many years to support racially diverse student populations, it is clear that supporting religious pluralism is also a consistent, albeit less outwardly visible, challenge. Numerous thorny issues related to deeply held convictions persist, be it beliefs around sexual orientation or the religious-political dimensions of conflicts in the Middle East. Some of these issues play out uniquely for religious communities and others cut across different faith traditions. A general consensus is that most colleges are ill equipped to recognize the relevance of religion and religious pluralism, let alone support it and harness it as one of richness in a diverse community. Engagement in interfaith activities has been linked to numerous positive outcomes,[39] and they are key to preparing students for citizenship in a diverse society.

Furthermore, recognizing the importance of religion and spirituality in students' lives is critical to supporting the needs of racially diverse populations, with many students of color reporting high levels of religious and spiritual engagement.[40] Religious and spiritual engagement are positive predictors of psychological well-being across racial/ethnic populations, and faith can play a particularly important role in fostering resilience among students of color.[41] Opening dialogue around religion and spirituality can also open the door for conversations around meaning and purpose, providing rich frameworks to help students explore issues of vocation, calling, and character as they seek to construct lives that will serve others.

There are no easy answers, but it is necessary for university leaders to be aware of the importance of supporting religious pluralism as part of a broader campus climate of diversity. Supporting religious pluralism does not mean watering down one's own faith or convictions or espousing a generic "lets all get along" rhetoric. It can actually lead to great moments of conflict, but it also opens the door to teach students how to engage in difficult dialogues with civility, understanding, and grace, all critically needed for citizenship in a diverse democracy. Organizations such as the InterFaith Youth Corps have taken leadership on this issue and have numerous materials and trainings that can support student affairs educators and faculty on how to engage around these issues both inside and outside of the classroom.

Religious diversity and pluralism are worth addressing because many faith traditions espouse frameworks around justice and equity. CIC institutions that are religiously affiliated in particular should pay careful attention to these principles and seek to live them out in their specific context. Such frameworks can provide a powerful foundation for students and educators to recognize the importance of diversity, equity, and justice for all students. Nonsectarian CIC institutions can also encourage students to recognize the mandate for justice that cuts across faith traditions, and spur conversations about how one's worldview paradigm connects to questions of meaning and purpose.

Conclusion: A Call to Equity-Mindedness

At one point it may have seemed that diversity was another to-do item on a task list that once completed could be checked off forever. However, it is clear that not only are needs related to student demography, equity, and climate never-ending, demanding constant attention, the needs themselves are always evolving as diverse student populations continue to evolve and new concerns arise. Given these key issues surrounding today's students, it is important for CIC institutions to adopt an equity-based perspective, or "equity-mindedness,"[42] to understand the challenges facing twenty-first-century student bodies. Equity-mindedness refers to the importance of looking at broader institutional, structural, and sociohistorical realities in understanding inequality, instead of putting the blame for such inequities on individual students and/or a particular cultural group's supposed deficiencies.[13] When addressing disparities that exist in college enrollment and graduation rates of diverse populations, it is easy for educators to invoke a deficit-based perspective, viewing disparities as largely stemming from the failure of the student or the student's culture to support enrollment and retention. In contrast, equity-mindedness takes into account "the sociohistorical context of exclusionary practices and racism in higher education and the impact of power asymmetries on opportunities and outcomes for [students of color]. Individuals who are equity-minded attribute unequal outcomes to institution-based dysfunctions."[44] Such a perspective widens understanding of the complex sociohistorical forces that influence student trajectories in higher education, and also emphasizes the institution's role and responsibility in ensuring student outcomes. In particular, Bensimon and colleagues[45] demonstrate how the prevalence of deficit-based perspectives among educators and practitioners have an adverse effect on students.

For CIC institutions, particularly those struggling to recruit and retain student body diversity, an equity-minded perspective can be a crucial paradigm shift. Instead of wondering what is wrong with students, or why certain populations might be lagging behind others, an equity-minded perspective shifts the responsibility to the institution. It requires institutions to understand their role—both the possibilities and potential limitations—in a society that continues to be stratified by race and class. Adopting an equity-minded perspective can disrupt the harmful myths relating diverse student populations on campus, such as the misconception that they or their families do not value or support education. It helps broaden one's focus beyond the student as the sole agent in his or her success to unveiling the complex ecosystem of social forces—from financial aid policy to community resources to employment opportunities—that shape the ability of students to flourish on college campuses. With students of color making up one-third (and growing) of the enrollment at private, four-year colleges,[46] recognizing the broader social forces that affect their success and engagement in higher education is vital.

Taking an equity-minded perspective into account, this chapter has highlighted the institution's responsibility in promoting a positive campus racial climate and making institutional-level reforms to better support diverse student populations. Prioritizing these issues and considering structural and institution-wide reforms is a first step in making sure that a commitment to diversity is accompanied by a commitment to equity. To further an equity-minded perspective on campus, CIC institutions might consider resources like the Center for Urban Education's Equity Scorecard, which could help facilitate critical conversations between faculty and practitioners to uncover the subtle but influential attitudes around students that hinder and inhibit success. Institutions have used the Equity Scorecard to help identify the barriers that deter student success and generate campus planning to address inequities between groups.

In line with equity-mindedness, institutions bear the majority of the responsibility for student success, and there is a particular need to invest resources in the students who may be a numeric minority but are greatly deserving of attention and time. In fact, under an equity-minded framework, these students may even need a greater amount of time and investment given the historic injustices that have been perpetuated throughout history and adversely affected educational opportunity and success. This overview can only provide a bird's-eye view of some of the issues paramount to campuses today, and certainly these issues (and others) will play out at different institutions due to campus context, history, and other dynamics. Institutions should consider how their unique campus cultures and institutional histories will shape both the way that diversity-related issues have manifest themselves on campus, as well as institutional responses in the past, present, and future. In a time when our country is seeing unprecedented diversity but our colleges and universities have not yet caught up, the urgency behind recruiting and retaining diverse and equitable student bodies is clear.

NOTES

1. "Racial and Ethnic Representation."
2. Ibid.
3. Sax, *Gender Gap in College*.
4. Harris III and Wood, "Student Success."
5. Council of Independent Colleges, "Enrollment by Race/Ethnicity."
6. Council of Independent Colleges, "Student of Color Graduation Rates."
7. Orfield, "Reviving the Dream."
8. Gurin et al., "Diversity and Higher Education."
9. Carnevale and Rose, "Socioeconomic Status, Race/Ethnicity."
10. Council of Independent Colleges, "Enrollment by Family Income."
11. Still, the percentage of students who come from affluent families ($120,000 or more of annual income) exceeds the percentage of low-income students across institutional type.
12. Park, Denson, and Bowman, "Does Socioeconomic Diversity."
13. Reardon et al., "Can Socioeconomic Status Substitute?"
14. Park, "It Takes a Village."
15. Byun and Park, "Academic Success."
16. Espinosa, Gaertner, and Orfield, "Race, Class, and College Access."
17. Reardon et al., "Can Socioeconomic Status Substitute?"
18. Espinosa, Gaertner, and Orfield, "Race, Class, and College Access."
19. Strauss, "What One College Discovered."
20. Park, Denson, and Bowman, "Does Socioeconomic Diversity."
21. Chang, "Does Racial Diversity Matter?"
22. Garces and Jayakumar, "Dynamic Diversity."
23. Park, "Are We Satisfied?"
24. Emerson and Smith, *Divided by Faith*.
25. Park, "Race and the Greek System."
26. Zúñiga, Naagda, and Sevig, "Intergroup Dialogues."
27. Bowman and Park, "Interracial Contact on College Campuses"; Kim, Park, and Koo, "Testing Self-Segregation."
28. Park, "Clubs and the Campus Racial Climate."
29. Williams and Wade-Golden, *Chief Diversity Officer*.
30. Smith, *Diversity's Promise*.
31. Antonio, "Faculty of Color Reconsidered."
32. Ward and Wolf-Wendel, *Academic Motherhood*.
33. Espinosa, Gaertner, and Orfield, "Race, Class, and College Access."
34. Hoxby and Avery, "Missing."
35. McDonough, *Choosing Colleges*.
36. Aries, *Race and Class Matters*.
37. Stephens, Hamedani, and Destin, "Closing the Social-Class Achievement Gap."
38. Ibid.
39. Mayhew, Rockenbach, and Bowman, "Connection between Interfaith Engagement."
40. Astin, Astin, and Lindholm, *Cultivating the Spirit*.
41. Park and Millora, "Psychological Well-Being."
42. Bensimon, Harris III, and Rueda, "Mediational Means."
43. Ibid.

44. Ibid., 9.
45. Ibid.
46. Council of Independent Colleges, "Enrollment by Race/Ethnicity."

REFERENCES

Antonio, Anthony L. "Faculty of Color Reconsidered: Retaining Scholars for the Future." *Journal of Higher Education* 73, no. 5 (2002): 582–602.

Aries, Elizabeth. *Race and Class Matters at an Elite College.* Philadelphia: Temple University Press, 2008.

Astin, Alexander W., Helen S. Astin, and Jennifer A. Lindholm. *Cultivating the Spirit: How College Can Enhance Students' Inner Lives.* San Francisco: Jossey-Bass, 2010.

Bensimon, Estela M., Frank Harris III, and Robert Rueda. "The Mediational Means of Enacting Equity-Mindedness among Community College Practitioners." Paper presented at the annual meeting of the Association for the Study of Higher Education. Louisville, KY, 2007.

Bowman, Nicholas A., and Julie J. Park. "Interracial Contact on College Campuses: Comparing and Contrasting Predictors of Cross-Racial Interaction and Interracial Friendship." *Journal of Higher Education* 85, no. 5 (September 1, 2014): 660–90. doi:10.1080/00221546.2014.11777344.

Byun, Soo-yong, and Hyunjoon Park. "The Academic Success of East Asian American Youth: The Role of Shadow Education." *Sociology of Education* 85, no. 1 (January 1, 2012): 40–60. doi:10.1177/0038040711417009.

Carnevale, Anthony P., and Stephen J. Rose. "Socioeconomic Status, Race/Ethnicity, and Selective College Admissions." New York: Century Foundation, 2003.

Chang, Mitchell J. "Does Racial Diversity Matter? The Educational Impact of a Racially Diverse Undergraduate Population." *Journal of College Student Development* 40, no. 4 (1999): 377–95.

Council of Independent Colleges. "Enrollment by Family Income." Making the Case, 2015. https://www.cic.edu/resources-research/charts-data?keyword=income. Accessed April 16, 2017.

———. "Enrollment by Race/Ethnicity." Making the Case, 2013. https://www.cic.edu/resources-research/charts-data?keyword=race. Accessed April 16, 2017.

———. "Student of Color Graduation Rates." Making the Case, 2014. https://www.cic.edu/resources-research/charts-data?keyword=graduation%20rates. Accessed April 27, 2017.

Emerson, Michael O., and Christian Smith. *Divided by Faith: Evangelical Religion and the Problem of Race in America.* Oxford: Oxford University Press, 2000.

Espinosa, Lorelle L., Matthew N. Gaertner, and Gary Orfield. "Race, Class, and College Access: Achieving Diversity in a Shifting Legal Landscape." Washington, DC: American Council on Education, 2015.

Garces, Liliana M., and Uma M. Jayakumar. "Dynamic Diversity: Toward a Contextual Understanding of Critical Mass." *Educational Researcher* 43, no. 3 (April 1, 2014): 115–24. doi:10.3102/0013189X14529814.

Gurin, Patricia, Eric Dey, Sylvia Hurtado, and Gerald Gurin. "Diversity and Higher Education: Theory and Impact on Educational Outcomes." *Harvard Educational Review* 72, no. 3 (September 1, 2002): 330–67. doi:10.17763/haer.72.3.01151786u134n051.

Harris III, Frank, and J. Luke Wood. "Student Success for Men of Color in Community

Colleges: A Review of Published Literature and Research, 1998–2012." *Journal of Diversity in Higher Education* 6, no. 3 (2013): 174–85. doi:10.1037/a0034224.

Hoxby, Caroline M., and Christopher Avery. "The Missing." Working Paper. National Bureau of Economic Research, December 2012. doi:10.3386/w18586.

Kim, Young K., Julie J. Park, and Katie K. Koo. "Testing Self-Segregation: Multiple-Group Structural Modeling of College Students' Interracial Friendship by Race." *Research in Higher Education* 56, no. 1 (February 1, 2015): 57–77. doi:10.1007/s11162-014-9337-8.

Mayhew, Matthew J., Alyssa N. Rockenbach, and Nicholas A. Bowman. "The Connection between Interfaith Engagement and Self-Authored Worldview Commitment." *Journal of College Student Development* 57, no. 4 (June 1, 2016): 362–79. doi:10.1353/csd.2016.0046.

McDonough, Patricia M. *Choosing Colleges: How Social Class and Schools Structure Opportunity.* Albany, NY: State University of New York Press, 1997.

Orfield, Gary. "Reviving the Dream of an Integrated Society: A 21st Century Challenge." Los Angeles: Civil Rights Project/Proyecto Derechos Civiles, 2009. https://escholarship.org/uc/item/2bw2s608. Accessed March 26, 2017.

Park, Julie J. "Are We Satisfied? A Look at Student Satisfaction with Diversity at Traditionally White Institutions." *Review of Higher Education* 32, no. 3 (March 8, 2009): 291–320. doi:10.1353/rhe.0.0071.

———. "Clubs and the Campus Racial Climate: Student Organizations and Interracial Friendship in College." *Journal of College Student Development* 55, no. 7 (November 3, 2014): 641–60. doi:10.1353/csd.2014.0076.

———. "It Takes a Village (or an Ethnic Economy): The Varying Roles of Socioeconomic Status, Religion, and Social Capital in SAT Preparation for Chinese and Korean American Students." *American Educational Research Journal* 49, no. 4 (August 1, 2012): 624–50. doi:10.3102/0002831211425609.

———. "Race and the Greek System in the 21st Century: Centering the Voices of Asian American Women." *Journal of Student Affairs Research and Practice* 45, no. 1 (April 8, 2008): 103–32. doi:10.2202/1949-6605.1909.

Park, Julie J., Nida Denson, and Nicholas A. Bowman. "Does Socioeconomic Diversity Make a Difference? Examining the Effects of Racial and Socioeconomic Diversity on the Campus Climate for Diversity." *American Educational Research Journal* 50, no. 3 (June 1, 2013): 466–96. doi:10.3102/0002831212468290.

Park, Julie J., and Melissa Millora. "Psychological Well-Being for White, Black, Latino/a, and Asian American Students: Considering Spirituality and Religion." *Journal of Student Affairs Research and Practice* 47, no. 4 (October 1, 2010): 445–61. doi:10.2202/1949-6605.6143.

"Racial and Ethnic Representation among College Students, by Type of Institution, 2012." *Chronicle of Higher Education*, August 18, 2014. http://chronicle.com/article/RacialEthnic/147373. Accessed April 21, 2017 (access for subscribers only).

Reardon, Sean F., Rachel Baker, Matt Kasman, Daniel Klasik, and Joseph B. Townsend. "Can Socioeconomic Status Substitute for Race in Affirmative Action College Admissions Policies? Evidence from a Simulation Mode." Washington, DC: Educational Testing Service, 2015.

Sax, Linda J. *The Gender Gap in College: Maximizing the Developmental Potential of Women and Men.* Vol. 25. San Francisco: Jossey-Bass, 2008.

Smith, Daryl G. *Diversity's Promise for Higher Education: Making It Work.* Baltimore: Johns Hopkins University Press, 2009.

Stephens, Nicole M., MarYam G. Hamedani, and Mesmin Destin. "Closing the Social-Class

Achievement Gap: A Difference-Education Intervention Improves First-Generation Students' Academic Performance and All Students' College Transition." *Psychological Science* 25, no. 4 (April 1, 2014): 943–53. doi:10.1177/0956797613518349.

Strauss, Valerie. "What One College Discovered When It Stopped Accepting SAT/ACT Scores." *Washington Post*, September 25, 2015. https://www.washingtonpost.com/news/answer-sheet/wp/2015/09/25/what-one-college-discovered-when-it-stopped-accepting-satact-scores. Accessed March 26, 2017.

Ward, Kelly, and Lisa Wolf-Wendel. *Academic Motherhood: How Faculty Manage Work and Family*. New Brunswick, NJ: Rutgers University Press, 2012.

Williams, Damon A., and Katrina C. Wade-Golden. *The Chief Diversity Officer: Strategy, Structure, and Change Management*. Sterling, VA: Stylus Publishers, n.d.

Zúñiga, Ximena, Biren (Ratnesh) A. Naagda, and Todd D. Sevig. "Intergroup Dialogues: An Educational Model for Cultivating Engagement across Differences." *Equity and Excellence in Education* 35, no. 1 (April 1, 2002): 7–17. doi:10.1080/713845248.

REACTION
Mary B. Marcy

The changing profile of contemporary students is a major issue for all people working in higher education and has particular resonance on Council of Independent Colleges (CIC) campuses that have long sought to provide opportunity and access. In this chapter, Julie J. Park provides a good summary of the challenges that all institutions of higher education face as the student profile evolves. She rightly highlights how an increasingly diverse student body demands that campuses assess their ability to support student success. Her comprehensive definition of diversity beyond race, which includes sexual orientation, gender identity, and religion, brings a broad perspective to the work.

Park lists numerous recommendations to support a racially diverse student body: addressing race relations on campus, encouraging supportive race relations, supporting low-income students, fostering religious pluralism, and creating a positive climate for sexual orientation, gender identity, and women. Her overview provides a valuable tool kit for leaders of colleges and universities, outlining not only challenges but also highlighting some of the most promising responses to supporting a diverse student body.

Many of these recommendations are fine examples of how institutions can provide broad opportunity. There are, however, two significant challenges for implementing these ideas at CIC institutions. First, approaches to diversity are most effective when undertaken in an integrated and comprehensive manner, no more so than at small independent colleges. Second, many of the approaches advocated in this chapter would demand significant new resources for implementation, also a challenge for many CIC institutions. Thus, I invite readers to embrace the outline of her well-researched chapter and think innovatively about their own campuses when considering implementation.

Most CIC institutions cannot approach these issues by adding staff, new programs, or physical space. The myriad challenges facing CIC institutions (including fiscal pressures, increased compliance, and enrollment concerns) require creativity and innovation more than addition. But the changing student demographic also represents a particular opportunity for CIC institutions.

The research presented by Park reinforces the notion that changing student profiles can be a path for CIC institutions to reconnect and reaffirm our mission. Many of our institutions were founded with a strong religious or values-based philosophy that challenged us to educate and elevate students in a spirit of inclusivity; today, we know that the percentage of underrepresented and low-income students at CIC institutions exceeds that of the rest of higher education. Our missions provide the framework for evolving in response to rapidly changing student demographics.

Park accurately describes CIC institutions' small scale, their focus on student learning, and their close-knit communities as attributes that will support diversity and inclusion on campus. Our relatively modest size allows for both nimbleness and integration. For example, interdisciplinary learning can be an effective model for diverse populations, as it invites faculty and students to make connections across difference. Similarly, service learning and co-curricular programming at CIC institutions have been shown to elevate student progress in areas such as cultural awareness tolerance, empathy, and the ability to relate to others. At many CIC institutions, including my own, such high-impact practices are central to the learning experience, fully integrated into the institution, and are particularly effective in supporting the educational attainment of diverse students.

It is important to read Park's recommendations with an eye toward the spirit of community central to our campuses, and to approach with caution those responses that will build or reinforce silos. For example, her recommendations to consider test-optional admissions and strengthen partnerships with community colleges are areas in which CIC campuses have been successful, and which can continue to strengthen their outreach. Her recommendations for providing leadership through a chief diversity officer are certainly possible, and this is an approach my own campus embraces. However, it is challenging for many CIC institutions to create multiple levels of diversity leadership and programming, given size and budget realities. Instead, my campus, as well as other highly diverse CIC campuses, can be most successful in ensuring broad ownership of diversity work not only through education but also through clear action. For example, consciously working to create a faculty, administration, and staff profile that reflects the diversity of our student body is a tangible means of supporting a diverse student body.

Park's call for "equity-mindedness" is particularly welcome in this context. Citing the work of Estela Bensimon and the Equity Scorecard Project at the University of Southern California, we are challenged to look at student outcomes as a pattern of institutional responsibility rather than only student responsibility. This approach requires that we adapt our systems and approaches to embrace the realities of today's students.

Many of our campuses have more diversity in the student body than in the communities in which we are located. Park mentions that this context means "fewer off-campus options for students to find support and community." Her point is well taken, but I would suggest that it is a larger issue than merely having fewer off-campus options. At Dominican University of California, our students come to a campus located in an affluent suburb populated primarily by older, more homogenous residents. Our diverse students are somewhat out of place in the neighborhood and may be treated differently by businesses, the police, and others. For these reasons, it is imperative for us to cultivate strong and proactive external relations with our neighbors in order to expand the university community to be a neighborhood community, which includes our students. At Dominican, this means student-neighbor meals, invitations to attend students' events, and regular communications with the neighborhood association. Our neighbors have offered to provide students with career advice and mentoring. In a partnership with neighbors, our students are better served and have the opportunity to reach across generational and class differences. Service learning projects and community engagement work tie our students to the local community and provide further forums for discussion across difference.

We have also actively established partnerships with the local police. We recently developed a memorandum of understanding (MOU) regarding sexual assault investigations, are in discussions to create a similar MOU regarding racial issues, and this work has led to other on-campus programming, providing students the opportunity to have a dialogue with the police department. This new partnership with the local police demonstrates how our institutions can be creative and innovative in our approaches to the multiple issues we face. This partnership is an opportunity for our students to engage in a meaningful dialogue on a national issue that affects many of them. For the police, they can begin to understand the fear and frustration experienced by communities of color when confronted by police officers. This programming is the kind of co-curricular dialogue that can readily occur on small campuses and leads to other discussions and student activity.

This chapter highlights an issue central to our campuses' identity and success: how we can effectively educate an increasingly diverse student body. The research and context are valuable tools for embracing the students of today—and of tomorrow.

7

Meaning Making and the Liberal Arts

CYNTHIA A. WELLS, DAVID GUTHRIE, AND DANIEL CUSTER

In an essay ominously entitled "How Liberal Arts Colleges Are Failing America," Scott Gerber[1] argues: "We keep telling young Americans that a bachelor's degree in history is as valuable as, say, a chemical engineering degree—but it's just not true anymore. All degrees are not created equal. And if we—parents, educators, entrepreneurs and nonprofit leaders—maintain this narrow-minded approach, then we are not just failing young indebted Americans and their families. We are harming the long-term vitality of our economy." Gerber's statement resonates well with the common statements that one hears with some frequency: "Yeah, my philosophy degree and 75 cents will buy me a cup of coffee"; or, "I really wanted to be an art major but my parents told me I wouldn't get a job, so I'm majoring in business instead"; or, "What do Western civilization and composition have to do with an engineering degree?" Such sentiments shed light on the pressures faced by independent colleges and universities with historic, missional commitments to liberal arts education, notably cultural skepticism regarding economic utility and employment outcomes.

Amid a backdrop of dismissal, however, a considerable number of compelling arguments are currently being made *for* an education grounded in the liberal arts.[2] For example, in a recent interview on *NPR*, Michael Roth, president of Wesleyan University, noted that "today, the shifts in the economy mean that technological change will only produce [an] accelerated pace of innovation of changing relations to audiences. A broad, wide-ranging education is the best way to be able to shape that change rather than just be victim [to] it."[3] Furthermore, reports consistently demonstrate the market's interest in and demand for broadly educated graduates.[4] A strong majority of employers (80 percent) believe every student should attain broad knowledge in the liberal arts.[5] Contrary to skeptics' beliefs, these arguments indicate that skills and abilities associated with a liberal arts education will only become increasingly more relevant—economically and otherwise—to the challenges faced in the workforce tomorrow.

The ultimate challenge facing independent colleges and those who value them is to expand cultural understanding regarding their worth, including among current and prospective students and their parents. The Council of Independent Colleges not only recognizes the weight and extent of this pressure on its members' educational commitments but also is vigorously championing the manifold benefits of independent higher education and the liberal arts, for both personal and societal welfare. A prime task toward this end is to make sense of the worth and relevance of the independent college and to widely disseminate our case in order to dispute the limited perspective as to their value that is too prominent. The future flourishing of the independent college hinges upon the collective institutional wisdom and requisite resolve to acknowledge and address the challenges, as well as to maximize and clearly articulate strengths. This chapter advances a more expansive narrative of value for the independent college that addresses the skeptics head-on. Essentially, it is critical to capitalize on the full meaning of an independent college degree. A degree in isolation has become conflated with the purpose of college. This is one interpretation that must be recognized and to which an adequate response is imperative. The full range of divergent perspectives—the varying degrees of meaning—must be articulated if prospective students, their parents, and the general populace are to better understand and even value independent higher education.

This chapter first outlines the interpretive queries that underlie the prominent critique facing independent colleges, followed by a response that identifies and describes key empirically verified benefits of an independent college education, including but not limited to employability. We emphasize the distinctive nature of independent higher education, rooted in particular and timely expressions of the liberal arts and tied clearly to the long-term employability of graduates. Finally, the chapter illustrates several important messages and related initiatives that college leaders may consider for expanding a narrative of the full value of the independent college.

Challenges of Meaning Facing Independent Colleges and Universities

Current beliefs in US culture regarding colleges and degrees present a tremendous challenge. The widespread social norm that the point of college is to graduate and be hired in a job that college has prepared one for has both primacy and power. Said another way, most believe college to be the *sine qua non* to gainful employment. The cultural conversation on the value of higher education in our current context has grown myopic in its focus on employment outcomes, particularly the economic variables attached to employment.[6] This is not to suggest that college graduates securing jobs is unimportant. Rather, we simply wish to argue that this cultural myopia has particularly troubling manifestations for the independent college; our hope in no small way is to offer a corrective to inadequate vision. More specifically, three critiques lobbed at independent colleges reflect this short-sightedness: concerns regarding employment outcomes, economic utility, and the notion that independent colleges are elitist. We consider each in turn.

The query of employment reflects a regnant cultural value that the sole purpose of a college education is career preparation. The vast majority of students place a higher premium on the employment-related outcomes of a college education than on the process and particular contents of higher education itself. The percentage of incoming first-year students citing "to be able to get a better job" as a very important reason for attending college recently reached an all-time high.[7] This myopia is unfortunately not limited to students. A recent poll suggested that gaining "skills and knowledge for a career" far outweighed gaining a "well-rounded general education" as a goal of higher education, not only among the general population, but also among college leaders.[8] This is not to say that broader outcomes do not result from a college education; however, it is to say that these aims are lost in the rhetoric of a narrow focus on perceived employability.

Independent colleges face real questions as to economic utility, more often framed as a "return on investment." Popular media suggests avoiding certain majors, including but not limited to psychology, art, theater, and sociology, based on the salaries offered to graduates within the first year after graduation.[9] Whether college is worth the significant investment of time and money is an important question.[10] However, reducing college to the size of the bill in proportion to salary associated with the first postcollege job skews the full value of a college education.

In particular, an excessive focus on economic utility has too often displaced attention to broader questions of meaning and purpose that include, but also transcend, one's future occupation and earning potential.[11] Moreover, the long-term economic strength of a degree from an independent college is often ignored. At one level, Gerber[12] is accurate in saying that "all degrees are not created equal." The question, however, is less about whether a chemical engineering and history major are the same but, rather, whether a nursing or English degree in isolation from a broader college experience is equal to any other.

Even if an independent education is truly desired, one may think that obtaining it is out of reach or even elitist, available only to those from more wealthy families. Blogger "Professor Quest,"[13] self-identified as a humanities professor from the Midwest, says it this way: "The idea that [students] need familiarity with literature, history, and science is merely an elitist bias perpetuated by academics whose paychecks are derived from forcing students to take courses in subjects they wouldn't otherwise pay for." The notion of a liberal arts education is perceived as an unnecessary hurdle at best and an elitist conspiracy at worst.

President Obama's highly publicized proposal to rate postsecondary institutions based on "measures such as the average tuition they charge, the share of low-income students they enroll and their effectiveness in ensuring students graduate without too much debt"[14] may serve to exacerbate the view that private colleges are elitist—no matter how unintended such a conclusion may be. The depiction of residential, private colleges as the "gold standard" in the documentary *Ivory Tower*[15] certainly fits the elitist narrative as well. And, given that the average total cost to attend a private, nonprofit institution now exceeds $43,000 per year, that tuition increases for the 2015–16 academic year at these institutions ranged between 3 percent and 6 percent, that the gap between actual price and "sticker price" of a college education has widened, and that the annual incomes for most Americans declined somewhat during the last decade,[16] the challenge for independent institutions to attract and retain students, much less to interest them in liberal arts fields for which students and their families believe the "return on investment" to be questionable, is daunting indeed.

Taken together, these concerns have raised troubling questions as to the very future of independent higher education as a viable institutional type. Twenty-five years ago, David Breneman conducted a study of independent liberal arts institutions to ascertain their relative status within the postsecondary landscape. In a recent update of Breneman's study, Vicki Baker, Roger Baldwin, and Sumedha Makker[17] testify, at least in part, to the relative impact of the challenges that are briefly highlighted above. For example, their analyses revealed that 130 institutions remain as "true liberal arts colleges" out of the 212

Breneman initially identified.[18] Echoing the challenges that we have already highlighted, they note that: "many liberal arts colleges have worked to update their educational strategies in order to remain competitive in an aggressive market for new students. While continuing to value the traditional goals of a liberal arts education . . . many liberal arts colleges have experimented with ways to adapt their educational model and to connect it more directly with the world beyond campus and with career opportunities." Baker, Baldwin, and Makker[19] identify compelling trends in degrees awarded over a 25-year period. These authors raise questions to which we must attend, including the pointed question of whether these data suggest the extent to which we may be "witnessing the gradual demise of the liberal arts college" or "merely seeing a normal evolutionary response that may lead to new or perhaps alternative (e.g., hybrid) models of a liberal arts college education." Ultimately, these innovative adaptations that draw on the strengths of the liberal arts but also clearly prepare graduates for gainful employment within a distinctive educational context must be part of the narrative about the value and relevance of the independent college.

Areas of Strength: A Narrative of Asset and Opportunity

The independent college has adapted to its social and educational context since its inception, even being recognized as an incubator for new ideas within the postsecondary landscape.[20] Today's context offers yet another opportunity to reaffirm and reimagine the strengths of the independent college with particular focus on how this institutional type uniquely serves persons and society. The strengths of the independent college stem from its rootedness in the liberal arts tradition and its ability to adapt liberal arts ideals to new contexts.

It is critical to both comprehend the history of the liberal arts and to frame this ideal in its contemporary context. The term "liberal arts" finds its origins in the concept of *artes liberalis*, connoting those branches of knowledge appropriate for a free individual. Initially, this ideal was composed of seven liberal arts. The first three, framed as the *trivium*, focused on cultivating an appreciation for language: grammar, rhetoric, and dialectic. To these were added the *quadrivium* focusing on the mathematical-physical arts: geometry, arithmetic, music, and astronomy. Today, the liberal arts have broadened to include the arts and sciences;[21] even more specifically, the liberal arts now encompass the humanities, natural sciences, and social sciences.[22]

The branches of knowledge associated with the liberal arts today are not only broader than the *quadrivium* and *trivium*, but also serve a broader function. The liberal arts and sciences provide breadth in undergraduate education. Unfortunately, "breadth" is often oversimplified and touted as a counterpoint to specialized knowledge.[23] This dichotomy does us a disservice amid the rapids of knowledge advancement we face today. Instead, we must lift up the ideals of the liberal arts as they connect with specialized knowledge and serve today's pressing educational and societal needs.

The liberal arts function in the present to consider knowledge in light of the larger question of "to what end," which is ultimately a question of meaning. The liberal arts provide an avenue to a "broad education" that allows students to contextualize rather than simply complement technical learning, thus enabling students to "place new and specialized knowledge within a larger mosaic."[24] In a world where not only jobs but careers change, where industries not only fail but also grow obsolete, college graduates need more than a degree to both secure gainful employment and also to maintain employment over the increasingly long lifespan. Toward this end, the independent college is uniquely situated to prepare graduates for success over the long haul; to prepare them not only for a first job after college, but for a fifth job after college as well because, ultimately, it prepares them for more than a job.

Empirical evidence supports the belief that independent colleges grounded in a liberal arts education provide a distinctive and highly beneficial form of undergraduate education.[25] Moreover, these benefits are grounded in attributes of the independent college that expand beyond types of degrees awarded, including "a strong emphasis on teaching and student development, a common valuing of the life of the mind, small size, a shared intellectual experience, high academic expectations, and frequent interactions inside and outside the classroom between students and faculty."[26] While a critical mass of liberal arts majors and exposure for all students to the liberal arts subjects, these broader attributes are equally critical for the independent college in helping the broader public make sense of its value.

In order to advance a more expansive narrative of the full value of the independent college for the present and future, it is time to evoke a both/and that is distinct to the independent college. The independent college sector is fully cognizant that focusing on employability is critical but incomplete. However, it is similarly critical to note that evoking the liberal arts as an ideal is important but insufficient. We must emphasize that this institutional type is rooted in particular ideals of the liberal arts *and* clarify how these attributes serve both persons and society. Three ideals are particularly salient for the independent college.

First, a liberal arts education affords students the opportunity to cultivate *critical thinking* abilities that are requisite for success beyond the academy.[27] Second, the liberal arts advance *personal meaning and purpose*.[28] Third, the liberal arts environment serves an *incubator for engaged citizenship*.[29] The full value of the independent college is embodied in these three frames of liberal arts education.

Critical Thinking

First, an education imbued in the liberal arts enables students to develop critical intellectual competencies. The list of basic competencies could almost certainly consume the remainder of this volume, but they typically include mastery of reading, communication, and critical thinking.[30] Moreover, these are the very skills that employers are looking for in college graduates.

Employers believe colleges and universities should place more emphasis on a variety of key learning outcomes in order to increase graduates' success in today's global economy. Employers express a need to increase the focus on active skills such as critical thinking, complex problem solving, communication, and applying knowledge to real-world settings. Eighty percent of employers want to see increased emphasis on critical thinking and analytical reasoning, complex problem solving and analysis, and written and oral communication.[31] Over 70 percent of employers want to see increased emphasis on the application of knowledge in real-world settings, the location, organization, and evaluation of information from multiple sources, and innovation and creativity.[32] In short, intellectual skills are marketable skills.

Independent colleges have the edge in helping students cultivate these skills. A recent report analyzing National Survey of Student Engagement (NSSE) data revealed that "private college students are more likely to experience courses that emphasize higher-order learning and reflective and integrative learning experiences as well as studying, writing, and reading."[33] Coursework at independent institutions was more likely to emphasize analyzing ideas or experiences, evaluating points of view and information sources and forming new ideas from various bits of information.[34] Seniors attending smaller, independent institutions were challenged to a greater extent in their courses to evaluate points of view and form new ideas. Private institution students on the whole had better regard for the progress they had made in learning and development. For example, college seniors at independent colleges and universities perceived greater gains in writing clearly and effectively, speaking clearly and effectively, and thinking critically and analytically.[35]

Employers strongly endorse educational practices that involve students in active, effortful work. Knowledge in isolation is less important to employers than intersecting skills, or questions that address a combination of knowledge and skills. Even where employers considered particular kinds of knowledge to be very important or somewhat important (e.g., global knowledge, science and technology), they still placed a higher priority on forms of learning that emphasize students' active development and application of intellectual and practical skills.[36] Employers highlight several educational practices as particularly helpful in preparing undergraduates for the workplace, including hands-on experience with the methods of science, developing research questions in their field and evidence-based analyses, conducting research collaboratively, completing an internship or community-based field project, and finishing a project prior to graduation that demonstrates their acquired knowledge and skills.[37] Again, small independent institutions have an edge in providing this type of learning.

Students at independent colleges participate in more high-impact educational practices (HIEPs). High-impact practices include such educational initiatives as undergraduate research, internships, capstone experiences, and common learning.[38] Across smaller independent institutions, a greater percentage (5 percent more) of first-year students participated in at least one HIEP. For example, at private institutions, 8 percent more seniors participated in service learning, 5 percent more worked on a research project with a faculty member, 8 percent more had an internship or field experience, and 11 percent more studied abroad. Consequently, 9 percent more seniors at independent institutions participated in at least two HIEPs during their college careers. Seniors attending smaller independent institutions were more likely to participate in *all* six high-impact educational practices. Finally, seniors at the smaller independent institutions were the *most* likely to complete a culminating senior experience. Research that focuses squarely on what employers need supports the liberal arts ideal of critical thinking and its prevalence in the small independent college.

Meaning and Purpose

Beyond the intellectual benefits, a curriculum that draws on the liberal arts provides opportunity for personal exploration of identity and meaning. A liberal arts education lays the groundwork for what Delbanco[39] refers to as the "fulfilled life." On the face of it, college as an avenue to a "fulfilled life" may smack of elitism or at least prefigure an elitist narrative. On the contrary, colleges and universities exist as places at which meaning making does not simply occur as a matter of course; they are contexts that intentionally advertise themselves to be places where meaning making not only happens but also is to be anticipated, including with particular, intentional ends in mind. Magolda and King[40] elaborate: "meaning making refers to the strategies students use to understand what and how they are learning. . . . It provides a way of weighing resources of information and insights (including texts, Web sites, professors, staff members, and peers) to decide what to believe." Meaning making is at the core of the college endeavor.

Unfortunately, higher education in the United States faces a flurry of critique for neglecting matters of meaning.[41] The independent college, however, maintains an emphasis on values and meaning better than other institutional types. Students enrolled in independent colleges are more likely to indicate they have made progress in clarifying personal values and ethical sensibilities.[42] Values and ethics are not simply pie-in-the-sky outcomes of the undergraduate degree; in fact, these are areas that directly impact employability. Employers point to a variety of types of knowledge and skills as important hiring considerations, but one of their greatest priorities is ethics.[43] In fact, 96 percent of employers rate the ability to "demonstrate ethical judgment and integrity" as important, with 76 percent rating it very important. Moreover, employers indicate that undergraduate education that allows students to work through ethical issues and to participate in debate in order to form their own judgments about consequential issues will help students succeed after graduation.[44] Ethical sensibilities are crucial to employability.

In addition, college students must engage queries of personal meaning in order to make sense of their degrees: Who am I? What are my convictions? How will I live and act? Graduates today need a deeply rooted inner compass to navigate society's relentless pace of change and disruption to the status quo; at the same time, it is crucial to cultivate college graduates who find meaning not simply in personal advancement but also in a commitment to the commons.[45] Toward that end, the independent college advances a sense of life's purpose by creating educational experiences that enable students to not only find meaning in their personal endeavors but also to contribute to the larger world. Students must consider questions of meaning within a context beyond the self: What are my obligations to others? What are theirs to me?[46] Finding personal identity and a commitment to the common good lie at the center of lives of purpose.

Again, the independent college provides an exemplary context for influencing lives of purpose. A recent study examining programs in independent college contexts demonstrated that conversations about purpose proved to develop "persistence and resilience" in college graduates that enabled them to weather life's inevitable storms.[47] Moreover, sustained conversations with students about questions of purpose resulted in a "recalibration of post-college trajectories" toward "journeys of significance and impact."[48] Lives of purpose are necessary not only for the first job but also to withstand the personal and social hurdles that can and will arise in a lifetime.

Engaged Citizenship

Extending from the intellectual benefits and opportunities for clarifying one's purpose, the independent college advances the liberal arts ideals of engaged citizenship. Such thoughtful attention to the common good is in too short supply in our society. As Chopp[49] asserts, "Our country is in desperate need of what the liberal arts can offer. A serious crisis deeply linked to the failure of individuals to find common ground is leading many citizens to lose faith in their leaders, in their democratic institutions, in their communities that are increasingly polarized, and in a long-held sense of the common good." The long-held sense of the common good is also disrupted by a polarized culture that hampers individuals' ability to talk with and understand each other and, most pointedly, to challenge professed "experts" on areas of common impact. The "dangerous and growing gap between public policy and public understanding"[50] is not new. However, the proliferation of professed experts and isolated mindsets perpetuating partial truths and limited perspectives within our current context of increasing global and technological complexity intensifies the gap. We run the risk of making critical decisions not on the basis of what is known but on the basis of blind faith in bits of information received from who we are told to trust.

An elemental aspect of engaged citizenship is the ability to understand and collaborate with those who hold differing perspectives. Bok[51] argues that "a successful democracy demands tolerance and mutual respect from different groups within its citizenry in order to contain the religious and ethnic tensions that have riven so many countries around the world." The independent college prepares students to meet these societal demands by presenting students with opposing philosophies and a forum for examining the rich cultures that surround us. In a residential college, such conversations occur not only in the classroom but also in the places where students share meals and living spaces. Conversations that cross philosophies and cultures include but expand beyond classroom dialogue. It is by living within these tensions that students learn to both walk in their neighbor's shoes and also appreciate the gifts of their neighbor's perspective. This aspect of engaged citizenship is important not only to democracy but also to employment.

As with intellectual capacity and cultivating meaning, the liberal arts ideal of engaged citizenship is not mere platitude but, rather, central to employment preparation. There is broad agreement among employers that all students, regardless of their chosen field of study, should have educational experiences that teach them about building civic capacity and cultures outside the United States. Large majorities of employers indicate that engaged citizenship is a crucial aim of a college education. Ninety-one percent of employers agree that all students should have undergraduate experiences that teach them how to solve problems with people whose views are different from their own. Eighty-six percent of employers indicate that an undergraduate education should ensure that college students gain experience working with others to solve important problems in their community.[52] Engaged citizenship, a liberal arts ideal, builds capacity for workplace success.

The full value of the independent college is found at the intersection of these three liberal arts ideals. The independent college helps students advance their intellectual capacity. Moreover, the independent college helps students to engage knowledge in a purposeful context, thus enabling students to make sense of their education and their lives, including but not limited to professional preparation. Finally, the independent college beckons students to explore inward while simultaneously engaging society. Students are prepared to pursue meaningful *and* lucrative careers while understanding their interconnectedness and responsibility to their neighbors. We must be sure to couch the value of the independent college in its fullest meaning in order to move forward.

Framing a More Expansive Narrative for the Independent College

The literature clearly offers a robust and empirically verified argument as to the value of independent higher education rooted in the liberal arts. Even as employers articulate the need for liberally educated graduates, and their desire to hire such graduates, the question as to how to shift the cultural mindset remains. The challenge is to cultivate an ethos of meaning for the independent college that includes but transcends employment outcomes. This will require both communicating the specifics of value as well as developing initiatives that draw upon the inherent benefits of an independent college education.

An expansive narrative of the value of the independent college needs to include but expand beyond the liberal arts disciplines. Moreover, it needs to address both the broader outcomes of the independent college alongside very pragmatic employment outcomes. It must also include robust but deeply intentional general education programs characteristic of the independent college. Finally, the narrative must articulate the full value of the residential experience.

While an exhaustive list of initiatives that would apply to every independent college is beyond the scope of this chapter, we provide the following exemplars in order to illustrate possibilities.

Beyond the Platitudes

The independent college must help its constituencies to make meaning of the liberal arts in a contemporary context. It is insufficient to market an institution with phrases like a "dynamic, liberal arts curriculum" without translating this phrase into terms that make sense to external constituencies. Moreover, institutions need to cast the various ideals of a liberal arts education—intellectual skills, meaning and purpose, and engaged citizenship—in a manner that applies to employment success. This is not to say that a dynamic liberal arts curriculum is not valuable; rather, it is to say that the independent college sector cannot leave these ideals up to interpretation. Fleshing out the full meaning of a liberal arts education in institution-specific as well as collective messaging will advance shared understanding and appreciation of this distinctive educational context.

Market Opportunities for Liberal Arts Majors

The future flourishing of the independent college depends upon greater understanding of the employment benefits of and opportunities for liberal arts majors. There is empirical evidence that liberal arts disciplines prepare graduates for long-term professional success.[53] At the same time, there are students who want to major in the liberal arts but their parents will not let them. A new narrative needs to tap into the aspirations of these prospective students while simultaneously responding to the employability concerns of their parents. Moreover, the utility-related concerns that students have internalized from their parents and the broader culture must be addressed.

The aim here is not to subvert the broader aims of the independent college by refocusing on the market. Rather, what is needed is a market correction of sorts: external constituencies need to have their initial economic concerns addressed in order to consider a liberal arts major or the independent college and, more importantly, to invest in the full value of their degree. David Kirp[54] frames the challenge this way: "Much like Swiss watchmakers, today's liberal arts professors offer what is widely regarded as a luxury item to a shrinking clientele. Because these academics treat the value of their subject as self-evident, not something that needs to be explained anew, in recent years they have lost much of their audience, as career minded undergraduates have shifted their allegiance to the 'practical arts.'" It is crucial to find persuasive ways to explain the enduring values of a liberal arts education to a new generation; its value is simply not self-evident in contemporary culture.

Whereas the common vernacular negates their value, liberal arts majors have actually been described as the most valuable in today's entrepreneurial, tech-heavy world. Liberal arts majors bring creativity and fresh ideas to companies.[55] Moreover, in an independent college context, liberal arts majors are coupled with opportunities for gaining practical experience; both liberal arts-inspired critical thinking and pragmatic experience advance employability.

Independent colleges can reframe existing scholarships to tap into humanities-based majors while creating initiatives for the recipients of those scholarships that help incentivize students to not just major in the humanities but to make the most out of their majors. Our culture questions whether one can translate an English major, as one example, into gainful employment, and independent colleges must clearly and articulately respond to this doubt.

Helene Meyers[56] illustrates her own experiment teaching English majors to "market themselves and their degrees with integrity." She created a course entitled "Novel English Majors" that allows students to think intentionally about their postgraduate lives and includes, as one learning objective, the ability to connect the "skills and mindsets of literary analysis to diverse career paths."[57] The course includes analysis of texts for the English major's marketable skills and incorporates first-person perspectives of English majors who credit specific aspects of their professional worlds to skills from the discipline. These activities helped students not only to "associate the [English] major with a narrative of professional plentitude rather than scarcity" but also to map out an impressive list of marketable skills, including writing, research, project management, listening, oral communication, creativity, innovation, and connecting details with the big picture. This is one example for clearly advancing the employability narrative for liberal arts disciplines.

Reimagine General Education

Even as understanding of the liberal arts major is expanded in the reasonable hope of attracting more students to these disciplines, colleges cannot ignore the reality that fewer students are majoring in the liberal arts disciplines.[58] As a result, all students need to be given meaningful opportunities to engage with the liberal arts regardless of major. In today's educational context, general education programs are the primary venue through which the liberal arts can be explored by all students. As specialized education became more common, the liberal arts were "retained in the general education program."[59]

Much like liberal arts majors, the value of general education is not self-evident. General education is, in fact, widely misunderstood.[60] We must carefully articulate the value of a general education in light of both its broad ideals and connections to employability. Moreover, general education must be reimagined and redesigned in order to realize the benefits of a general education in the current context. General education has long adapted to societal changes.[61] As one example, the distribution model of general education in which students select disciplinary courses among a menu of options was designed in the mid-twentieth century and yet remains the most widely used model of general education.[62] While the distribution model has many strengths, it does not offer an avenue for students to make interdisciplinary connections except on their own. To fulfill the ideals of a liberal education, curricular avenues for helping students make connections across disciplines is crucial.[63] Moreover, in our cultural context where not only every college but also every credit is examined for its cost, it is critical to make the most of the credits afforded to general education. This is typically one-third of the credits toward a baccalaureate degree; the stakes are high and the task is large. Fortunately, the independent college can take the lead in these adaptations.

Articulate the Value of the Residential Environment

The residential environment enables students to live in close quarters with others from different walks of life and whose budding expertise is in different disciplines. The engineering major connecting with the English major and with the business major in conversation about solving problems large and small emulates the work world. By learning to appreciate the interconnectedness of the world, graduates emerge with a richer understanding of complexity and the ability to collaborate toward solving society's vexing problems.

Degrees of Meaning

As we have emphasized, the challenges independent colleges face and the response to these challenges are queries of meaning. Human beings, by their very nature, are meaning makers.[64] Institutions of higher education, the students that inhabit them, and the aspects of broader culture that depend on them are consciously (and unconsciously) engaged in a meaning-making process that impacts the perceived value of higher education and various avenues toward the baccalaureate degree.

Although we can acknowledge the connection between meaning making and higher education, not all institutions or constituencies that comprise higher education make meaning in the same way or with the same ends in mind. That is, the primary meaning that one student associates with higher education may be career preparation, while for another it may be learning for its own sake. Similarly, the central meaning of the learning enterprise for one institution may be framed around the development of critical thinking skills, while for another institution it may emphasize the cultivation of citizenship. Meaning making in higher education—as regards its institutions as well as its respective constituencies—is not a monolith. Tapping into and expanding meaning without downplaying or denigrating existing ways of making meaning (e.g., the point of a degree is gainful employment) is our primary task.

We believe that the meaning of an undergraduate degree from independent colleges and universities has particular, noteworthy characteristics. These characteristics reflect a certain distinctiveness that must not be overlooked amid the seeming primacy of other meaning-making narratives surrounding the purpose of a degree. The way to create a shared appreciation of a more expansive narrative of value for independent higher education will require the very liberal arts–inspired creativity and critical thinking that we have advocated. After all, the "ability to understand the world through different lenses and turn competing or disparate viewpoints into a compelling narrative" requires an "intuitive understanding of the world that comes from a deep immersion in the liberal arts."[65] In essence, there are varying degrees of meaning for undergraduate education. There are divergent viewpoints in our culture regarding the value of liberal arts majors, general education, residential colleges, and independent higher education as a whole. The ultimate challenge is to create and communicate a compelling narrative that articulates the full value and meaning of a degree from an independent college rooted in the liberal arts.

NOTES

1. Gerber, "How Liberal Arts Colleges."
2. Ferrall, *Liberal Arts at the Brink*; Chopp, "Remaking, Renewing, Reimagining"; Deblanco, *College*; Lewis, *Excellence without a Soul*; Roche, *Why Choose the Liberal Arts*; Zakaria, *Defense of a Liberal Education.*
3. Quoted in Westervelt, "Amid Rising College Costs."
4. American Association of Colleges and Universities, "Liberal Arts Graduates and Employment"; Humphreys, "Making the Case for Liberal Education."
5. Association of American Colleges and Universities, "More than a Major."
6. Donoghue, *Last Professors.*
7. In 2012, this percentage was 87.9 percent, which was up from 67 percent in 1976. Pryor et al., *American Freshman 2012*, 4. In 2013, this percentage showed a slight decline to 86.3 percent. Eagan et al., *American Freshman 2013*, 35.
8. Ripley, "College Is Dead."
9. Bui, "Most and Least Lucrative Majors"; Goudreau, "10 Worst College Majors."
10. Bennett and Wilezol, *Is College Worth It?*; Selingo, *College (Un)bound.*
11. Kronman, *Education's End.*
12. Gerber, "How Liberal Arts Colleges."
13. Professor Quest, "Four Arguments."
14. See Anderson and Rucker, "Obama Proposes College-Rating System."
15. Rossi, *Ivory Tower.*
16. College Board, "Trends in College Pricing 2015."
17. Baker, Baldwin, and Makker, "Where Are They Now?"
18. Brenneman's ("Are We Losing?") definition of a true liberal arts college was based on degrees awarded in fields considered to be "traditional liberal arts," including history, psychology, the sciences (natural and social), foreign languages, religion, the arts, and English. Professional fields include business/management, communications, education, engineering, nursing, and computer sciences. A Liberal Arts I classification indicated that 50 percent or more of degrees awarded were in traditional liberal arts fields and a Liberal Arts II classification indicated that more than 50 percent but less than 60 percent of degrees were awarded in traditional liberal arts fields. Baker, Baldwin, and Makker ("Where Are They Now?") used these degree classifications in determining that 130 out of the 212 institutions identified in 1990 remained "true liberal arts colleges" in 2012.
19. Baker, Baldwin, and Makker, "Where Are They Now?"
20. Chopp, "Remaking, Renewing, Reimagining."
21. Roche, *Why Choose the Liberal Arts.*
22. Deresiewicz, *Excellent Sheep.*
23. Taylor, *Crisis on Campus.*
24. Roche, *Why Choose the Liberal Arts*, 6.
25. Astin, "How the Liberal Arts College"; Hu and Kuh, "Being (Dis)Engaged"; Pascarella and Terenzini, *How College Affects Students.*
26. Pascarella and Terenzini, *How College Affects Students*, 12.
27. Chopp, "Remaking, Renewing, Reimagining"; Roche, *Why Choose the Liberal Arts.*
28. Chopp, "Remaking, Renewing, Reimagining"; Deblanco, *College.*
29. Chopp, "Remaking, Renewing, Reimagining"; Deblanco, *College.*
30. Bok, *Higher Education in America*; Boyer, "General Education."
31. Hart Research Associates, "Falling Short?"
32. Ibid.

33. Gonyea and Kinzie, "Independent Colleges and Student Engagement," 4.
34. Ibid.
35. Ibid.
36. Hart Research Associates, "Falling Short?"
37. Ibid.
38. Kuh, "High-Impact Educational Practices."
39. Deblanco, *College.*
40. Baxter Magolda and King, "Assessing Meaning Making," 2.
41. Deresiewicz, *Excellent Sheep*; Kronman, *Education's End*; Lewis, *Excellence without a Soul.*
42. Gonyea and Kinzie, "Independent Colleges and Student Engagement."
43. Hart Research Associates, "Falling Short?"
44. Ibid.
45. Parks, *Big Questions, Worthy Dreams.*
46. Questions are drawn from the work of Boyer, *College*; Hahnenberg, *Awakening Vocation*; Roche, *Why Choose the Liberal Arts.*
47. Clydesdale, *Purposeful Graduate.*
48. Ibid., xvii.
49. Chopp, "Remaking, Renewing, Reimagining," 21.
50. Boyer, *College*, 279.
51. Bok, *Our Underachieving Colleges*, 195.
52. Hart Research Associates, "Falling Short?
53. American Association of Colleges and Universities, "New Report."
54. Kirp, *Shakespeare, Einstein, Bottom Line*, 258–59.
55. Sportelli, "Liberal Arts Majors."
56. Meyers, "Feeding English Majors," para. 3.
57. Ibid., para. 7.
58. Ferrall, *Liberal Arts at the Brink*; Zakaria, *Defense of a Liberal Education.*
59. Fant, "Heartbeat of Christian Higher Education," 34.
60. Mannoia, *Christian Liberal Arts*; Wells, "General Education"; Wells, "Realizing General Education."
61. Wells, "Realizing General Education."
62. Handstedt, *General Education Essentials.*
63. Cronon, "'Only Connect.'"
64. Berger, *Sacred Canopy*; Kegan, *Evolving Self.*
65. Perrault, "Digital Companies," para. 140.

REFERENCES

Association of American Colleges and Universities. "Liberal Arts Graduates and Employment: Setting the Record Straight." 2014. http://www.aacu.org/sites/default/files/files/LEAP/nchems.pdf. Accessed March 29, 2017.
———. "New Report Documents That Liberal Arts Disciplines Prepare Graduates for Long-Term Professional Success." Press release, January 22, 2014. http://www.aacu.org/press/press-releases/new-report-documents-liberal-arts-disciplines-prepare-graduates-long-term. Accessed March 29, 2017.
Anderson, Nick, and Philip Rucker. "Obama Proposes College-Rating System in Bid to Increase Affordability." *Washington Post*, August 22, 2013. https://www.washington

post.com/politics/obama-to-propose-college-ranking-system-that-could-increase
-affordability/2013/08/22/73e674c0-0b17-11e3-b87c-476db8ac34cd_story.html. Accessed
March 29, 2017.

Association of American Colleges and Universities. "It Takes More than a Major: Employer Priorities for College Learning and Student Success." *Liberal Education* 99,
no. 2 (Spring 2013). https://www.aacu.org/publications-research/periodicals/it-takes
-more-major-employer-priorities-college-learning-and. Accessed April 24, 2017.

Astin, Alexander W. "How the Liberal Arts College Affects Students." *Daedalus* 128, no.
1 (1999): 77–100.

Baker, Vicki L., Roger G. Baldwin, and Sumedha Makker. "Where Are They Now? Revisiting Breneman's Study of Liberal Arts Colleges." *Liberal Education* 98, no. 3 (2012):
48–53.

Baxter Magolda, Marcia, and Patricia M. King. "Assessing Meaning Making and Self-
Authorship: Theory, Research, and Application." *ASHE Higher Education Report* 38,
no. 3 (September 27, 2012).

Bennett, William John, and David Wilezol. *Is College Worth It? A Former United States
Secretary of Education and a Liberal Arts Graduate Expose the Broken Promise of Higher
Education.* Nashville: Thomas Nelson, 2013.

Berger, Peter. *The Sacred Canopy: Elements of a Sociological Theory of Religion.* New York:
Doubleday, 1967.

Bok, Derek C. *Higher Education in America.* Princeton, NJ: Princeton University Press,
2013.

———. *Our Underachieving Colleges: A Candid Look at How Much Students Learn and Why
They Should Be Learning More.* Princeton, NJ: Princeton University Press, 2006.

Boyer, Ernest L. *College: The Undergraduate Experience in America.* New York: Harper and
Row, 1987.

———. "General Education: The Integrated Core." Text of speech delivered as Academic
Convocation Address of the University of San Francisco, San Francisco, April 11, 1988.

Breneman, David. "Are We Losing Our Liberal Arts Colleges?" *AAHE Bulletin* 43, no.
2 (1990): 3–6.

Bui, Q. "The Most and Least Lucrative College Majors, in 2 Graphs." *NPR*, October 22,
2013. http://www.npr.org/sections/money/2013/10/22/239698749/the-most-and-least
-lucrative-college-majors-in-2-graphs. Accessed March 29, 2017.

Chopp, Rebecca. "Remaking, Renewing, Reimagining: The Liberal Arts College Takes
Advantage of Change." In *Remaking College: Innovation and the Liberal Arts*, edited by
Rebecca Chopp, Susan Frost, and Daniel H. Weiss, 13–24. Baltimore: Johns Hopkins
University Press, 2014.

Clydesdale, Tim. *The Purposeful Graduate: Why Colleges Must Talk to Students about Vocation.* Chicago: University of Chicago Press, 2015.

College Board. "Trends in College Pricing 2015." New York: College Board, 2015.

Cronon, William. "'Only Connect . . .' The Goals of a Liberal Education." *American
Scholar* 67, no. 4 (1998): 73–80.

Delbanco, Andrew. *College: What It Was, Is, and Should Be.* Princeton, NJ: Princeton University Press, 2012.

Deresiewicz, William. *Excellent Sheep: The Miseducation of the American Elite and the Way
to a Meaningful Life.* New York: Free Press, 2014.

Donoghue, Frank. *The Last Professors: The Corporate University and the Fate of the Humanities.* New York: Fordham University Press, 2008.

Fant, Gene C. "The Heartbeat of Christian Higher Education: The Core Curriculum."

In *Faith and Learning: A Handbook for Christian Higher Education*, edited by David S. Dockery, 27–49. Nashville: B&H, 2012.

Ferrall, Victor E. *Liberal Arts at the Brink*. Cambridge, MA: Harvard University Press, 2011.

Gerber, Scott. "How Liberal Arts Colleges Are Failing America." *Atlantic*, September 24, 2012. http://www.theatlantic.com/business/archive/2012/09/how-liberal-arts-colleges -are-failing-america/262711. Accessed March 29, 2017.

Gonyea, Robert M., and Jillian Kinzie. "Independent Colleges and Student Engagement: Descriptive Analysis by Institutional Type." Washington, DC: Council of Independent Colleges, 2015.

Goudreau, Jenna. "The 10 Worst College Majors." *Forbes*, October 11, 2012. http://www .forbes.com/sites/jennagoudreau/2012/10/11/the-10-worst-college-majors/#2715e 4857a0b4cbac75353c9. Accessed March 29, 2017.

Hahnenberg, Edward P. *Awakening Vocation: A Theology of Christian Call*. Collegeville, MN: Liturgical Press, 2010.

Handstedt, Paul. *General Education Essentials: A Guide for Faculty*. San Franscisco: Jossey Bass, 2012.

Hart Research Associates. "Falling Short? College Learning and Career Success. Selected Findings from Online Surveys of Employers and College Students Conducted on Behalf of the Association of American Colleges and Universities." 2013. https://www .aacu.org/sites/default/files/files/LEAP/2013_EmployerSurvey.pdf. Accessed March 29, 2017.

Hu, Shouping, and George D. Kuh. "Being (Dis)Engaged in Educationally Purposeful Activities: The Influences of Student and Institutional Characteristics." *Research in Higher Education* 43, no. 5 (October 1, 2002): 555–75. doi:10.1023/A:1020114231387.

Humphreys, Debra. "Making the Case for Liberal Education: Responding to Challenges." Washington, DC: Association of American Colleges and Universities, 2006. http:// www.aacu.org/sites/default/files/files/LEAP/MakingtheCase.pdf. Accessed March 29, 2017.

Kegan, Robert. *The Evolving Self: Problem and Process in Human Development*. Cambridge, MA: Harvard University Press, 1982.

Kirp, David L. *Shakespeare, Einstein, and the Bottom Line: The Marketing of Higher Education*. Cambridge, MA: Harvard University Press, 2003.

Kronman, Anthony T. *Education's End: Why Our Colleges and Universities Have Given Up on the Meaning of Life*. New Haven, CT: Yale University Press, 2007.

Kuh, George D. "High-Impact Educational Practices: What They Are, Who Has Access to Them, and Why They Matter." Washington, DC: Association of American Colleges and Universities, 2008.

Lewis, Harry R. *Excellence without a Soul: How a Great University Forgot Education*. New York: Public Affairs, 2006.

Mannoia Jr., James V. *Christian Liberal Arts: An Education That Goes Beyond*. New York: Rowman and Littlefield, 2000.

Meyers, Helene. "Feeding English Majors in the 21st Century." *Chronicle of Higher Education*, January 25, 2016. http://chronicle.com/article/Feeding-English-Majors-in -the/235042. Accessed March 29, 2017.

Parks, Sharon Daloz. *Big Questions, Worthy Dreams: Mentoring Emerging Adults in Their Search for Meaning, Purpose, and Faith*. San Francisco: Jossey-Bass, 2011.

Pascarella, Ernest T., and Patrick T. Terenzini. *How College Affects Students: A Third Decade of Research*. Vol. 2. San Francisco: Jossey-Bass, 2005.

———. *How College Affects Students: Findings and Insights from Twenty Years of Research*. San Francisco: Jossey-Bass, 1991.

Perrault, Tom. "Digital Companies Need More Liberal Arts Majors." *Harvard Business Review*, January 29, 2016. https://hbr.org/2016/01/digital-companies-need-more-lib eral-arts-majors. Accessed March 29, 2017.

Professor Quest. "Four Arguments for the Elimination of the Liberal Arts." *My Fall Semester Periodic: Reflection on Teaching at a Small Liberal Arts College*. November 20, 2009. http://myfallsemester.blogspot.com/2009/11/four-arguments-for-elimination-of .html. Accessed March 29, 2017.

Pryor, John, H., Kevin Eagan, Laura Palucki Blake, Sylvia Hurtado, Jennifer Burdan, and Matthew H. Case. *The American Freshman 2012: National Norms Fall 2012*. Los Angeles: Higher Education Research Institute, 2013.

Ripley, Amanda. "College Is Dead. Long Live College!" *Time*, October 18, 2012. http://nation.time.com/2012/10/18/college-is-dead-long-live-college. Accessed March 29, 2017.

Roche, Mark W. *Why Choose the Liberal Arts*. South Bend, IN: University of Notre Dame Press, 2010.

Rossi, Andrew. *Ivory Tower*. Motion picture on DVD. CNN Films, 2014.

Selingo, Jeffrey J. *College (Un)bound: The Future of Higher Education and What It Means for Students*. Boston: Houghton Mifflin Harcourt, 2013.

Sportelli, Natalie. "Liberal Arts Majors Are 'the Most Desirable Employees': Boom Brands Talk Road to Millennial Success." *Forbes*, April 13, 2015. http://www.forbes.com/sites/nataliesportelli/2015/04/13/liberal-arts-majors-are-the-most-desirable-employ ees-boom-brands-talk-millennial-success/#13df24d5741a. Accessed March 29, 2017.

Taylor, Mark C. *Crisis on Campus: A Bold Plan for Reforming Our Colleges and Universities*. New York: Alfred A. Knopf, 2010.

Wells, Cynthia A. "General Education and the Quest for Purpose." In *Ernest L. Boyer: Hope for Today's Universities*, edited by Todd C. Ream and John M. Braxton, 35–66. Albany: State University of New York Press, 2015.

———. "Realizing General Education: Reconsidering Conceptions and Renewing Practice." *ASHE Higher Education Report* 42, no. 2 (January 1, 2016): 1–85. doi:10.1002/aehe .20068.

Westervelt, Eric. "Amid Rising College Costs, a Defense of the Liberal Arts." *NPR*, "All Things Considered," August 3, 2014.

Zakaria, Fareed. *In Defense of a Liberal Education*. New York: W. W. Norton, 2015.

REACTION
Linda McMillin

This chapter by Cynthia A. Wells, David Guthrie, and Daniel Custer identifies issues connected to the core mission of liberal arts institutions and the value of liberal education writ large. It points out the enduring significance and import of a liberal education: critical thinking, vocation formation, engaged citizenship, and exploration of identity and meaning. It also outlines the skepticism of our modern culture that casts this education as nice but esoteric and evaluates educational investments by their immediate pragmatic and economic return.

I come to my reading of this chapter from two vantage points. I have spent my career at a small liberal arts college, Susquehanna University, and have served as its provost for over a decade. Consequently, I grapple daily with the economic and demographic realities that are confronting our business model. I am also a medieval historian. As such, I am steeped in the history of the "university," especially its twelfth- and thirteenth-century manifestations. I can assure you that in this argument over the pragmatic versus the intellectual outcomes of higher education, there is "nothing new under the sun." Indeed, I can point to medieval correspondence between parents and students debating the return on investment (ROI) of continuing to commit family treasure to educational endeavors (especially in light of said student's consumption of alcohol or propensity for brawling).

Consequently, I am impatient at times with our conversation about the "purity" of the liberal arts—as if such hyacinth pasts existed. Susquehanna has been awarding degrees in accounting since the 1920s and education since the 1960s. Sister Council of Independent Colleges (CIC) institutions have long-standing programs in nursing and engineering. Even those higher up the food chain who claim the most purity have habitually covered a multitude of pragmatism under the departmental heading of "economics." We need to stop fretting about purity—the "either/or" of liberal arts versus pragmatic education—and embrace a "both/and" model. We need to recognize our long history and strength in doing so. As the chapter points out, higher education needs to do both, and the liberal arts college can lead the way. Indeed, we have been doing so for some time.

So what does "both/and" look like? All of our promotional literatures tell stories about student outcomes. Our admissions staffs have convinced us, and rightly so, that we ignore family interest in vocationalism at our peril. Thus our career development centers facilitate the first destinations—graduate and professional school or job—of our students. However, we do not stop there. We are also telling stories about larger career arcs that extend into true vocations. And we connect the breadth of the liberal arts experience to creating lives of meaning and purpose. In this endeavor, our alumni play an increasingly important role. The myriad ways they have created lives of "achievement, leadership, and service" are the best proof points of the value of a Susquehanna educational experience. Thus alumni who donate time, advice, mentoring, as well as facilitate internships and entry-level opportunities are as valuable as those who write checks to the endowment.

When it comes to traditional liberal arts majors, "both/and" has been boosted by student desire for multiple credentials. On my campus, nimble departments have introduced enough program flexibility to survive as second majors—starting decades ago in modern languages. More recently, and fueled by funding from A. W. Mellon, we have deliberately created interdisciplinary minors with a pragmatic bent that complement particular liberal arts disciplines. Publishing and editing connects to English, museum studies to history and art, and arts management to theater. This has allowed students to pursue their passions and still have an answer when asked, "What are you going to do with that!?!" at Thanksgiving dinner.

"Both/and" plays out to its fullest potential, or should, in the ongoing discipline and focus the liberal arts tradition brings to general education. It is through strengthening and enriching our core requirements—which touch every student regardless of major—that we most live out our missions as liberal arts colleges. In its latest iteration at Susquehanna, implemented in 2007, we again affirmed the breadth of a liberal arts education by continuing to require the basic array: literature, history, science, ethics, fine arts, social science, and so on. We also, however, explicitly called out those skills associated with the liberal arts by requiring intensive courses in writing, teamwork, and oral presentation. And we began to articulate emerging liberal arts foci in diversity and cross-cultural competency—the former through both theoretical and applied coursework and the latter by a required off-campus immersion framed by academic reflection. Our shaping and reshaping of the core continues. Led in part by the flowering of the digital humanities and our participation in CIC's Consortium for Online Humanities Instruction, we are exploring how to empower our students to wield the tools and values of the liberal arts as they create and curate their own presence in the exploding digital universe.

Finally, "both/and" moves us beyond the classroom and into the intentional residential communities at the heart of our campuses. Creating these imperfect but redemptive spaces for young people to explore their own identities and attempt to craft relationships across difference is an ongoing challenge. We sometimes succeed but often come up short as the student protests of this past fall have shown us. Nevertheless, the liberal arts call on us to continue to help our students find the grace and skills to build and sustain the kinds of communities our world so desperately needs.

In the end, this chapter encourages us to embrace "both/and." As the authors note, "The full value of the independent college is found at the intersection . . . [and] beckons students to explore inward while simultaneously engaging society. Students are prepared to pursue meaningful *and* lucrative careers while understanding their interconnectedness and responsibility to their neighbors. We must be sure to couch the value of the independent college in its fullest meaning in order to move forward."

8

The Faculty Role in the Smaller Private College

JOHN M. BRAXTON

Faculty members represent a key component of private colleges, including those colleges that are members of the Council of Independent Colleges (CIC). The faculty define the core characteristics of such colleges through their performance of the professorial roles of scholars and teachers. The curriculum also functions as an instrument of professorial practice.[1] Put differently, faculties constitute the core of colleges and universities.[2] The leaders of CIC affiliated colleges and universities shoulder a responsibility for the stewardship of their faculty and of the roles they perform. The use of scholarly literature to guide institutional policy and practice best serves such a stewardship.

Accordingly, I provide a targeted review of the scholarly literature on particular topics of central importance among college and university faculty. These topics include the graduate school socialization process, the employment status of members of the faculty, the academic reward structure, and supportive teaching cultures as an organizational source of influence on college teaching. I then delineate the challenges this review presents to leaders of CIC affiliated colleges and universities. Finally, I will present recommendations for policies and practices that institutions might use to address the delineated challenges. This chapter seeks to strike at the crux of faculty work and the contribution of this work to the achievement of the goals of private small colleges.

The Graduate School Socialization Process

Through graduate study, graduate students acquire attitudes, values, norms, and disciplinary knowledge and skill required for faculty research and teaching role performance.[3] This potent socialization process also shapes graduate students' impressions of the professorial role's styles of work and standards of performance that will guide their subsequent career as members of the professoriate.[4] As a consequence, the outcomes of this socialization hold important implications for small private colleges and the faculty members they appoint.

The research of Ann Austin[5] on the graduate school socialization process sheds light on some of these outcomes. Austin conducted in-depth personal interviews with 79 graduate students. These participants were studying at two large research universities and represented a range of clusters of academic fields such as the humanities, the sciences, the social sciences, and professional fields. These in-depth personal interviews took place every six months over a four-year period.

Austin's research indicates that graduate study prepares students for faculty careers marked by research and publication. However, the socialization process neglects teaching and other professorial responsibilities. The outcomes for teaching are particularly problematic as Austin notes that students report receiving mixed messages about the value placed on teaching. Although some graduate students report encouragement to value teaching, other students come to devalue teaching based on their observations of graduate professors who devote little time to helping graduate students with their teaching and some who urge their teaching assistants not to spend much time on teaching.

In addition, Austin points to some important shortcomings of the teaching assistant experience for graduate students. Such shortcomings begin with the view that the role of the teaching assistant is to help the department staff course sections. Moreover, Austin observes that the teaching assistant experience is not viewed as a development process for preparing faculty to teach because few teaching assistants progress from grading papers to teaching their own course. Moreover, teaching assistants report that they infrequently receive feedback about their teaching practices. Taken together, these findings suggest that the teaching assistant experience fails to provide preparation for the role of college teaching.

Austin's other findings include graduate students' lack of understanding about the roles faculty play beyond teaching and research, such as advising and institutional service. She also found that although graduate students comprehend success in research, they are less certain about success in other faculty roles. Austin also notes that graduate students receive little assistance concerning academic careers in different types of colleges and universities because most graduate students lean toward a career at a research university.

Challenges to Small Private Colleges

This configuration of findings presents significant challenges to the teaching-oriented colleges and universities that make up the membership of CIC. Newly minted PhD faculty hires may value research over teaching and have received little or no preparation for their teaching roles other than knowledge of their academic discipline. Thus, the presence of such faculty may disrupt the teaching-oriented culture of CIC colleges.

Recommendations for Policy and Practice

These challenges carry implications for the faculty search and selection process and for new faculty orientation. I offer the following recommendations for institutional policy and practice at CIC member institutions.

- *Faculty selection committees should determine if candidates have participated in a Preparing Future Faculty Program at their university of doctoral origin.* The Preparing Future Faculty Program focuses on the professorial roles of teaching, research, and service in a variety of colleges and universities.[6] This program also gives opportunities to advanced doctoral students to participate in a mentored internship at a college or university located near their doctoral university.[7] Faculty candidates who participate in a Preparing Future Faculty program likely will be better prepared for a faculty position at a CIC institution than candidates who have not participated in this program.
- *Policies on on-campus interviews for faculty candidates should include a requirement that all candidates give a teaching demonstration or a pedagogical colloquium.* Lee S. Shulman[8] suggests three models for a pedagogical colloquium. The first model he terms the "course narrative or course argument" approach, which involves the candidates' use of a syllabus to explain how they would teach a course, the topics they would cover, and the nature of the experience for both students and faculty. This model provides an opportunity for a candidate to display their philosophy about teaching and learning. The second approach delineated by Shulman entails a colloquium centered on an essential idea or topic. The candidate selects a difficult disciplinary concept for students to learn. The candidate then describes the approaches he or she would use to help students learn the concept. Shulman labels the third approach a "dilemma-centered colloquium." In this approach, a candidate is asked

to "think out loud" about a problem in teaching the discipline (e.g., the balance between breadth and depth in an introductory course). These three approaches provide a search committee with an opportunity to observe the teaching ability of the faculty candidate. Moreover, an institutional policy that requires a teaching demonstration as part of the on-campus interview signals to the candidate the high value the CIC institution places on teaching. This particular recommendation also stands as the fourth defining characteristics of strong teaching cultures delineated by Michael Paulsen and Kenneth Feldman.[9]

- *New faculty orientation programs at CIC institutions should include presentations on the history and culture of the college as well as on the assessment of teaching.* Presentations on the history and culture of the college would provide new faculty members with an understanding of their new institutional context and how it differs from their doctoral origin. A presentation on the various approaches the institution uses to assess faculty teaching performance would provide new faculty members with a knowledge of the methods the institution uses to determine effective teaching.

Faculty Employment Status

Scholars such as Jack Schuster and Adrianna Kezar and Cecile Sam[10] bring attention to the alarming change in the composition of faculty in US colleges and universities that has occurred over the past 25 years. Schuster describes the emergence of contingent faculty appointments or full- and part-time faculty in non-tenure-track positions as the predominant form of faculty employment status in higher education. He points out that "now approximately two-thirds of all faculty appointments take the form of contingent faculty appointments."[11] Research reviewed by Sean Gehrke and Adrianna Kezar[12] suggests that such an upsurge in non-tenure-track faculty has resulted in an unbundling of the faculty role into "teaching only contingent positions." Thus, a stratified faculty structure emerges that is composed of faculty in tenure-track positions and faculty who are in contingent or non-tenure-track positions.[13]

Economic reasons account for the ascendance of contingent faculty, whose primary economic benefits are cost effectiveness and flexibility in staffing.[14] The use of contingent faculty allows colleges and universities to hire more non-tenure-track faculty to teach more courses than tenure-track faculty would be able to cover.[15] Contingent faculty appointments provide the flexibility for colleges and universities to adjust to institutional budget reductions and changing enrollment patterns across different academic fields.[16] Underlying these economic reasons rests a deeper sense of economic uncertainty about the US economy and competition between higher education and other social needs for scarce financial resources.[17]

The unbundling of the faculty role into teaching-only contingent positions presents some problems to colleges and universities. Such problems pertain to student success, as research reviewed by Gehrke and Kezar[18] indicates that students who take more courses from contingent faculty than from tenure-track faculty suffer lower graduation rates and lower levels of academic performance in subsequent courses. Moreover, the instructional practices of part-time faculty include less emphasis on active learning, service learning, and culturally sensitive teaching approaches.[19] Other problems include lack of involvement in institutional governance and curriculum planning.[20] Contingent faculty also have few opportunities for professional development and limited access to campus resources or secretarial support.[21] Gehrke and Kezar[22] also indicate that contingent faculty are uninvolved in curricular design and lack awareness of institutional goals and outcomes.

Challenges to Small Private Colleges

Kezar and Sam[23] report that 22 percent of the full-time faculty at private master's and baccalaureate colleges and universities hold contingent appointments. This percentage lies considerably below the 66 percent of all faculty appointments that take the form of contingent faculty noted by Schuster.[24] Nevertheless, a policy point for small private colleges springs forth: *CIC member colleges and universities must work to assure that contingent faculty remain a minority of the full-time faculty members at their institution.*

Recommendations for Policy and Practice

In addition to the above policy point, I offer recommendations that work to ameliorate the negative effects associated with the employment of contingency faculty. CIC colleges should consider these recommendations regardless of the percent of full-time contingent faculty at their institution. The following recommendations echo those of Kezar and Sam:[25]

- *Contingent faculty should be treated with respect.* The central administration of CIC colleges should communicate to contingent faculty that they are valued and respected at the CIC college. This recommendation works to blunt some of the status differentials created by the stratified ranks of faculty into tenure-track and non-tenure-track tiers.

- *CIC colleges and universities should provide professional development opportunities for contingent faculty.* In particular, Roger Baldwin and Jay Chronister and Judith Gappa and David Leslie[26] put forth this particular recommendation. Although other types of professional development activities should be provided, funds to attend teaching-oriented conferences and workshops to learn about instructional practices such as active learning, service learning, and teaching diverse students are also needed to address some of the instructional problematics of contingent faculty.
- *CIC colleges and universities should include contingent faculty in institutional governance.* Contingent faculty should be afforded full participation and not token representation in the institutional governance process.[27] Full participation entails voting rights and involvement in such matters as the curriculum, teaching and learning.[28]

The Academic Reward System

Important dimensions of the academic reward system at the level of the individual college or university include reappointment of untenured faculty members, tenure, promotion, and annual increases in pay. KerryAnn O'Meara's[29] research indicates that regardless of institutional type, research and publication receive the greatest emphasis in tenure, promotion, and annual increases in pay. She views Fairweather's[30] body of work as central to her conclusions about the weight placed on research and publication in pay. However, the expectations for the quantity and quality of research differ greatly by institutional type.[31] The emphasis placed on research in teaching-oriented colleges and universities receives reinforcement through O'Meara's observation that when teaching portfolios and research activities are jointly assessed, research receives greater emphasis in tenure and promotion decisions in such colleges and universities.

Moreover, O'Meara points out the misalignment between institutional mission and the emphases of the academic reward system. She states that a majority of institutional reward systems are not in alignment with institutional mission and rhetoric or the time faculty spend on teaching, research, and service.[32] However, Boyer[33] views misalignment between reward systems and institutional mission as pertaining to the predominant emphasis on the scholarship of discovery rather than other domains of scholarship more befitting the institutional missions of small independent colleges and universities. Boyer advances prescriptions for individual faculty domain engagement by institutional type. For liberal arts colleges, he posits that faculty engagement in the scholarship of integration and the scholarship of teaching befits the mission of this type of institution of higher education. The scholarship of integration involves interpretation of pieces of literature and "fitting one's own work and the work of others into larger intellectual patterns."[34]

The scholarship of teaching seeks to develop and improve pedagogical practices.[35] Braxton, Luckey, and Helland[36] found that faculty members in research and doctoral-granting universities tended to publish more scholarship reflective of the scholarship of integration than did faculty in liberal arts colleges. However, they failed to observe institutional differences in publication levels for the scholarship of teaching. Regardless of Boyer's institutional prescriptions for domain emphasis, Braxton, Luckey, and Helland[37] learned that faculty in liberal arts colleges tended to publish more discovery-oriented scholarship than scholarship reflective of the domains of integration and teaching. Nevertheless, Toby Park and John Braxton[38] empirically identify scholars of pedagogical practice and localized scholars as two distinct types of faculty in liberal arts colleges. The scholarship of scholars of pedagogical practice focuses on the development and improvement of pedagogical practice, whereas the scholarship of localized scholars consists of a mixture of activities focused on the scholarship of application and the scholarship of integration.[39]

Challenges to Small Private Colleges

These findings regarding the academic reward systems present a clear-cut challenge to CIC member institutions to assure that their academic reward systems align with their espoused teaching-oriented missions. The properties of this challenge to each CIC college may emerge from institutional responses to four questions delineated in paragraphs below.

The work of scholars of pedagogical practice aligns with the teaching-oriented missions of liberal arts colleges. Given the presence of scholars of pedagogical practice in liberal arts colleges,[40] a possible alignment between institutional mission and the academic reward system of such colleges may exist provided faculty scholars of pedagogical practice reap the rewards of their scholarship in the form of reappointments, tenure, promotion, and annual salary increases. For each CIC member institution, two questions spring forth: *Are some members of the faculty scholars of pedagogical practice? If yes, are such scholars rewarded for their scholarship in the form of reappointment or tenure for untenured faculty, and promotion and annual salary increments for tenured faculty?*

In addition to Boyer's perspective on the misalignment between institutional mission and the academic reward system, misalignment also pertains to the emphasis on research and not teaching in the allocation of rewards to faculty members, as noted by O'Meara.[41] Given the teaching-oriented mission of CIC member institutions, two questions for each institution emerge from O'Meara's review: *How much weight does teaching receive in such key faculty personnel decisions as reappointment or tenure for untenured faculty, and promotion and annual salary increments for tenured faculty? Does research receive more weight than teaching in the allocation of such academic rewards?*

Recommendations for Policy and Practice

CIC member institutions should work to ensure that their academic reward system aligns with their teaching-oriented mission. Accordingly, I recommend that each CIC member institution engage in institutional research to address the four questions posed above. The findings of such institutional research should provide a basis for actions needed by CIC member institutions to redress any identified imbalances in their academic reward structures.

Regardless of the outcomes of such institutional research, CIC should give serious consideration to enact the following imperative that I recommend: *to safeguard the teaching mission of CIC member institutions, effective teaching should constitute an indispensable criterion for reappointment, tenure, promotion, and annual salary increments.* Put differently, only faculty members assessed as effective in their teaching role should be reappointed, tenured, promoted, or given salary increases. This criterion of effective teaching should also apply to contingent faculty members. Adherence to this policy would serve to ensure an alignment between the teaching-focused mission of CIC member institutions and their academic reward systems.

However, I also concur with Boyer[42] by positing that an institutional mission that aligns well with its academic reward system does not preclude an academic reward system that rewards faculty who engage in the scholarship of teaching. Given that the scholarship of teaching endeavors to develop and improve pedagogical practice,[43] it aligns with and supports the teaching-oriented mission of CIC member institutions. Lee Shulman and Pat Hutchings[44] view the scholarship of teaching as the process through which the profession of teaching advances itself. Accordingly, I present a set of three recommendations focused on encouraging faculty engagement in the scholarship of teaching. I encourage CIC member institutions to implement these recommendations regardless of the outcomes of the institutional research recommended above.

- *The mission statements of CIC member institutions should emphasize an institutional commitment to faculty engagement in the scholarship of teaching.* An espoused emphasis on the scholarship of teaching fully resonates with the teaching-oriented mission of CIC member institutions given that the scholarship of teaching strives to develop and improve pedagogical practice.[45]
- *In addition to viewing effective teaching as an indispensable criterion, the academic reward systems of CIC member institutions should give considerable weight to the scholarship of faculty focused on the development and improvement of pedagogical practice.* To elaborate, reappointments of untenured faculty, tenure and promotion decisions, and annual salary increments should be based, in part, on faculty engagement in the scholarship of teaching.
- *CIC member institutions should support of the work of scholars of pedagogical practice.* Such support should take the form of travel monies for faculty to attend teaching-oriented conferences as well as the provision of library resources in the form of books and journals focused on college teaching. Examples of journals include the *Journal of Chemical Education*, the *Journal of Economic Education*, *Teaching Sociology*, *Teaching of Psychology*, and the *Journal of Excellence in College Teaching*.

Teaching Cultures as an Organizational Source of Influence on Teaching

Paulsen and Feldman[46] assert that college teaching does not take place in a vacuum, as college and university faculty members are part of an organization and that the culture of that organization can positively or negatively influence their teaching. Teaching cultures place a high value on college teaching and can exist at the level of the college or university or at the level of the academic department. Paulsen and Feldman derive eight defining characteristics of supportive teaching cultures from the research literature.

1. High-level administrators of the institution should be clear about their commitment to and support for placing a high value on teaching. Senior

administrators communicate the high value the institution places on teaching and accord visibility to efforts focused on the improvement of teaching. Moreover, faculty must perceive that the value being placed on teaching is not mere lip service.

2. The involvement of faculty in every aspect of the planning and implementation of efforts to improve teaching should be prevalent. Such extensive faculty involvement contributes to the formation of shared values about teaching between faculty and administrators. Through such extensive involvement and the sharing of values, faculty come to view themselves as having ownership of efforts to improve teaching.

3. Paulsen and Feldman delineate the adoption of a broader definition of scholarship by the institution. This particular characteristic is manifested in an institution's academic reward structure, which creates an appropriate balance between teaching and research. Such reward structures also give weight to faculty engagement in the scholarship of teaching, especially as it relates to the faculty member's academic discipline. This defining characteristic resonates with the recommendations I advanced in the previous section of this chapter.

4. Use of the faculty selection process should include a teaching demonstration or pedagogical colloquium because it demonstrates the importance the college or university places on teaching. These would also provide an opportunity to gauge a faculty candidate's teaching ability.[47]

5. Paulsen and Feldman[48] posit that faculty should engage in frequent interaction, collaboration, and community about issues pertaining to teaching, and intrinsic rewards arise from this interaction. One method of collaboration takes the form of team teaching.[49] Another is the formation of a community of college teachers.[50] Characteristics of such a community include the sharing of ideas about teaching, intellectual stimulation around teaching, and a reduction in the isolation many faculty members interested in teaching frequently experience.[51]

6. Paulsen and Feldman[52] point out that the existence of a faculty development program or campus teaching center signifies that a high value is placed on teaching.

7. Chairpersons must be encouraging and effective in order to promote a supportive teaching culture.[53] Such chairpersons communicate the high value they place on teaching through actions such providing their de-

partmental colleagues with information on how teaching is valued, how one can use their time most effectively, and how rewards are allocated.[54]

8. A relationship between a rigorous evaluation of teaching and decisions about tenure and promotion can indicate a supportive teaching culture.[55] Rigorous evaluations of teaching make use of peer and student evaluations and the outcomes of such evaluations carry some weight in tenure and promotion decisions.

Paulsen and Feldman present each of these eight defining characteristics as equal in importance for shaping a supportive teaching culture. Institutional actions and behaviors involved in the enactment of these eight defining characteristics strongly communicate the prominence of teaching to the institution and the high value the institution places on it.

Challenges to Small Private Colleges

The notion of supportive teaching cultures provides CIC member institutions with both an opportunity and a challenge. Because their institutional missions place high value on teaching, CIC member institutions stand on firm ground to work toward the development of strong teaching cultures. However, the challenge to CIC member colleges centers on the development and maintenance of an abiding institutional commitment to ensuring the presence of all eight of the defining characteristics of strong teaching cultures at their institution.

Recommendations for Policy and Practice

Some recommendations for policy and practice offered in previous sections of this report contribute to the shaping of a strong teaching culture. However, I present the following additional recommendations:

- *The president, chief academic affairs officer, and academic deans of CIC member institutions should publicly express their commitment and support for excellence in undergraduate college teaching.* Public speeches, speeches made before university assemblies, memoranda, and day-to-day conversations of such members of the central administration should express the high value the institution places on teaching.
- *CIC member institutions that do not currently have centers for teaching or faculty development programs should establish them.* Centers for teaching and faculty development programs could offer courses and workshops that would work to remedy some of the pedagogical shortcomings of

the graduate school socialization process previously outlined. These activities should be made available to both tenure-stream and contingent
faculty members.

- *Symposiums or colloquiums on undergraduate college teaching should become
  a routine feature of both institutional and departmental life at CIC colleges
  and universities.* Although speakers external to the institution can be
  selected, the basic idea is to provide CIC faculty members with an opportunity to make presentations on their teaching and discuss various
  topics related to undergraduate college teaching. Such presentations
  could include the outcomes of faculty engagement in the scholarship of
  teaching. Such symposia or colloquia would provide CIC faculty with
  an opportunity to discuss teaching with one another. A reduction in
  isolation among faculty interested in teaching might also result, a benefit noted by Mary Deane Sorcinelli and Norman Aitken.[56]

Conclusions

In this chapter, I presented the results of a targeted review of the scholarly
literature on the graduate school socialization process, contingent faculty
members, the academic reward structure, and teaching cultures. I identified
challenges to CIC member institutions and provided some recommendations
for policy and practice to address these challenges. The most significant of the
challenges I delineated pertains to the proportion of faculty members in CIC
institutions that are contingent, teaching-only faculty members. CIC member
colleges and universities must work to assure that teaching-only contingent
faculty remain a minority of full-time faculty members at their institution. A
majority of contingent teaching-only faculty would seriously undermine the
tightly woven fabric of the culture of CIC colleges and universities.

The recommendations for policy and practice that I presented in this chapter should not be viewed as exhaustive. Nevertheless, I believe these recommendations are central to effectively addressing the identified challenges. I also
offer these recommendations as a stimulant to individual CIC member colleges
and universities to develop policies and actions that meet their particular institutional needs.

Faculty members reside at the core of private colleges such as those that hold
membership in the Council of Independent Colleges (CIC). As a consequence,
the stewardship of faculty and the roles they perform stand as abiding concerns
of the leaders of CIC affiliated colleges and universities. Meeting the chal-

lenges and enacting the recommendations for institutional policy and action will go a long way to equipping CIC institutional leaders to effectively serve as stewards of their faculties' welfare.

NOTES

1. Toombs and Tierney, "Meeting the Mandate."
2. Clark, *Academic Life.*
3. Austin and Wulff, "Challenge to Prepare"; Merton, Reader, and Kendall, *Student Physician.*
4. Zuckerman, "Deviant Behavior and Social Control"; Fox, "Publication, Performance, and Reward."
5. Austin, "Preparing the Next Generation."
6. "Preparing Future Faculty Program."
7. Pruitt-Logan and Graff, "Preparing Future Faculty."
8. Shulman, "Pedagogical Colloquium."
9. Paulsen and Feldman, "Taking Teaching Seriously."
10. Schuster, "Professoriate's Perilous Path"; Kezar and Sam, "Understanding the New Majority."
11. Schuster, "Professoriate's Perilous Path," 2.
12. Gehrke and Kezar, "Supporting Non-Tenure-Track Faculty," 51.
13. Schuster, "Professoriate's Perilous Path."
14. Kezar and Sam, "Understanding the New Majority."
15. Cross and Goldenberg, *Off-Track Profs.*
16. Gappa and Leslie, *Invisible Faculty*; Baldwin, "Technology's Impact."
17. Schuster, "Professoriate's Perilous Path."
18. Gehrke and Kezar, "Supporting Non-Tenure-Track Faculty."
19. Ibid.; Baldwin and Wawrzynski, "Contingent Faculty as Teachers"; Jacoby, "Effects of Part-Time Faculty Employment"; Umbach, "How Effective Are They?"
20. Gehrke and Kezar, "Supporting Non-Tenure-Track Faculty"; Kezar and Sam, "Understanding the New Majority."
21. Gehrke and Kezar, "Supporting Non-Tenure-Track Faculty"; Kezar and Sam, "Understanding the New Majority."
22. Gehrke and Kezar, "Supporting Non-Tenure-Track Faculty."
23. Kezar and Sam, "Understanding the New Majority."
24. Schuster, "Professoriate's Perilous Path."
25. Kezar and Sam, "Understanding the New Majority."
26. Baldwin and Chronister, *Teaching without Tenure*; Gappa and Leslie, *Invisible Faculty.*
27. Baldwin and Chronister, *Teaching without Tenure.*
28. Kezar and Sam, "Understanding the New Majority."
29. O'Meara, "Inside the Panopticon."
30. Fairweather, "Teaching, Research and Faculty Rewards"; *Faculty Work and Public Trust*; and "Beyond the Rhetoric."
31. O'Meara, "Inside the Panopticon."
32. Boyer, *Scholarship Reconsidered*; Diamond, *Aligning Faculty Rewards*; Fairweather, "Ultimate Faculty Evaluation; Finnegan and Gamson, "Disciplinary Adaptations."
33. Boyer, *Scholarship Reconsidered.*

34. Ibid., 19.
35. Braxton, Luckey, and Helland, "Institutionalizing a Broader View."
36. Ibid.
37. Ibid.
38. Park and Braxton, "Delineating Scholarly Types."
39. Ibid.
40. Ibid.
41. O'Meara, "Inside the Panopticon."
42. Boyer, *Scholarship Reconsidered.*
43. Braxton, Luckey, and Helland, "Institutionalizing a Broader View."
44. Shulman and Hutchings, "About the Scholarship of Teaching."
45. Braxton, Luckey, and Helland, "Institutionalizing a Broader View."
46. Paulsen and Feldman, "Taking Teaching Seriously."
47. Shulman, "Pedagogical Colloquium," describes three models for a pedagogical colloquium, which I previously described in this chapter.
48. Ibid.
49. Lacelle-Peterson and Finkelstein, "Institutions Matter."
50. Paulsen and Feldman, "Taking Teaching Seriously."
51. Sorcinelli and Aitken, "Academic Leaders and Faculty Developers."
52. Paulsen and Feldman, "Taking Teaching Seriously."
53. Ibid.
54. Rice and Austin, "Organizational Impacts on Faculty Morale."
55. Paulsen and Feldman, "Taking Teaching Seriously."
56. Sorcinelli and Aitken, "Academic Leaders and Faculty Developers."

REFERENCES

Austin, Ann E. "Preparing the Next Generation of Faculty: Graduate School as Socialization to the Academic Career." *Journal of Higher Education* 73, no. 1 (January 1, 2002): 94–122. doi:10.1080/00221546.2002.11777132.
Austin, Ann E., and Donald H. Wulff. "The Challenge to Prepare the Next Generation of Faculty." In *Paths to the Professoriate: Strategies for Enriching the Preparation of Future Faculty*, edited by Ann E. Austin and Donald H. Wulff, 3–16. San Francisco: Jossey-Bass, 2004.
Baldwin, Roger G. "Technology's Impact on Faculty Life and Work." *New Directions for Teaching and Learning* 1998, no. 76 (December 1, 1998): 7–21. doi:10.1002/tl.7601.
Baldwin, Roger G., and Jay L. Chronister. *Teaching without Tenure: Practices and Policies for a New Era.* Baltimore: Johns Hopkins University Press, 2001.
Baldwin, Roger G., and Matthew R. Wawrzynski. "Contingent Faculty as Teachers: What We Know; What We Need to Know." *American Behavioral Scientist* 55, no. 11 (November 1, 2011): 1485–1509. doi:10.1177/0002764211409194.
Boyer, Ernest L. *Scholarship Reconsidered: Priorities of the Professoriate.* Princeton, NJ: Princeton University Press, 1990. https://eric.ed.gov/?id=ED326149.
Braxton, John M., William Luckey, and Patricia Helland. "Institutionalizing a Broader View of Scholarship through Boyer's Four Domains." In *Institutionalizing a Broader View of Scholarship through Boyer's Four Domains*, vol. 29. ASHE-ERIC Higher Education Report. San Francisco: Jossey-Bass, 2002. https://eric.ed.gov/?id=ED468779.

Clark, Burton R. *The Academic Life: Small Worlds, Different Worlds.* Princeton, NJ: Carnegie Foundation for the Advancement of Teaching, 1987.

Cross, John G., and Edie N. Goldenberg. *Off-Track Profs: Nontenured Teachers in Higher Education.* Cambridge, MA: MIT Press, 2009.

Diamond, Robert M. *Aligning Faculty Rewards with Institutional Mission.* Bolton, MA: Anker, 1999. https://eric.ed.gov/?id=ED432178.

Fairweather, James S. "Beyond the Rhetoric: Trends in the Relative Value of Teaching and Research in Faculty Salaries." *Journal of Higher Education* 76, no. 4 (July 1, 2005): 401–22. doi:10.1080/00221546.2005.11772290.

———. *Faculty Work and Public Trust: Restoring the Value of Teaching and Public Service in American Academic Life.* Boston: Allyn and Bacon, 1996.

———. "Teaching, Research and Faculty Rewards." University Park, PA: National Center on Postsecondary Teaching, Learning, and Assessment, 1993.

———. "The Ultimate Faculty Evaluation: Promotion and Tenure Decisions." *New Directions for Institutional Research* 2002, no. 114 (June 1, 2002): 97–108. doi:10.1002/ir.50.

Finnegan, Dorothy E., and Zelda F. Gamson. "Disciplinary Adaptations to Research Culture in Comprehensive Institutions." *Review of Higher Education* 19, no. 2 (1996): 141–77.

Fox, Mary F. "Publication, Performance, and Reward in Science and Scholarship." In *Higher Education: Handbook of Theory and Research*, edited by John C. Smart, 1:225–82. New York: Agathon Press, 1985.

Gappa, Judith M., and David W. Leslie. *The Invisible Faculty: Improving the Status of Part-Timers in Higher Education.* San Francisco: Jossey-Bass, 1993. https://eric.ed.gov/?id=ED358756.

Gehrke, Sean J., and Adrianna Kezar. "Supporting Non-Tenure-Track Faculty at 4-Year Colleges and Universities: A National Study of Deans' Values and Decisions." *Educational Policy* 29, no. 6 (September 1, 2015): 926–60. doi:10.1177/0895904814531651.

Jacoby, Daniel. "Effects of Part-Time Faculty Employment on Community College Graduation Rates." *Journal of Higher Education* 77, no. 6 (November 1, 2006): 1081–1103. doi:10.1080/00221546.2006.11778957.

Kezar, Adrianna J., and Cecile Sam. "Understanding the New Majority: Contingent Faculty in Higher Education." In *ASHE Higher Education Report Series*, vol. 36. San Francisco: Jossey-Bass, 2010.

Lacelle-Peterson, Mark W., and Martin J. Finkelstein. "Institutions Matter: Campus Teaching Environments' Impact on Senior Faculty." *New Directions for Teaching and Learning* 1993, no. 55 (September 1, 1993): 21–32. doi:10.1002/tl.37219935504.

Merton, Robert K., George G. Reader, and Patricia L. Kendall. *The Student Physician.* Cambridge, MA: Harvard University Press, 1957.

O'Meara, KerryAnn. "Inside the Panopticon: Studying Academic Reward Systems." In *Higher Education: Handbook of Theory and Research*, edited by John C. Smart and Michael B. Paulsen, 161–220. Higher Education: Handbook of Theory and Research 26. New York, NY: Springer Netherlands, 2011. doi:10.1007/978-94-007-0702-3_5.

Park, Toby J., and John M. Braxton. "Delineating Scholarly Types of College and University Faculty Members." *Journal of Higher Education* 84, no. 3 (May 1, 2013): 301–28. doi:10.1080/00221546.2013.11777291.

Paulsen, Michael B., and Kenneth A. Feldman. "Taking Teaching Seriously: Meeting the Challenge of Instructional Improvement." In *ASHE-ERIC Higher Education Report*, vol. 2. Washington, DC: George Washington University, 1995.

The Preparing Future Faculty Program. *PFF Web.* N.d. http://www.preparing-faculty
.org.

Pruitt-Logan, Anne S., and Jerry G. Graff. "Preparing Future Faculty: Changing the
Culture of Doctoral Education." In *Paths to the Professoriate: Strategies for Enriching
the Preparation of Future Faculty,* edited by Donald H. Wulff and Ann E. Austin. San
Francisco: Jossey-Bass, 2004.

Rice, R. Eugene, and Ann E. Austin. "Organizational Impacts on Faculty Morale and
Motivation to Teach." In *How Administrators Can Improve Teaching,* edited by Peter
Sedlin. San Francisco: Jossey-Bass, 1990.

Schuster, Jack H. "The Professoriate's Perilous Path." In *The American Academic Profession: Transformation in Contemporary Higher Education,* edited by Joseph C. Hermanowicz. Baltimore: Johns Hopkins University Press, 2011.

Shulman, Lee S. "The Pedagogical Colloquium: Three Models." *AAHE Bulletin* 41, no.
10 (1995): 6–9.

Shulman, Lee S., and Pat Hutchings. "About the Scholarship of Teaching and Learning:
The Pew Scholars National Fellowship Program." Carnegie Foundation for the Advancement of Teaching, 1998.

Sorcinelli, Mary Deane, and Norman D. Aitken. "Academic Leaders and Faculty Developers: Creating an Institutional Culture That Values Teaching." *To Improve the
Academy* 13 (1994): 63–77.

Toombs, William, and William G. Tierney. "Meeting the Mandate: Renewing the College and Departmental Curriculum." In *ASHE Higher Education Report* 6. Washington, DC: George Washington University, 1991.

Umbach, Paul D. "How Effective Are They? Exploring the Impact of Contingent Faculty on Undergraduate Education." *Review of Higher Education* 30, no. 2 (November 7,
2006): 91–123. doi:10.1353/rhe.2006.0080.

Zuckerman, Harriet. "Deviant Behavior and Social Control in Science." In *Deviance and
Social Change,* edited by Edward Sagarin, 87–138. Beverly Hills, CA: Sage, 1977.

REACTION

Carolyn J. Stefanco

The summaries of research and recommendations by John M. Braxton provide
a springboard for leaders of American independent colleges and universities
to contemplate where their institutions fit today among the diversity of CIC
members, and, as higher education continues to be transformed, how they want
to work with their stakeholders to lead change to support students, prioritize
teaching, and foster research.

Braxton uses descriptors such as "smaller private colleges" and "CIC institutions" interchangeably and refers to "liberal arts colleges" when discussing
Ernest Boyer's[1] model of scholarship. CIC institutions are clearly independent,
private, and not public. They are not research institutions, not primarily doctoral, and not large, but they are also not all focused solely on teaching, not all

undergraduate only, and not all small. While 53 percent of CIC institutions fit the Carnegie classification category of baccalaureate, 41 percent fit the classification of master's. The CIC uses the phrase "small and mid-sized" to describe its members, and while most member institutions have student enrollment up to about 4,000, CIC does not have a membership criteria pertaining to size, and the largest CIC member institution has more than 21,000 students. No matter what their degree offerings and size, CIC institutions value the liberal arts at the undergraduate level. Declining revenue and increasing expenses, changes in student demand for particular academic programs, and the desire to create greater distinctiveness to attract students from outside traditional recruitment areas, however, have led many independent colleges and universities to make changes in the broad range of liberal arts and sciences majors they offer at the undergraduate level. Some institutions that focus on the liberal arts continue to call themselves liberal arts colleges, but others, especially those with robust graduate enrollment; professional degree programs in fields such as education, business, and nursing; and an organizational structure that includes schools and colleges, call themselves comprehensive institutions. Many have also become "universities" to better reflect the evolution in their missions and to more effectively recruit graduate and international students.

Even more significant than current institutional profiles, the challenges we face in the independent sector demand that we work closely with our boards of trustees, our alumni, our external partners, and, most significantly, our internal community—and especially the faculty—to serve students. Doing so requires that we continue to offer a personalized learning environment where excellent teaching is the first priority.

Privileging teaching in the independent sector has meant that, despite the ability to reduce costs by hiring a greater percentage of contingent faculty, only "22 percent of the full-time faculty at private masters and baccalaureate colleges and universities hold contingent appointments," compared to the 66 percent Braxton cites for higher education as a whole in research by Schuster.[2] No matter what their proportion of the teaching faculty, the role and responsibilities of contingent faculty is in contention. Braxton recommends that contingent faculty be shown respect and offered professional development funds, especially in the area of pedagogy. This makes perfect sense, especially if institutions allocate funds for workshops on teaching that benefit all faculty, tenured, tenure-track, and contingent. His declaration that "contingent faculty should be afforded full participation and not token representation in the institutional governance process," however, requires greater consideration. The ranks of contingent faculty vary greatly, and include, among others, full-time hires who serve for decades, full-time professionals in the community who teach an occasional course, advanced doctoral students who are gaining teaching experience while searching for tenure-track positions, and part-time faculty who may or may not have terminal degrees and who try to support themselves by teaching at numerous, nearby institutions and, when possible, online. Should individuals in each group participate equally in institutional governance with tenured and tenure-track faculty? With increasing efforts around the country to unionize contingent faculty, will collective bargaining agreements that are negotiated by administrators and union representatives and approved by boards make such determinations? Although the national higher education press tends to focus on disagreements over shared governance between tenured and tenure-track faculty and senior administrators, we need to think seriously about the potential changes to the "faculty" side of the equation in shared governance if contingent faculty, especially those who teach part-time at multiple institutions, become institutional stakeholders with the same roles and responsibilities as tenured and tenure-track faculty.

While tenured and tenure-track faculty and contingent faculty should demonstrate excellence in teaching and should be supported by academic leaders in this pursuit, only tenured and tenure-track faculty are usually engaged in research as part of their college and university assignments. Braxton notes that "scholars of pedagogical practice" align best with the "teaching-oriented missions of liberal arts colleges." Yet, after serving at three CIC institutions and studying many others, the role of research, and particularly what Boyer calls the scholarship of discovery, is generally believed to be an essential component of excellent teaching and is required to win and maintain accreditation. While tenured and tenure-track faculty at CIC institutions generally teach more courses per year and spend less time on sponsored research and creative and publication projects in comparison to their colleagues at research institutions, their work is valued for its own sake. Additionally, this work is an essential component of faculty-mentored undergraduate research, which is focused on the scholarship of discovery, not teaching or integration. Of course, faculty at many independent colleges and universities also teach graduate students, and their continuing involvement in research is expected for this reason as well. Accrediting bodies also require faculty scholarship. To maintain scholarly academic status at CIC institutions with largely teaching missions, for example, the Association to Advance Collegiate Schools of Business (AACSB) requires business faculty to produce work that includes peer-reviewed journal articles that are discipline based and, as of 2013, asks that the impact of scholarship be measured. Similarly, the National Council for Accreditation of Teacher Education[3] (NCATE) requires that institutions maintain a database of each faculty member's scholarly activities. While scholarship is broadly defined, it includes "knowledge generation," and education faculty who teach in graduate programs and in certain undergraduate academic programs are expected to conduct traditional research.

Braxton's chapter on how PhD students are prepared in graduate school, the roles and responsibilities of faculty and their employment status, and the appropriate place of research at CIC institutions provides senior administrators with much food for thought.

NOTES

1. Boyer, *Scholarship Reconsidered.*
2. Schuster, "Professoriate's Perilous Path."
3. National Council for Accreditation of Teacher Education, "Professional Standards."

REFERENCES

Boyer, Ernest L. *Scholarship Reconsidered: Priorities of the Professoriate.* Princeton, NJ: Princeton University Press, 1990. https://eric.ed.gov/?id=ED326149.
National Council for Accreditation of Teacher Education. "Professional Standards for the Accreditation of Teacher Preparation Institutions." Washington, DC: National Council for Accreditation of Teacher Education, 2008.
Schuster, Jack H. "The Professoriate's Perilous Path." In *The American Academic Profession: Transformation in Contemporary Higher Education*, edited by Joseph C. Hermanowicz. Baltimore: Johns Hopkins University Press, 2011.

9

Institutional Strategy and Adaptation

JAMES C. HEARN AND ERIN B. CIARIMBOLI

Strategy and Adaptation in Independent Colleges

Recently, when asked what has been his school's strategy for adapting to difficult circumstances, the president of a small independent college told us:

> Survival, to be blunt. If you go back to the 2009 time-frame, with the Great Recession, the *Chronicle of Higher Ed, Inside Higher Ed*, everyone was publishing . . . "stress tests" for private colleges: if you had an enrollment below 1,000, if you're in rural America, if you're in small communities, small endowment. . . . And . . . you would go through that list, and it's like, "Hmm, [our school, our school, our school]." And some of those things you're not going to change. Certainly we're trying to grow enrollment . . . but we're not going to change the fact that we're in a community of 3,500, dead center in rural [state]—those aren't going to change. So I say "survival" seriously but also tongue-in-cheek . . . it is who we are, so [the question is] what are we going to do about it?[1]

The end of the recession has not brought an end to such challenges. During the past two years, tales of Sweet Briar College's apparent demise (and possible rebirth) filled the pages of the *New York Times* and other outlets, and the *Chronicle of Higher Education* published what it called "A Survival Guide for Small Colleges." Many other publications and associations have offered advice and opinions for college leaders as they approach their schools' uncertain futures. Without question, threatening conditions are dramatically testing the adaptive capacities of smaller institutions.

The particular challenges facing independent colleges have been well detailed. Prospective students and their families are increasingly concerned about the economic returns to college and stability of their future careers, making "practical" degrees in fields such as business or education more attractive, while likely creating resistance to relatively high tuition costs.[2] These attitudes tend to disfavor smaller private colleges, which lack both the public subsidies and large number of practically focused degree programs of public institutions.[3] In concert, many such colleges are finding that substantial tuition discounts are requisite to bring in the students needed to fill their classes, and, consequently, those discounts potentially remove significant revenues from college coffers.[4] What is more, as growing numbers of students are drawn to the wide variety of activities and entertainment available on larger campuses, the long-revered ideal of the small, engaging campus removed from bustling urban life[5] may have declining appeal for current students. In short, the traditional business model of the classic liberal arts college appears endangered.

For many institutions, these very real problems are compounded by feverish accounts in the popular and professional press suggesting that the entire independent college sector is on the brink of collapse. As inaccurate as those portraits may be in individual cases, contemporary independent college leaders are finding that they unquestionably shape larger public perceptions of all colleges in the sector.[6]

Missing from the current conventional storyline, however, is the simple fact that many institutions in the sector are financially and academically healthy and in no imminent danger.[7] Also missing from the conventional wisdom is something more fundamental: small private colleges are not helpless, passive victims awaiting impending doom. In fact, the nation's current stock of such institutions is largely composed of survivors of several earlier waves of doomsayers.

Writing in 1984, Allan Pfnister identified three distinct periods of doubt about these colleges earlier in US history. In the early and middle years of the nineteenth century, Pfnister notes, virtually every frontier settlement seemed to initiate a newspaper, a hotel, and an academy as necessary hallmarks of the newfound community's legitimacy. Not surprisingly, the mortality rate of such schools was extraordinarily high. Later in that century, the improvement in secondary schooling and the rise of the new land-grant universities brought further questions: "To many of the educational leaders of the country, the liberal arts college had become anachronistic . . . there seemed little place for a four-year independent college that was neither secondary school nor university."[8] Finally, a third challenge began in the 1970s, when demographic and financial challenges partnered with increasing vocationalism among students to threaten the sector. Despite the dire prognostications of the experts of these prior eras, the great majority of small colleges have survived, and many have grown more robust.

Edward St. John, David Leslie and E. K. Fretwell, Douglas Toma,[9] and many others argue that timely and assertive transformational thinking has contributed to the endurance of most schools through tough times. For example, Morphew[10] examines initiatives by some colleges to rename themselves "universities," signaling to potential students their commitment to move beyond undergraduate liberal arts programming. Conversely, an absence of such thinking can contribute to difficulties. Bacow and Bowen[11] suggest, for example, that Cooper Union faculty and students were jolted when that institutions' administrators and trustees moved to charge tuition for the first time in the school's history. What, then, are the key ingredients of successful strategic planning and management?

The literature is disparate and diverse on that question but largely emphasizes the need to focus first on the core mission and business model of the college. What are our institutional mission and goals? Who are we targeting for enrollment? How will we organize classes and the curriculum? Who will be our faculty? How will we price our services and bring in revenue? Operationally, the strategic approach entails analysis of the institution's current and potential contexts, commitment to ongoing planning and management with those contexts in mind, attentiveness to the historic culture of the institution, and the exercise of directive, politically sensitive leadership. This chapter reviews what research suggests about strategic change and adaptation in higher education and points toward further extensions of that work in the emerging context of independent colleges.

Strategy and Adaptation in Higher Education: The Literature

Strategy and adaptation became prominent concerns for colleges and universities in the United States in the 1970s and 1980s, largely in response to increasingly complex and foreboding environmental conditions. As the baby boom generation began to move past the traditional college-going years and government student aid funding slowed in growth, many leaders worried about their institutions' future viability. Such concerns ran especially high in the independent college sector. Prominent analysts of that time[12] emphasized the need for college leaders first to identify their institutions' core missions and business models, then the need for leaders to

1. assess systematically both their current academic "portfolios" and their emerging external environments, using institutional research as well as external research on similar contexts to optimally position the institution for the future;
2. embed strategic thinking and activity as ongoing rather than periodic processes, thus ensuring regular reconsideration of institutional missions and goals;
3. understand and respect the critical role of institutions' academic and decision-making culture in constraining or facilitating organizational change in colleges; and
4. exhibit mission-centered directive leadership while remaining sensitive to internal and external political contexts.

Because the importance of these points has only grown over recent years, and because each can entail a special (and difficult) challenge for institutional leaders, a detailed review of each is presented below.

Assessment and Research

The 1970s and 1980s brought the first systematic strategic reviews of academic offerings in higher education. Led by presidents and provosts, these early processes aimed to enable holistic institutional decision making regarding which programs to maintain, which to target for additional investment, and which to consider for elimination. Analysts argued that leaders should array an institution's academic programs along a vertical axis, then grade each academic program on factors such as quality, costs, centrality to campus mission, connectedness to other campus programs, comparative advantage in the market, and current and anticipated demand.[13] At the same time, research suggested that institutions should engage in ongoing study of their social, technological, economic, and political environments, anticipating both threats to existing programming and opportunities for new and expanded programming.[14]

As the strategic movement in higher education has grown and matured in subsequent years, one research-related development merits particular attention: the growth of strategic enrollment management (SEM). One of the pioneering insights of the early years of strategic thinking and research in higher education was the recognition of the need for holistic "systems thinking."[15] Prior to the 1980s, colleges' core activities were highly compartmentalized. That is, fiscal planning and management were the province of the business office; academic planning and management fell under the authority of the provost, deans, and faculty; the admissions, student affairs, and registrar's offices took care of students; alumni and development offices managed outside friends and sponsors of the school. This historic separation of authority was seen as an asset, as dedicated professionals reigned over their own specialized domains. However, the advent of external threats to the survival of small private colleges in the 1980s brought a felt need to shake up that model's reliance on distinct, atomized centers of decision making.

College admissions and enrollment models also began to shift as institutions realized that it would not suffice to simply recruit and retain talented, diverse students that fit with the school's mission. Rather, they also needed to recruit and retain students in ways that contributed to the college's short- and long-term financial health. The answer lay in integrated, fiscally sound enrollment management systems shaped by institutions' core missions. Offices and workflows were restructured and administrative roles created as a result of this new approach, including a dramatic growth in the number of positions with titles such as vice president for enrollment management.[16] In concert, sophisticated research expertise was brought to campuses, either via newly created positions or consulting arrangements. Complex statistical analyses have become essential to many institutions' academic and fiscal health. From its beginnings in small private colleges over three decades ago, SEM's design and growth has been led by higher-education researchers in academic, administrative, and consulting positions.[17] Today, SEM is an institutionalized feature of the "new normal" in colleges.

Embedded, Ongoing Processes

Strategic advocates' early arguments have had mixed success in higher education. Some of the movement's favored techniques have never achieved widespread adoption. Structural factors appear to play a role in these outcomes: faculty and administrators are busy and often operate within tight budget and time constraints. Constructing elaborate "probability/impact matrices" or pursuing highly detailed and formalized "environmental scanning" may make little sense in cost-effectiveness terms on most campuses.

Still, several somewhat stalled tenets of the original strategic movement merit contemporary support. Notably, from the beginning, the strategic movement in higher education called on institutions to abandon the traditional "five-year plan" and other highly periodicized planning approaches in favor of embedded, ongoing efforts. As long ago as the 1970s, organizational theorist James March observed that, when he asked presidents whether their college had a plan, he received one of four kinds of responses: "1) Yes, we have a plan. It is used in capital budget and physical location decisions; 2) Yes, we have a plan. Here it is. It was made during the administration of our last president. We are working on a new one; 3) No, we do not have a plan. We should. We are working on one; or 4) I think there's a plan around here someplace. Miss Jones, do we have a copy of our comprehensive 10-year plan?" Now, four decades past March's presidential interviews, planning limited in both scope and duration shows little sign of disappearing. Accreditors, public and private funders, and boards have persisted in demanding periodicized planning processes, so such practices are far from dead.

Nonetheless, researchers and veterans of campus reform efforts continue to make the case for deeply rooted strategic planning and management. The pace of environmental change has accelerated in recent years, and institutions content to remain idle are likely to miss potential moves that may be critical to their ability to survive and thrive. In 1984, Kim S. Cameron[18] wrote that colleges must be "tight enough to implement [multiple adaptations] quickly and to change major components of the organization as needed." More recently, Toma[19] noted that institutions must be not only mission-centered but also nimble if they wish to establish and sustain initiatives to reach their vision. Embedded, ongoing processes help ensure that necessary change can happen quickly on campuses.

Sensitivity to Culture

As the strategic approach transitioned from military and business usage into higher education, seasoned analysts anticipated some difficulties. There is little question that all organizations must be ready to change with their environments, but that observation must be somewhat tempered in colleges and universities. More than in purely profit-oriented or strictly hierarchical settings (such as corporations and public agencies), change efforts in higher education must acknowledge and embrace the critical role of institutional culture. Institutions' long-standing value commitments to faculty autonomy and consensual decision making have the potential to work against solely leader-driven strategic efforts.

Strategic change is unlikely to be embraced and implemented successfully on a campus without close attention to its fit with that school's historically institutionalized mission, values, norms, symbols, rituals, and myths.[20] It has always been essential that change efforts take into account how institutions can respond to shifting environments without threatening key aspects of a college's mission and strengths. "The key is to understand and build upon past achievements while being forward looking," write Clayton M. Christensen and Henry J. Eyring.[21] That is not always easy: faculty cultures can inhibit academic success, and dominant interpretations of past history can overwhelm the rationalist logic behind potentially effective current actions, including the choice of new leaders.[22] The turbulent history of Antioch College and, more recently, Sweet Briar College arguably fit that pattern.

Mission-Centered, Directive Leadership

It is no surprise that leadership has been viewed as critical in strategic efforts from the beginning. Unfortunately, it is also no surprise that leadership was (and remains) the least understood aspect of successful organizational change efforts in higher education.

The case for attention to directive leadership on private college campuses is clear-cut. Whether attempting to raise new forms of revenue, increase rankings and prestige, or serve some other goal, many schools have been expanding beyond their traditional liberal arts missions and growing in scope as they respond to changing student demographics and market demands. Today's colleges have been "acting in an entrepreneurial manner that has never been more characteristic of American higher education," writes Toma.[23] Doing so often requires challenging aspects of tradition while remaining true to others. As Jeffrey Alstete[24] observes, "Modern leaders must think beyond traditional income sources and improve institutional effectiveness while being mindful of the value of faculty and the collegiate culture."

Leaders must thus be both culturally and politically sensitive.[25] Research has consistently emphasized the importance of leaders remaining cognizant of institutional identity, campus culture, and stakeholder attitudes, perceptions, and values as they respond to changing student markets and adapt institutional preferences and strategies.[26] As Anna Neumann[27] suggests, leaders can play a major role in helping a campus understand its resource challenges and respond strategically and effectively.

Central to leaders' success is close attention not just to establishing and communicating the primary objectives determined through strategic planning, but also setting up processes to implement and pursue those objectives.[28] The president's cabinet or executive council can be critical to an effective strategic process both early and late, as can thoughtfully involving widely respected faculty leaders, including unit heads and faculty senate leaders.

What kind of leader can succeed in these conditions? Perhaps the most integrated advice has been that from Daniel Julius, Victor Baldridge, and Jeffrey Pfeffer.[29] In a pointed essay taking the form of advice from Machiavelli for "presidents, senior administrators, and faculty leaders who would seek change,"[30] the authors distill decades of thinking and empirical research on the art of higher-education leadership in the complex political, cultural, and bureaucratic contexts of colleges and universities. Especially striking are their prescriptions that new leaders learn institutional history and employ that knowledge wisely, plan strategically with clearly defined short-term and long-term objectives, concentrate their efforts and follow-through persistence on their highest strategic priorities, and evaluate political odds as well as strategic outcomes in order to better know when to retreat.

Strategy in a Time of Challenge

Today's higher education environment imposes daunting challenges on institutions and their leaders. With these challenges, however, also come opportunities. It is instructive to look back on other industries confronted by environmental difficulties. In a classic contribution to the corporate strategy literature, Robert H. Miles and Kim Cameron[31] examine how US tobacco companies addressed the surgeon general's report of the 1960s declaring smoking harmful to health. Their analysis suggested that the most successful companies looked beyond merely claiming the healthiness of cigarettes, their traditional mainstay product. While these companies did aggressively defend their smoking products in the United States, they also began marketing in new outlets overseas and expanding their product lines into new, non-smoking-related arenas. In other words, faced with crisis, successful companies creatively identified new market niches for development and exploitation.

That pioneering work, along with later additions to the management literature,[32] suggests that organizational leaders tend to implement specific "domain strategies" in response to certain external conditions threatening their traditional niches:

- *Domain defense*: protecting the legitimacy of organizations' core activities, typically chosen in the face of a rapid contraction in the size of their market niche

- *Domain consolidation*: eliminating activities to focus on those best aligned with counteracting conditions, also typically chosen in the face of a rapid contraction in the size of an organization's market niche
- *Domain offense*: pursuing activities that maintain and enhance viability, typically chosen in the face of a continuously eroding niche
- *Domain creation:* expanding activities in new arenas that broaden portfolios, typically chosen in conditions of slow, incremental change to the shape of a niche (e.g., one niche slowly morphing into another)
- *Domain substitution*: switching one set of activities for another, typically chosen when the shape of a niche is changing rapidly and unexpectedly

Matching strategies to appropriately fitting conditions has been effective in business settings, and there is some evidence that well-chosen strategic approaches may be effective in colleges during times of major challenges, such as those currently facing independent institutions.[33] For example, when Ellen Earle Chaffee[34] assayed strategic responses to prospective students' shifting academic preferences in 14 threatened small liberal arts institutions, she found that the most successfully adaptive colleges created new academic programs and often also dropped languishing programs. In keeping with the conceptualization of Cameron and his colleagues (noted above) Chaffee's work suggests the effectiveness of well-targeted efforts in domain creation, consolidation, offense, and substitution. Especially notable in more recent years have been efforts by both individual colleges and groups of colleges, which have begun major domain defense efforts,[35] all emphasizing the importance and effectiveness of a liberal arts education.

Some colleges adopted systematic strategic planning efforts in the 1980s and 1990s, but the pace of change now seems to be quickening. A recent survey of independent college presidents found that *every* responding president had undertaken either a cost containment and reduction effort or a revenue enhancement and diversification effort on his or her campus over the past five years, and 92 percent of the respondents reported that they had undertaken *both* cost and revenue initiatives on their campuses.[36] Behind these efforts lay virtually uniform presidential perceptions that market forces and economic pressures were driving their institutions toward strategic change and innovation.

These leaders' responses suggest that they viewed their reform efforts as largely mission-centered, that they perceived broad institutional and constituent support for their change efforts, and that they felt a general sense of optimism for their institutions' futures. These sentiments were seemingly affirmed in a recent study by Moody's Investors Service[37] suggesting that the outlook for US higher education has moved from negative to stable, reflecting slow yet stable tuition revenue growth in the sector.

Thus, despite continuing pessimism among many of the public and much of the press, there are hints that many independent colleges are actively adapting to their pressing challenges, and to good effect. Whether driven by strategic positioning or purely by institutional survival, some are displaying characteristics of adaptive, deliberate, and responsive organizations.[38] Lawrence Biemiller[39] captures this changing dynamic quite powerfully, stating, "Small colleges are discovering—some faster than others—that they have to be acutely sensitive to the evolving whims of students and the concerns of parents, as well as nimble enough to meet the marketplace on its terms." Nearly all schools within the sector are innovating or cutting costs as they adapt to changing environmental demands. These adaptations can be classified within three broad categories: revenue enhancement and diversification, cost-focused measures, and other initiatives and programs.

Revenue Enhancement and Diversification

Efforts to improve revenues are abundant within the small college sector, including the addition of new undergraduate and graduate programs, development of online curricula, and transformation of approaches to institutional fundraising.[40] New academic programs, which are most common, frequently include more vocational, high-demand majors, such as education, business, or health care, or appear as more flexible hybrid or online programs that appeal to a wider range of students, including adult learners.[41]

Moves to establish new majors and new required courses in such non-liberal-arts areas as business and education may mean de-emphasizing units and courses in areas like religion or history. If resources follow students and students are responding to new offerings at the expense of older, more established ones, such curricular and enrollment changes can compel a redistribution of budget allocations. Those fiscal changes can, in turn, raise questions about the maintenance of the core historic values of the institution and also threaten the interests and even the historic hegemony of certain groups on campuses. Dealing with such resistance requires political as well as interpersonal skills.

In a further departure from their undergraduate liberal arts focus, many schools are also developing graduate programs, which increase tuition revenue without the additional costs of student services and residential facilities associated with traditional undergraduates.[42] For example, Wheaton College in Massachusetts, a traditional undergraduate liberal arts college, is one of many institutions to add a business and management major to its offerings,[43] while New England College has created online and hybrid graduate programs in health care and fine arts.[44] Benedictine College of Illinois has recently launched a new campus in Mesa, Arizona, far from its main campus in Illinois, leveraging its religious mission in an attempt to capture an underserved Catholic and Latino population in the Southwest.[45] Finally, many schools have turned to nonacademic areas, such as bookstores, events, and facilities, to generate new revenue. Numerous independent colleges offer summer programs and short courses on their campuses—for example, Ohio's Kenyon College provides "a true education vacation"—taught by popular faculty members and professionals.[46]

Cost-Focused Measures

A second area of strategic adaptation focuses on cost reduction measures, including merging or cutting academic programs, freezing salaries, reducing staff, cutting athletics budgets, sharing resources among institutions or departments, or outsourcing operations.[47] Again, academic areas have been frequent targets of these adaptive efforts, including consolidating academic majors or cutting low-enrollment programs altogether as schools evaluate the efficiency of their programs.[48] For example, Centenary College of Louisiana decreased its academic major offerings by half, from 44 to 22, and Houghton College in upstate New York reduced its number of academic departments from 18 to 12.[49]

Although attention to costs can be painful, there are examples of institutions benefitting substantially from reconsidering long-established ways of doing business in the interest of cost control. The Associated Colleges of the South (ACS) is perhaps the best-known example of institutions banding together collaboratively to form consortia addressing shared strategic dilemmas.[50] By the end of the 1980s, it was becoming clear that liberal arts colleges in the southern United States would be unable to maintain full staffing and curricula in the classics and related humanities fields. Student demand was insufficient on individual campuses to warrant continuing existing commitments to these fields. Faced with the prospect of closing academic units and programs historically closely associated with their schools and the liberal arts sector more broadly, institutional leaders at Davidson, Morehouse, Rhodes, Sewanee, Spelman, Centre, and similar schools came together to form the ACS,[51] which persists to this day and offers advanced coursework in the fields as an interinstitutional consortium. With substantial foundation support, ACS, in turn, led efforts to initiate Sunoikisis, a national consortium of classics programs. In 2016, ACS will celebrate the twenty-fifth anniversary of its founding. Liberal arts education in the United States has unquestionably been enriched through creative collaborative efforts like ACS, an effort begun in large part to control costs.

Other cost containment actions in the sector have focused on staffing and human resource areas, whether reducing staff and faculty hours, reevaluating employee benefit packages, or eliminating faculty, staff, or administrative positions as part of a strategic change process. As part of its recent "realignment" process, Houghton also eliminated an academic dean's position, cut back on part-time faculty and teaching overloads, and deferred hiring in some areas.[52] Other schools are realizing cost savings by reducing their athletics budgets, including Centenary, which recently changed its athletic affiliation from NCAA Division I to Division III.[53]

Of course, like efforts in revenue diversification, aggressive cost-containment efforts can run the risk of moving institutions so far away from historical values, traditions, and commitments as to threaten the cultures that previously built and sustained the schools. Striking in that light are almost universal comments from academic leaders (including those we have interviewed as well as those interviewed for the articles we cite in this chapter) to the effect that cultural attentiveness was a core element in the financially driven change processes they initiated. In an interview for a recent Council of Independent Colleges (CIC) research project, the president of Houghton College in New York suggested the concurrent roles of institutional culture, history, and locale in shaping her community's response to recent strategic changes on her campus.

> Houghton, like many small residential colleges, has not had a lot of experience in dealing with drastic change. Houghton is a very small college town with a very small college, so because we're the only game in town, the fear of change has been a huge part of this, and even though we have not, in fact, dealt with some of the drastic changes that some of our sister colleges have had to deal with, I would say it doesn't take as much change here to engender the kind of fear or wondering, "How's all this going to look when we're done with things?"

Unfortunately, hard evidence on the success of such leaders' efforts to adapt culture for dramatically new times is lacking.

Other Initiatives and Programs

Nearly all small private schools are looking beyond revenue diversification and cost containment. Among the other campus-specific strategic changes being pursued are organizational and governance realignment, revising admissions and enrollment strategies, reevaluating financial aid practices, and expanding athletics programs in order to reach a more diverse and targeted group of prospective students. For example, New England College in New Hampshire recently reorganized its faculty governance system in order to allow for more collaborative, holistic, and timely decision making, allowing for faculty meetings to be called with only a day's notice. In our interview for the aforementioned CIC research project, the institution's provost stressed the flexibility and timeliness of this process as critical in the school's curricular redesign process. "There was a strong belief that institutions like ours are in a fragile condition, and we really wanted to be proactive and position ourselves from a point of strength," he noted. As part of this process, the institution invested in resources to provide their faculty with more competitive, market-driven data, which then enabled them to make informed decisions and accelerate the pace of curricular change. Consequently, the school has made significant investments in both online education and curricular redesign in a very short period of time, which he attributes to a shared commitment to institutional goals, positioning, and quick decision making enabled by the faculty governance process.

Also common among these institutions is an increase in tuition discounting and merit aid, in hopes of enticing high-achieving, wealthier students to enroll, while simultaneously raising the schools' academic profiles.[54] Wilson College (Pennsylvania) recently announced both a $5,000 reduction in annual tuition, as well as a unique loan-buyback program for on-time completion of undergraduate degrees.[55] Coupled with the admittance of men to undergraduate programs, this previously female-only institution recently enrolled its largest class in 40 years.[56] Other institutions have attempted to propel enrollment shifts by reaching new populations of students, including both international students and adult learners.

Recommendations

Leaders undertaking strategic change and adaptation on independent college campuses must press decision making in several domains simultaneously. Cameron and David O. Ulrich[57] identified seven domains for the attention of leaders seeking effective transformational change: strategy, structure, systems, style, staff, skills, and shared values. St. John[58] suggests that the successfully adapting schools he studied pursued "action strategies" in six domains: academic, management, enrollment management, pricing, alternative revenue streams, and leadership. These typologies are useful, but it is difficult to definitively classify initiatives for independent colleges because they often touch on several areas at once. For example, tuition discounting efforts touch on strategy, systems, staffing, revenues, and, of course, mission. With this in mind, we instead present below ten recommendations, with each addressing such core institutional aspects as evaluation and assessment, enrollment management, structure, process, mission, culture, and leadership.

Recommendation 1: Systematically review institutional opportunities and challenges on an ongoing basis. Leaders inevitably vary in their decision-making styles, but there should be little variation in their commitment to data-based analysis and decision making. In the current, variable environment for independent colleges, cultivating "reflective practitioners" has never been so important. Evaluation, assessment, and other analytic activities must be supported. Ensuring that the campus has adequate capacity in this domain is essential.

Recommendation 2: Involve multiple offices and individuals in evaluating programs, assessing performance, and researching opportunities and challenges. Historically, assessment of levels of student qualifications, performance, completion, persistence, and satisfaction has largely been the function of a college's institutional research office. Developing a strong IR office is critical and necessary. At the same time, data and analytic skills are increasingly widely distributed on campuses, and there is much to be gained by expanding participation from both faculty and administrative staff in strategically critical studies. Beyond bringing new expertise to the table, such an approach may help build engagement and support beyond the administrative ranks.

Recommendation 3: Periodically review earlier established initiatives to ensure that empirical evidence supports their continuation. Programs and actions do not always turn out as earlier envisioned, but tight budgets, pride of creation, and political sensitivities often lead to a lack of attention to follow up. Notable cost and revenue returns can be realized, however, by investing in this data-based "feedback loop." This loop is the final stage of an implementation process, with results accumulated thoroughly and implications integrated into decisions regarding program termination and refinement.

Recommendation 4: Develop benchmarking systems to alert leadership to perfor-

mance in key academic and financial domains. Building a system that accumulates historic and current data on those domains and provides means for comparing such data to that in other schools is essential. Among the many factors to be included in an effective benchmarking system are application and yield rates, first-year students' qualifications, tuition discount levels, student diversity, year-to-year progression rates, current financial ratios, endowment returns, and job placement patterns. When selected indicators move out of historically or comparatively favorable zones, a benchmarking system can help leaders more immediately and more effectively diagnose and address the problems.

Recommendation 5: Identify colleges' central strategic priorities and challenges and attach people and resources to associated analyses. For example, in some schools, a prominent concern may be the equity and diversity consequences (e.g., low-income student enrollment) of increased tuition discounting and focus on targeted merit aid. Can scenarios and trade-offs be quantified for differing student aid approaches as they relate to the varying aspects of institutional mission? At some institutions, primary concerns may focus on the accumulation and presentation of evidence on the college's quality of educational programming, both traditional and online. At other schools, the nature, productivity, and satisfaction of the faculty may be the primary concern, as contract hiring increases, online offerings are encouraged, salaries are restrained, and teaching loads increased. Taking the same question to the organizational level, some leaders may wish to examine the implications of expanding non-tenure-track faculty hiring: how are the changed hiring patterns affecting students' academic outcomes and the institution's governance, responsiveness, fiscal health, and survival? That is, some schools may wish to study whether increasing use of non-tenure-track faculty are "paying off" in cost-effectiveness terms for small independent colleges. Once leaders have identified the central strategic foci for their institutions, it then becomes critical to determine the specific people and action plans most appropriate for enacting such analyses on their campuses.

Recommendation 6: Thoroughly analyze the costs and effects of strategic enrollment management systems. As Don Hossler[59] notes, in just three decades, SEM went "from a strategy practiced at a small number of private colleges to standard procedure at most public and private institutions." In the current "new normal" of higher education institutions straining for resources and public support, it is unlikely that SEM will disappear. Thus, the details of SEM—in particular, the effects of its implicit and explicit incentives—warrant careful attention. A prominent area for attention is tuition discounting: Enrollment challenges can lead institutions toward a destructive cycle of ever-increasing discounting.[60] Careful quantitative analysis of student demand (inquiry volume, application volume, yields, price sensitivity, etc.) is imperative to avoid the traps that some recently endangered colleges have encountered.

In analyses of SEMs, attention to costs should not be limited to existing out-of-pocket expenditures for staff, data, information systems, and consultants but should also include attention to potential alternative approaches, such as consortial efforts with other institutions. For a comprehensive cost-effectiveness analysis, institutions should also consider the opportunity costs of *not* choosing alternatives to the current approach. For example, aggressive commitment to certain aspects of enrollment management systems can work against the attainment of established missions and goals, such as diversity. Conceptually and practically, retreat from such goals can incur real costs. These trade-offs can be difficult to quantify, and many SEMs do not incorporate attention to questions of values and mission. Still, the trade-offs merit attention: what seems economically sensible in the shorter term may be economically harmful in the longer term.

Recommendation 7: Creatively explore alternative structures and processes to control costs and generate new revenues. There is nothing sacrosanct about the inherited structures and processes of colleges. While certain organizational forms appear to be required in the marketplace (a library, an English department, intercollegiate sports, a bachelor's degree program, etc.), others may be less obligatory. Some strategic priorities (such as moving academic programs online) require additional front-end financial investment, but others may not require much. Schools may be able to utilize existing human resources or realign offices and responsibilities in order to meet strategic needs or changing environmental demands.

As noted earlier, leaders pursuing important strategic emphases need to consider the relative value of deploying their current cabinet-level leaders and their staffs versus establishing new, targeted task forces made up of staff and faculty. Concurrently, leaders need to evaluate existing governance and management approaches as elements in their efforts to frame, consider, and progress on change initiatives. As Cameron and Ulrich and St. John[61] stress, leaders need to consider how and to what extent other members of the campus community (faculty, staff, students, alumni) are taking part in dialogue regarding institutional adaptation. Similarly, leaders need to consider the role of each of the various parties in contributing to implementation of those efforts. In short, the successful leader must determine which adaptive structures and processes appear to be working well, which may need reform, and who will lead the charge in implementing such reforms.

Thus, if assessment becomes a priority, presidents may be able to identify faculty and staff to lead this strategic process. As a result, they might generate a greater acceptance of the need for change on their campuses. Or, if online education is a priority, experts, advocates, and leaders may be identified within the current faculty and staff workforce without necessitating new hiring. If costs are becoming prohibitive, leaders may want to explore abandoning existing arrangements to form or join across-institution academic or business collaborations. In each case, creative leaders supported by a savvy exploration of the costs and effects may succeed in innovating without major financial investments.

Recommendation 8: Make strategic thinking, planning, and management an everyday feature of their college. Institutional leaders should embrace the notion that no school is safe; independent colleges need to be attuned to their environment and prepared to be entrepreneurial, whatever that means in their unique context and culture. Crisis is not essential for undertaking strategic change; an ongoing, constant strategic orientation may help forestall or prevent crisis when environmental conditions change. The goal is "nimbleness" rather than complacency.

St. John[62] studied transformational efforts at Pomona College in the 1980s, noting that it was not threatened at the time but undertook significant strategic adaptations nonetheless. In doing so, leaders refined and improved the college's marketplace posture. As a result, Pomona strengthened its endowment, grew alternative revenue sources, constructed or renovated several buildings, and, consequently, positioned itself to increase its reputation and attract new students. Leaders should consistently take advantage of any opportunity arising to reposition and strengthen their institutions, regardless of resources or ranking.

Recommendation 9: Place a high priority on enabling and encouraging stakeholder acceptance into change initiatives. Research has repeatedly suggested that cultivating a widely shared perception of the need for institutional change is a critical ingredient in successful strategic change. Central to building that perception is leaders' sharing and shaping of a coherent and compelling case for transformation. When campus stakeholders understand specific resource challenges and the logic of potential solutions, they may become less likely to resist. While a college's faculty are rarely unanimous in supporting strategic reforms, cultivating the support of these critical allies can raise the odds for success.

Recommendation 10: Treat existing institutional missions as constraints but not barriers. In building support for a change argument, there is a critical need to keep the institutional mission at the forefront, while allowing for some flexibility in terms of interpretation. As noted earlier, faculty cultures and overly rigid interpretations of past history can inhibit strategic success. Alternatively, openness to mission expansion and adaptation can be critical to success.

Benedictine College is a prime example of an institution with deep Christian mission, roots, and traditions. In recent years, however, it has welcomed new groups of students to its campuses, including Muslims. In an interview, the former president of Benedictine College told us, "The key is, you've got to stay true to yourself and your mission, but you have to differentiate. And I think we do that quite well." In making the change, the school's provost placed the move to admit Muslim students within the boundaries of the school's traditions, noting that one of the main hallmarks of Benedictine tradition is being welcoming to strangers:

> It's the real world. We have to teach our students to be in a multicultural, multi-faith environment, and the best way to teach them how to live and be good citizens there is to do it here, within the context of the Catholic faith. . . . We see that as part of our mission, to educate all types of students, and to offer students an environment that teaches them how to be good Catholic citizens—or whatever they are . . . Muslim citizens . . . and know how to deal with and relate to people of other faiths and cultures.

Similarly, at New England College, when internal constituents initially questioned the school's innovative efforts in online education and other arenas, the president referenced their mission and founding as an entrepreneurial institution: "We were innovative from the moment of our founding. . . . We were entrepreneurial from the get-go. You have to make sure people don't lose that memory."

Conclusions

Despite their numerous and varied efforts at innovation, skepticism remains regarding the future and sustainability of many private colleges. While more prestigious and wealthier institutions seem to be protected from recent enrollment shifts and revenue shortfalls—and indeed, many are flourishing—less resourced and lower-ranked colleges still seem to be at risk. Citing recent examples of the closing of small, nonprofit colleges, William Tierney and James Ward[63] call today's liberal arts college "an endangered species" and caution that these campuses "should be viewed as canaries in the expanding small-college coal mine."[64] Some enrollment management officials project that as many as 30 percent of the schools in this sector may not exist in a decade,[65] while others have appealed to the leading private institutions to lead the charge in investing in innovations and solutions that will secure the future of the sector rather than using their resources to protect the status quo and their own place in it.[66] Finally, despite the improvement in outlook for US higher education, the aforementioned Moody's announcement[67] cautioned that "pockets of stress" would continue to exist in small, private schools with less than $200 million in revenue. In sum, it seems that many independent colleges are at a critical crossroads, with deliberate, mission-driven adaptation and innovation essential to ensuring their survival.

One might easily dismiss these perspectives, given the resilience of the independent college sector through past crises and the unreliability of dire forecasts in the past.[68] But to do so would be to gainsay the possibility that this time the forecasters will get it right, as well as to downplay the role of active change efforts on campuses in response to the earlier forecasts. It seems wiser to accept that independent colleges are now facing real and diverse difficulties. There is little question that existing research on strategic planning and management can contribute to addressing those challenges. And there remains little doubt that fruitful new research can be undertaken. Ideally, the results of such work will add to the tool kits of those asked to lead in the sector.

Still, research can guide strategic change only so far. There is wisdom in the words of Julius, Baldridge, and Pfeffer,[69] writing as Machiavelli:

> There are many books that concern themselves with leadership and mountains of articles. Much of what is written is valuable but it is written, by and large, by those who study the topic. As you are no doubt aware, there is a big difference. My concept of leadership is simple and direct—leaders identify an issue that is perceived by the larger community as an important dilemma or a critical problem. The true leader offers (and implements) a solution. For example, Moses conceived of freedom and a vision of the promised land—and led a group of former slaves through the desert (and even Moses was allowed only to see Israel, never to set foot there!). Leaders are those who identify and articulate a vision and successfully manage a solution.

In the end, leaders able to act boldly on not only their own vision but also on insights distilled from higher education research will be best equipped to maintain and increase the vitality of the threatened independent college sector.

NOTES

This work is based in part on earlier work supported by the Council of Independent Colleges, the TIAA-CREF Institute, and the Lumina Foundation. We gratefully acknowledge that support. The views expressed are those of the authors alone, however.

1. Comment made to interview team for a recent research project sponsored by the Council of Independent Colleges (CIC).
2. Silver, "As More Attend."
3. Neely, "Threats to Liberal Arts Colleges."
4. Lapovsky, "Tale of Three Campuses"; Woodhouse, "What It Might Mean."
5. E.g., see Koblik and Graubard, *Distinctively American.*
6. E.g., see Kiley, "Another Liberal Arts Critic"; Lewin, "As Interest Fades."
7. Hearn and Belasco, "Commitment to the Core."
8. Pfnister, "Role of Liberal Arts College," 149.
9. St. John, "Transformation"; Leslie and Fretwell, *Wise Moves in Hard Times*; Toma, "Institutional Strategy."
10. Morphew, "Rose by Any Other Name."
11. Bacow and Bowen, "Double Trouble."
12. E.g., Chaffee, "Successful Strategic Management"; Chaffee, "Concept of Strategy"; Chaffee, "Three Models of Strategy"; Hardy et al., "Strategy Formation"; Peterson and Spencer, "Understanding Academic Culture and Climate."
13. E.g., see Keller, *Academic Strategy.*
14. E.g., see Hearn and Heydinger, "Scanning the External Environment"; Rowley, Lujan, and Dolence, *Strategic Change.*
15. Cope, "Strategic Planning"; Kotler and Murphy, "Strategic Planning for Higher Education."
16. Kraatz, Ventresca, and Deng, "Precarious Values and Mundane Innovations."
17. Hossler, "Enrollment Management"; Hossler, "How Enrollment Management Has Transformed"; Hossler and Bontrager, *Handbook of Strategic Enrollment Management.*
18. Cameron, "Organizational Adaptation and Higher Education," 138.
19. Toma, *Building Organizational Capacity.*
20. Chaffee, "Three Models of Strategy"; Dill, "Management of Academic Culture"; Drake and Sparks, "Transforming Private Universities"; Kezar and Eckel, "Effect of Institutional Culture"; Masland, "Organizational Culture"; Tierney, "Organizational Culture in Higher Education."
21. Christensen and Eyring, "Innovative University," 52.
22. Kempner, "Faculty Culture"; Gioia and Thomas, "Identity, Image, and Issue Interpretation"; Kolman and Hossler, "Influence of Institutional Culture."
23. Toma, *Building Organizational Capacity*, 4.
24. Alstete, "Revenue Generation Strategies," 4.
25. Birnbaum, *How Academic Leadership Works.*
26. Cameron, "Organizational Adaptation and Higher Education"; Chaffee, "Successful Strategic Management"; Kezar and Eckel, "Effect of Institutional Culture."

27. Neumann, "On the Making of Hard Times."

28. Galbraith, "Designing the Innovating Organization"; Morphew, "Realities of Strategic Planning."

29. Julius, Baldridge, and Pfeffer, "Memo from Machiavelli."

30. Ibid., 113.

31. Miles and Cameron, *Coffin Nails and Corporate Strategies.*

32. Including Cameron, "Organizational Adaptation and Higher Education"; Cameron and Zammuto, "Matching Managerial Strategies."

33. Hearn, "Strategy and Resources."

34. Chaffee, "Successful Strategic Management in Small Private Colleges."

35. E.g., see the national "Power of Liberal Arts" campaign at http://www.liberal artspower.org.

36. Hearn and Warshaw, "Mission-Driven Innovation."

37. Moody's Investor Service, "US Higher Education Outlook."

38. Toner, "Highly Endangered Higher Education."

39. Biemiller, "Survival at Stake," para. 5.

40. Alstete, "Revenue Generation Strategies"; Hearn and Warshaw, "Mission-Driven Innovation."

41. Alstete, "Revenue Generation Strategies."

42. Drake and Sparks, "Transforming Private Universities."

43. Marcus, "Why Some Small Colleges."

44. Alstete, "Revenue Generation Strategies."

45. Benedictine University, "Benedictine Promise."

46. Kenyon College, "Education Vacation."

47. Hearn and Warshaw, "Mission-Driven Innovation."

48. Rivard, "Private Colleges Remain."

49. Green, "Houghton Announces Strategic Realignment." On Centenary College, see Biemiller, "How 3 Colleges."

50. Forcier, "Innovation through Collaboration," comprehensively reviews several prominent consortial efforts.

51. See Associated Colleges of the South., "ACS Strengthens and Showcases."

52. Green, "Houghton Announces Strategic Realignment."

53. Biemiller, "How 3 Colleges."

54. Alstete, "Revenue Generation Strategies"; Marcus, "Why Some Small Colleges"; Toma, "Positioning for Prestige"; Toma, "Institutional Strategy."

55. Biemiller, "Armed with Data."

56. Biemiller, "How 3 Colleges."

57. Cameron and Ulrich, "Transformational Leadership."

58. St. John, "Transformation."

59. Hossler, "How Enrollment Management Has Transformed," B3.

60. See Woodhouse, "What It Might Mean."

61. Cameron and Ulrich, "Transformational Leadership"; St. John, "Transformation."

62. St. John, "Transformation."

63. Tierney and Ward, "Demise of Small Liberal Arts," para. 1.

64. Ibid., 2.

65. Belkin, "U.S. Private Colleges."

66. Kirschner, "Innovations in Higher Education? Hah!"

67. Moody's Investor Service, "US Higher Education Outlook."

68. Pfnister, "Role of Liberal Arts College."
69. Julius, Baldridge, and Pfeffer, "Memo from Machiavelli," 129.

REFERENCES

Alstete, Jeffrey W. "Revenue Generation Strategies: Leveraging Higher Education Resources for Increased Income." *ASHE Higher Education Report* 41, no. 1 (December 1, 2014): 1–138. doi:10.1002/aehe.20019.
Associated Colleges of the South. "ACS Strengthens and Showcases Liberal Arts Education through Collaboration." http://colleges.org/about. Accessed April 4, 2017.
Bacow, Lawrence S., and William G. Bowen. "Double Trouble: Sweetbriar College and Cooper Union." *Ithaka S+R*, September 21, 2015. http://www.sr.ithaka.org/blog/double-trouble. Accessed April 3, 2017.
Belkin, Douglas. "U.S. Private Colleges Face Enrollment Decline." *Wall Street Journal*, November 11, 2013. https://www.wsj.com/articles/SB10001424052702304672404579186153175094892. Accessed April 3, 2017.
Benedictine University. "The Benedictine Promise." 2017. https://www.ben.edu/mesa/promise. Accessed April 3, 2017.
Biemiller, Lawrence. "Armed with Data, a Women's College Tries a Transformation." *Chronicle of Higher Education*, February 4, 2013. http://www.chronicle.com/article/A-Womens-College-Tries-a/136969. Accessed April 3, 2017.
———. "How 3 Colleges Made Tough Choices." *Chronicle of Higher Education*, March 2, 2015. http://www.chronicle.com/article/How-3-Colleges-Made-Tough/190493. Accessed April 3, 2017.
———. "Survival at Stake." *Chronicle of Higher Education*, March 2, 2015. http://www.chronicle.com/article/With-Survival-at-Stake-Small/190491. Accessed April 3, 2017.
Birnbaum, Robert. *How Academic Leadership Works: Understanding Success and Failure in the College Presidency*. San Francisco: Jossey-Bass, 1992. https://eric.ed.gov/?id=ED349923. Accessed April 3, 2017.
Cameron, Kim S. "Organizational Adaptation and Higher Education." *Journal of Higher Education* 55, no. 2 (March 1, 1984): 122–44. doi:10.1080/00221546.1984.11778679.
Cameron, Kim S., and David O. Ulrich. "Transformational Leadership in Colleges and Universities." In *Higher Education: Handbook of Theory and Research*, edited by John C. Smart, 2:1–42. New York: Agathon Press, 1986.
Cameron, Kim S., and Raymond F. Zammuto. "Matching Managerial Strategies to Conditions of Decline." In *Readings in Organizational Decline: Frameworks, Research, and Prescriptions*, edited by Kim S. Cameron, Robert I. Sutton, and David A. Whettern, 117–28. Cambridge, MA: Ballinger, 1988.
Chaffee, Ellen Earle. "The Concept of Strategy: From Business to Higher Education." In *Higher Education: Handbook of Theory and Research*, edited by John C. Smart, 1:133–72. New York: Agathon Press, 1985.
———. "Successful Strategic Management in Small Private Colleges." *Journal of Higher Education* 55, no. 2 (March 1, 1984): 212–41. doi:10.1080/00221546.1984.11778683.
———. "Three Models of Strategy." *Academy of Management Review* 10, no. 1 (January 1, 1985): 89–98. doi:10.5465/AMR.1985.4277354.
Christensen, Clayton M., and Henry J. Eyring. *The Innovative University: Changing the DNA of Higher Education from the Inside Out*. San Francisco: Jossey-Bass, 2011.
Cope, Robert G. "Strategic Planning, Management, and Decision Making." ASHE-

ERIC Research Report. Washington, DC: American Association for the Study of Higher Education, 1981.

Dill, David D. "The Management of Academic Culture: Notes on the Management of Meaning and Social Integration." *Higher Education* 11, no. 3 (May 1, 1982): 303–20. doi:10.1007/BF00155621.

Drake, Anna P., and William L. Sparks. "Transforming Private Universities: An Exploratory Study." *International Journal of Humanities and Social Science* 2, no. 23 (2012): 6–17.

Forcier, Mary Frances. "Innovation through Collaboration: New Pathways to Success." *Trusteeship* 19, no. 5 (2011): 8–12.

Galbraith, Jay R. "Designing the Innovating Organization." *Organizational Dynamics* 10, no. 3 (December 1, 1982): 5–25. doi:10.1016/0090-2616(82)90033-X.

Gioia, Dennis A., and James B. Thomas. "Identity, Image, and Issue Interpretation: Sensemaking during Strategic Change in Academia." *Administrative Science Quarterly* 41, no. 3 (1996): 370–403. doi:10.2307/2393936.

Green, Marshall. "Houghton Announces Strategic Realignment of Academic Programs." October 2, 2013. http://www.houghton.edu/news-media/recent-news/houghton-announces-strategic-realignment-of-academic-programs/335. Accessed April 4, 2017.

Hardy, Cynthia, Ann Langley, Henry Mintzberg, and Janet Rose. "Strategy Formation in the University Setting." *Review of Higher Education* 6, no. 4 (1983): 407–33.

Hearn, James C. "Strategy and Resources: Economic Issues in Strategic Planning and Management in Higher Education." In *Higher Education: Handbook of Theory and Research*, edited by John C. Smart, 4:212–81. New York: Agathon Press, 1988.

Hearn, James C., and Andrew S. Belasco. "Commitment to the Core: A Longitudinal Analysis of Humanities Degree Production in Four-Year Colleges." *Journal of Higher Education* 86, no. 3 (May 1, 2015): 387–416. doi:10.1080/00221546.2015.11777369.

Hearn, James C., and Jarrett B. Warshaw. "Mission-Driven Innovation: An Empirical Study of Adaptation and Change among Independent Colleges." Washington, DC: Council of Independent Colleges, 2015.

Hearn, James C., and Richard B. Heydinger. "Scanning the External Environment of a University: Objectives, Constraints, and Possibilities." *Journal of Higher Education* 56, no. 4 (1985): 419–45.

Hossler, Don. "Enrollment Management: An Integrated Approach." New York: College Board, 1984.

———. "How Enrollment Management Has Transformed—or Ruined—Higher Education." *Chronicle of Higher Education*, April 30, 2004. http://www.chronicle.com/article/How-Enrollment-Management-Has/29115. Accessed April 4, 2017.

Hossler, Don, and Bob Bontrager. *Handbook of Strategic Enrollment Management*. San Francisco: Jossey-Bass, 2014.

Julius, Daniel J., J. Victor Baldridge, and Jeffrey Pfeffer. "A Memo from Machiavelli." *Journal of Higher Education* 70, no. 2 (March 1, 1999): 113–33. doi:10.1080/00221546.1999.11780758.

Keller, George. *Academic Strategy: The Management Revolution in Higher Education*. Washington, DC: American Association of Higher Education, 1983.

Kempner, Ken. "Faculty Culture in the Community College: Facilitating or Hindering Learning." *Review of Higher Education* 13, no. 2 (1990): 215–35.

Kenyon College. "Education Vacation." 2013. http://www.kenyon.edu/middle-path/story/education-vacation. Accessed April 10, 2017.

Kezar, Adrianna, and Peter D. Eckel. "The Effect of Institutional Culture on Change

Strategies in Higher Education." *Journal of Higher Education* 73, no. 4 (July 1, 2002): 435–60. doi:10.1080/00221546.2002.11777159.

Kiley, Kevin. "Another Liberal Arts Critic." *Inside Higher Ed*, January 30, 2013. https://www.insidehighered.com/news/2013/01/30/north-carolina-governor-joins-chorus-republicans-critical-liberal-arts. Accessed April 4, 2017.

Kirschner, Ann. "Innovations in Higher Education? Hah!" *Chronicle of Higher Education*, April 8, 2012. http://chronicle.com/article/Innovations-in-Higher/131424 Accessed April 4, 2017.

Koblik, Steven, and Stephen Richards Graubard, eds. *Distinctively American: The Residential Liberal Arts Colleges.* Brunswick, NJ: Transaction, 2000.

Kolman, Eileen M., and Don Hossler. "The Influence of Institutional Culture on Presidential Selection." *Review of Higher Education* 10, no. 4 (1987): 319–32.

Kotler, Philip, and Patrick E. Murphy. "Strategic Planning for Higher Education." *Journal of Higher Education* 52, no. 5 (September 1, 1981): 470–89. doi:10.1080/00221546.1981.11778119.

Kraatz, Matthew S., Marc J. Ventresca, and Lina Deng. "Precarious Values and Mundane Innovations: Enrollment Management in American Liberal Arts Colleges." *Academy of Management Journal* 53, no. 6 (December 1, 2010): 1521–45. doi:10.5465/AMJ.2010.57319260.

Lapovsky, Lucie. "Tale of Three Campuses: A Comparison of Three Small Liberal Arts Colleges." Unpublished manuscript, 2012.

Leslie, David W., and E. K. Fretwell Jr. *Wise Moves in Hard Times: Creating and Managing Resilient Colleges and Universities.* San Francisco: Jossey-Bass, 1996. https://eric.ed.gov/?id=ED392352. Accessed April 4, 2017.

Lewin, Tamar. "As Interest Fades in the Humanities, Colleges Worry." *New York Times*, October 30, 2013. http://www.nytimes.com/2013/10/31/education/as-interest-fades-in-the-humanities-colleges-worry.html. Accessed April 4, 2017.

Marcus, Jon. "Why Some Small Colleges Are in Big Trouble." *Boston Globe*, April 14, 2013. http://www.bostonglobe.com/magazine/2013/04/13/are-small-private-colleges-trouble/ndlYSWVGFAUjYVVWkqnjfK/story.html. Accessed April 4, 2017.

Masland, Andrew T. "Organizational Culture in the Study of Higher Education." *Review of Higher Education* 8, no. 2 (1985): 157–68.

Miles, Robert H., and Kim S. Cameron. *Coffin Nails and Corporate Strategies.* Englewood Cliffs, NJ: Prentice Hall, 1982.

Moody's Investor Service. "US Higher Education Outlook Revised to Stable as Revenues Stabilize." July 20, 2015. https://www.moodys.com/research/Moodys-US-higher-education-outlook-revised-to-stable-as-revenues—PR_330530. Accessed April 4, 2017.

Morphew, Christopher C. "The Realities of Strategic Planning: Program Termination at East Central University." *Review of Higher Education* 23, no. 3 (March 1, 2000): 257–80. doi:10.1353/rhe.2000.0011.

———. " 'A Rose by Any Other Name': Which Colleges Became Universities." *Review of Higher Education* 25, no. 2 (January 1, 2002): 207–23. doi:10.1353/rhe.2002.0005.

Neely, Paul. "The Threats to Liberal Arts Colleges." *Daedalus* 128, no. 1 (1999): 27–45.

Neumann, Anna. "On the Making of Hard Times and Good Times." *Journal of Higher Education* 66, no. 1 (January 1, 1995): 3–31. doi:10.1080/00221546.1995.11774755.

Peterson, Marvin W., and Melinda G. Spencer. "Understanding Academic Culture and Climate." *New Directions for Institutional Research* 1990, no. 68 (December 1, 1990): 3–18. doi:10.1002/ir.37019906803.

Pfnister, Allan O. "The Role of the Liberal Arts College." *Journal of Higher Education* 55, no. 2 (March 1, 1984): 145–70. doi:10.1080/00221546.1984.11778680.

Rivard, Ry. "Private Colleges Remain under the Weather." *Inside Higher Ed*, December 9, 2013. https://www.insidehighered.com/news/2013/12/09/private-colleges-remain-un der-weather. Accessed April 4, 2017.

Rowley, Daniel J., Herman D. Lujan, and Michael G. Dolence. *Strategic Change in Colleges and Universities: Planning to Survive and Prosper.* San Francisco: Jossey-Bass, 1997.

Silver, Nate. "As More Attend, Majors Are Becoming More Career-Focused." *New York Times*, June 26, 2013. http://fivethirtyeight.blogs.nytimes.com/2013/06/25/as-more -attend-college-majors-become-more-career-focused. Accessed April 4, 2017.

St. John, Edward P. "The Transformation of Private Liberal Arts Colleges." *Review of Higher Education* 15, no. 1 (1991): 83–106.

Tierney, William G. "Organizational Culture in Higher Education." *Journal of Higher Education* 59, no. 1 (January 1, 1988): 2–21. doi:10.1080/00221546.1988.11778301.

Tierney, William G., and James D. Ward. "The Demise of Small Liberal Arts Colleges." *21st Century Scholar*, May 11, 2015. http://21stcenturyscholar.org/2015/05/11/the-de mise-of-small-liberal-arts-colleges. Accessed April 4, 2017.

Toma, J. Douglas. *Building Organizational Capacity: Strategic Management in Higher Education.* Baltimore: Johns Hopkins University Press, 2010.

———. "Institutional Strategy: Positioning for Prestige." In *The Organization of Higher Education: Managing Colleges for a New Era*, edited by Michael N. Bastedo, 118–59. Baltimore: Johns Hopkins University Press, 2012.

———. "Positioning for Prestige in American Higher Education: Case Studies of Strategies at Four Public Institutions toward 'Getting to the Next Level.'" Paper prepared as part of the research grant program, Center for Enrollment Research. University of Southern California, 2009.

Toner, Mark. "The Highly Endangered Higher Education Business Model (and How to Fix It)." *Innovative Practices*, June 12, 2015. http://www.acenet.edu/the-presidency/ columns-and-features/Pages/The-Highly-Endangered-Higher-Education-Business -Model.aspx. Accessed April 4, 2017.

Woodhouse, Kellie. "What It Might Mean When a College's Discount Rate Tops 60 Percent." *Inside Higher Ed*, November 25, 2015. https://www.insidehighered.com/ news/2015/11/25/what-it-might-mean-when-colleges-discount-rate-tops-60-percent. Accessed April 4, 2017.

REACTION
Richard H. Dorman

This chapter provides a well-crafted overview of the challenges facing many smaller independent liberal arts colleges and offers useful and concrete recommendations to achieve solutions to those challenges. Most noteworthy within the document was the reference to institutional mission, which is central to providing a unifying vision to help guide college presidents and boards of trustees in directing the varied institutional constituencies toward future institutional growth and stability. The authors astutely point out the difficulty in managing change in a cultural and tradition-bound organizational environment, an environment in which the primary indispensable constituency—the faculty—directly benefits from adherence to those traditions. Related to this fact, the chapter neglects an adequate exposition of the most salient feature of the changes now occurring within our profession.

The authors assert that three distinct periods in American higher education caused existential crises for the small private liberal arts sector. And though a noteworthy number of schools did not survive these periods, the sector, as a whole, continued to operate effectively. The premise of the chapter suggests that through continued adaptation and effective leadership on matters of process and structure, the viability of the sector will again remain, save for the relatively few institutions whose circumstances today are sufficiently compromised that survival is all but impossible. But I believe the authors neglect to adequately address the two main conditions that prevail in this dialogue, and because of that the utility of the recommendations rendered are only partially beneficial to the reader and to those leaders responsible for the welfare of these institutions.

The first condition relates to the center of control in academic decision making. During the three tumultuous periods identified by the authors, one factor remained constant: the academic enterprise was defined and controlled by the faculty, vigorously protecting traditions and practices that date back even to the ancient medieval guilds. Throughout the history of American higher education, matters of curriculum, pedagogy, academic schedule and year, majors offered, tenure, teaching load, and numerous other variables that define the academic experience were—and are—defined by the faculty. Today, the locus of control is slowly but assuredly shifting from the faculty to the market. Largely this is being brought about by technology and emerging forms of education apart from the more traditional classroom experience. And as students of tomorrow enjoy greater levels of choice in how they access information and find faster, cheaper, and more highly tailored curricula to meet their specific needs, the relevancy of faculty will wane. The rapidity in which it wanes depends upon the second, and next, condition.

The practice of tuition discounting could be the undoing of many institutions in our sector. Discounting has opened the small private liberal arts colleges to the masses, and given the quality of the outcomes derived from a small school education due to the personalized attention students receive, independent higher education now serves in many states as a proxy for the educational mission formerly given public institutions. That is certainly true in Pennsylvania, where the socioeconomic profile of the students attending state-related institutions is wealthier than those attending the schools of the independent sector. Yet, as middle incomes continue to decline relative to inflation, and costs to attend college rise significantly, the current model is unsustainable for our sector. Addressing this requires a vast overhaul of the manner in which education is delivered and priced at our private colleges in order to achieve the cost reductions necessary to sustain affordability. Yet the manner in which education is delivered is controlled by the faculty through our system of shared governance, and, as mentioned above and in the chapter itself, faculty can be the most rigid in their desire or ability to change.

The chapter correctly argues for adaptation and provides concrete and helpful recommendations for leaders to consider as they strategically and thoughtfully move their respective organizations through the inevitable change process. The challenge, however, comes in recognizing that the paradigm of higher education is significantly changing and no one is quite sure what it is changing to. Changes advocated in the chapter, then, use the methods, practices, and language of our *existing* view of the higher education world. The chapter is a functional and helpful guide to looking at the problem through the prism of our traditions and current condition. But any discourse on strategy or adaptation is not fully complete without a recognition of the impact by the two challenges mentioned above, which, if not addressed, will render all conventional strategies we currently use less than fully effective in bringing about the long-term resurgence our independent higher education sector seeks.

10

Trusses and Gaps in the Bridge from Research to Practice

CHRISTOPHER C. MORPHEW AND JOHN M. BRAXTON

This book's innovative design was devised as means of explicitly connecting the work of prominent higher education scholars to the everyday experiences of senior leaders on campuses representative of the independent sector. Our hope is that the juxtaposition of research highlighting the challenges and opportunities at private colleges with responses from practitioners will highlight what we know and what we need to know about this important higher education sector. We believe the work of our authors—scholars and practitioners—has done that. This chapter will highlight the common elements identified by our scholars, patterns in the reactions of our Council of Independent College (CIC) leaders, and, as a result, a description of where our research to practice bridge has good support and where it needs more work.

Opportunities for the Independent Sector: Suggestions from Our Scholars

Several themes emerged among the chapters of our scholars. In each case, the themes suggest that, even across the diverse topics covered, there are consistencies in the research that predict organizational effective and innovative responses for private colleges and universities.

Create Partnerships That Save Money and Provide Other Dividends

A message our scholars frequently communicated was that the challenges being experienced in the private higher education sector required the establishment of new partnerships that would serve several purposes. Barrett Taylor and David Weerts, in chapter 1, suggest that private colleges seeking to control costs would be wise to create strategic relationships with other colleges with similar profiles and missions that serve the needs of both institutions. Areas for partnerships include international programming for students and working with local nonprofits that share private colleges' historic mission for civic engagement. Tulane University's post-Katrina efforts are a prime example of how a university and its community have worked together to produce tangible benefits for their community and unique learning opportunities for students. Similarly, CIC's recent report on "Strategic Change and Innovation in Independent Colleges" describes an example of a partnership between CIC member Valparaiso University and several area health care providers that produces tuition revenue, provides employment opportunities for students, and meets the needs of other nonprofits.

Julie Park (chapter 6) and Nicholas Hillman and Valerie Crespín-Trujillo (chapter 2) suggest other types of partnerships that private colleges and universities should consider pursuing. Both chapters focus on the importance of reaching out to organizations where future students reside. Implementing peer mentor relationships with incoming students or high school students from the local area, for example, may be a productive way of better informing prospective students on how to prepare for college and educating lower-income or first generation students about the advantages of attending a smaller, teaching-focused college. Because identifying students' unique talents and needs immediately is so important for student success, as Laurie Schreiner (chapter 5) notes, these partnerships can be used to produce information about incoming students that better position colleges to meet students' needs during the crucial first-year experience. As Park notes, fast-changing demographic realities should cause leaders of private colleges without a "name brand" to identify strategies to reach out to new populations of students and parents. Partnerships are a cost-effective way of reaching out to new populations of students and parents.

Reimagine and Leverage Historical Mission as Competitive Advantage

Our scholars challenge leaders in this sector to consider how their historic mission and identity can be reimagined and leveraged to better position the institution for contemporary challenges. Cynthia Wells, David Guthrie, and Daniel Custer (chapter 7) point out, for example, that even as fewer students profess a desire to major in the liberal arts nationally, these programs can and should be part of the strategic advantage that private colleges leverage. This may result in thinking creatively about the general education curriculum such as Bethany College (Kansas) did in creating its Core Experience program.[1] This program is a fresh take on Bethany's historical liberal arts mission that differentiates Bethany from other colleges by combining the expertise of existing faculty and programs to create unique interdisciplinary courses that showcase the value of disciplines that students might not otherwise connect to their career goals. The Core Experience is innovative by also requiring students to reach a level of "religious literacy" that clearly demonstrates how this institution is different from many others. Most CIC members, like Bethany, come from a history that features unique founding principles that, if dusted off and repurposed, could be used to differentiate the college and make its identity stand out in an increasingly crowded marketplace.

Contemporary civic learning shares a common kinship with many private colleges' and universities' religious identities, as Weerts and Taylor (chapter 1) note. This may be another opportunity for institutions to connect what they've done historically with what they can do for students and parents today and simultaneously develop sustainable revenue streams. Connecting religious identity with career goals is not a stretch, as evinced by the Lilly Endowment's Programs for the Theological Exploration of Vocation initiative. This program has invested more than $200 million in private colleges' efforts to, among other things, "help students examine the relationship between their faith and vocational choices." CIC member Simpson College (Iowa), for example, used its Lilly grant to identify and bring to campus high school juniors and seniors interested in exploring their religious identity.

Private colleges and universities have an engaged faculty with a primary focus on teaching and student development. This presents a significant opportunity. Jillian Kinzie and Cynthia Cogswell (chapter 3) remind us of this built-in advantage and encourage private college leaders to make the best use of this historical asset by actively involving faculty in the development of interdisciplinary teaching cohorts and assessment work. Research clearly indicates that involved faculty are a key to student engagement, which is an increasingly marketable feature. The relatively small size of institutions in the independent sector is another advantage to exploit; faculty at these campuses have intimate knowledge of students' development and relative ability to engage in assessment practices using tools such as portfolios that can demonstrate students' learning.

Distance learning may not be the first thought that comes to mind when considering the mission and identity of private colleges and universities, but Matthew Mayhew and Stephen Vassallo remind us in chapter 4 that this is another potential opportunity for institutions to replicate the intensive student-faculty interaction that is a calling card of the independent college sector. They argue that distance learning can approximate the traditional liberal arts college classroom environment, but private college leaders must be thoughtful about implementing distance learning technologies. This can be done with a focus on good teaching practices and by ensuring all faculty—full- and part-time—are trained in using learning technologies. If done correctly, this can be another way that independent colleges can leverage their brand to enroll and serve students who seek out institutions that use distance learning.

Invest in Systematic Assessment Practices

Assessment is a key strategy for many of the research-based recommendations made by our scholars. Smaller private colleges are in a unique position to do assessments on their campuses. Kinzie and Cogswell, for example, mention how CIC members Franklin Pierce University (New Hampshire) and St. Olaf College (Minnesota) use student researchers in their assessment efforts. This innovative idea accomplishes a number of things. First, it involves students in the institution's assessment, which provides a unique perspective on which data to collect that might otherwise be ignored. Second, it provides students with an extraordinary learning opportunity tied to both mission and employment-related skills. Franklin Pierce's Sophomore Assessment Seminar course for English majors, for example, has learning objectives that include students gaining a "working understanding" of the department's learning goals and using information technology as an assessment tool.[2] This is exactly the type of strategy that Schreiner suggests when she argues that private colleges and universities need to take advantage of their small size and existing successes in student outcomes. Finally, adding student members to the assessment team may be a cost-saving measure for the institution.

James Hearn and Erin Ciarimboli (chapter 9) spend a great deal of their chapter on institutional strategy, focusing on the importance of assessment and techniques that colleges in this sector might best employ. Their argument might be described as "make no assumptions; instead, assess." This means not only assessing newer efforts to improve student learning and realize cost savings, it also means assessing strategies and practices that have been employed for years or decades. Examples of this type of thinking at CIC campuses include Stetson University (Florida), which has a systematic process to evaluate all staffing opportunities where a universitywide committee reviews requests from units. This process requires units to consider "alternative solutions" to simply replacing the staff member they have lost, including opportunities that involve using new technologies or reorganization.[3]

Hearn and Ciarimboli astutely define assessment as a strategy in and of itself. As part of that strategy, they suggest that hiring and orientation practices include an assessment component. At small colleges, where the tradition is that everyone wears more than one hat, assessment must be everyone's job, and private colleges and universities must select and train those who are capable of doing it inside and outside the classroom. Wells, Guthrie, and Custer's suggestion that the residential nature of CIC members be utilized to differentiate the student experience is apropos here as well. The fact that students live on campus is another opportunity to build in assessment strategies that demonstrate the value of co-curricular learning that has historically been the calling card of smaller private colleges and universities.

Reactions from Our Campus Leaders

We invited presidents and provosts from nine colleges and universities that hold membership in the CIC to write their reactions to the nine chapters that compose this book. We asked that these reactions address the utility of the information contained in each chapter, with particular attention to how the information contained in the assigned chapter might be used by institutional leaders to make decisions. Put differently, we asked these institutional leaders to assess how the content of the chapter might assist leaders at small independent colleges.

The reactions of our campus leaders provide us with an opportunity to learn how practitioners engage with the work of scholars by assessing how the contents of these chapters might be used by them. In this section of this chapter, we provide some observations from these chapter reactions. These observations fall into two broad categories: shortcomings of the chapters and the value of the chapters to institutional leaders at small independent colleges.

Shortcomings

We derived five categories of shortcomings from the chapter reactions. These categories include lack of attention to institutional variation within the category of independent colleges and universities, a need to prioritize strategies, neglected considerations, difficult-to-implement recommendations, and inaccuracies about institutional realities. We describe each of these categories.

Institutional Variations

One shortcoming pertains to the range of different types of colleges and universities within the category of independent colleges and universities that some chapter authors failed to acknowledge. This particular shortcoming was noted by chapter reactors Roger Drake, Kevin Ross, and Carolyn Stefanco, who are all college presidents. Drake points out that this category of independent colleges and universities includes institutions of varying degrees of admissions selectivity, urban or rural location, secular or religiously affiliated, and institutional mission such as liberal arts and technical. To these differences, Stefanco adds size and whether only undergraduate education is emphasized. Ross adds additional nuance by stating that "each independent institution has a distinct nature."

These chapter reactors appear to be calling for research and scholarship that fits the characteristics of their particular college or university. That is, the utility of the recommendations of research and scholarship to institutional leaders depends on how closely the institutional context of such research and scholarship matches the characteristics of their college or university. Drake elaborates on this point as he asserts that different types of colleges and universities "face somewhat different challenges to accessibility and affordability while possessing vastly different assets that may be leveraged to provide solutions." Ross also emphasizes the importance of institutional matching as he states that "detailed prescriptions on how to create and administer a new online program may or may not be effective across independent institutions. Faculty development strategies and incentives may be effective at one institution but not work well at another due to institutional culture, history, and leadership."

A Need to Prioritize Strategies

In his reaction to the Schreiner chapter titled "Ensuring Student Success," Charlie McCormick (provost of Schreiner University) notes that the author does not prioritize the order of the implementation of the strategies for student success. McCormick explains the need for a "priority order" because of the limited institutional resources independent colleges have available to implement student success strategies. He further states that "deciding which strategies to implement first—rather than adopting an approach that assumes they can all be accomplished at once—requires institutional leaders to be diligent in the assessment effort that Schreiner identifies as being preliminary to any student success efforts."

McCormick's comments suggest that scholars need to prioritize the order of the institution's implementation of the recommendations they make for institutional policy and practice. The specification of such a priority order works to increase the utility of research and scholarship to institutional leaders.

Neglected Considerations

Several reactors suggested that the scholars' contributions neglected important considerations that may get in the way of strategic adaptation. For example, in his reaction to the chapter by Hearn and Ciarimboli titled "Institutional Strategy and Adaptation," Richard Dorman, a college president, posits "that the utility of the recommendations rendered are only partially beneficial to the reader" because the authors neglected to discuss two main conditions important to adaptation and survival of small independent colleges. Dorman describes these two conditions—the tradition of academic governance and enrollment management—in his reaction.

Recommendations Difficult to Implement

Three chapter reactors argue that the recommendations of our scholars may be difficult for independent colleges and universities to implement. In his assessment of the utility of the recommendations offered by Hillman and Crespín-Trujillo in their chapter "Access and Affordability," Drake, for example, states that "the recommendations in the area of campus financial aid may provide less practical solutions for the practitioner." He further notes that their suggestion to replace loans with grants is not a financially feasible option for financially challenged independent colleges and universities.

McCormick outlines another difficult recommendation to implement as he points to the importance Schreiner places on campus integration and alignment needed to achieve the goal of student success. McCormick contends that the integration and alignment needed to implement the strategies do not currently exist at many small independent college and universities. He reinforces his assertion by stating, "until that happens, it will be difficult to fully experience all of the benefits of the strategies Schreiner identifies."

In her chapter "Student Demographics and Equity," Park offers recommendations for how independent colleges and universities can meet the challenges of student diversity. However, Mary Marcy, in her reaction to Park's chapter, asserts that many of Park's recommendations would require significant new resources for their implementation. She reinforces this point by stating "most CIC institutions cannot approach these issues by adding staff, new programs, or physical space."

Inaccuracies about Institutional Realities

The last category of shortcomings noted by chapter reactors pertains to inaccuracies about the institutional realities of small independent colleges and universities held by some of the chapter authors. For example, McCormick notes that Schreiner contends that faculty have intentionally opted to work at small independent colleges. However, McCormick states that his experience suggests that faculty seldom intentionally select this type of college or university. Consequently, he posits that institutional leaders must create and provide incentives for faculty to interact with students in ways that graduate school did not prepare them to do.

Stefanco also identifies some inaccuracies about the scholarly and research activities of faculty in independent colleges and universities. These inaccuracies stem from John M. Braxton's contention that "scholars of pedagogical practice," or faculty engagement in Boyer's scholarship of teaching, align best with the teaching mission of such colleges and universities. Sefanco states that "after serving at three CIC institutions and studying many others, the role of research, and particularly what Boyer calls the scholarship of discovery, is generally believed to be an essential component of excellent teaching and is required to win and maintain accreditation.

Finally, Marc Roy, in his reaction to the Weerts and Taylor chapter titled "Public Purposes and Benefits of Independent Higher Education," comments on their recommendation that independent colleges work to enroll more students from underrepresented populations and different religious faiths than they have in the past. He indicates that "many independent faith-based colleges have accepted students of other faiths for decades." Roy also states that it is common practice at these institutions to recruit students from underrepresented backgrounds and low-income families.

Value

The chapter reactors also found much of value in some of the chapters they reviewed. The value of some chapters fall into two categories: useful recommendations and new understandings.

Useful Recommendations

In his comments on Hillman and Crespín-Trujillo's chapter "Access and Affordability," Drake regards their recommendation of removing transportation and child-care barriers to improve student access as likely to have a positive impact on improving access. He also points to their recommendation of using alumni networks and community-based organizations as insightful and noted that it could improve access as well as affect alumni involvement and institutional advancement in a positive manner.

Ross also finds utility in recommendations advanced by Mayhew and Vassallo in their chapter "Leveraging Learning Technologies at Liberal Arts Colleges and Universities" as he refers to the possibility of implementing these technologies for students as a "remarkable opportunity" for independent colleges and universities. He contends that "new and expanded programs on ground and online will likely result in additional revenue to support traditional and expanded mission-based activities, ensuring continued institutional health."

In their chapter "Public Purposes and Benefits of Independent Higher Education," Weerts and Taylor put forth suggestions or opportunities for independent colleges to pursue that might help them confront the challenges they face. These recommendations take the form of reinterpreting mission to speak to the American public, clearly articulate the institution's contribution to the public good, and seek partners that can share costs. In his reaction to this chapter, Roy states that these recommendations are "necessary for independent colleges to thrive and to continue as an important sector of American higher education."

McCormick views the "thriving framework" advanced by Schreiner in her chapter "Ensuring Student Success" as particularly useful to independent colleges. He states that the thriving framework "encourages institutional leaders to think about student success across a variety of domains (cognitive, behavioral, and psychological), while drawing attention to the possibility that these domains can be shaped by intentional interventions." McCormick also highlights as a contribution Schreiner's contention that rather than being selective in the student admissions process independent colleges need to be deliberate in their creation of excellence by design.

Although not centered on a specific recommendation, Marcy finds value in the contents of Park's chapter, titled "Student Demographics and Equity." More specifically, Marcy regards the overview of challenges and recommendations involving increasing student diversity provided by Park as offering a "valuable tool kit for leaders of colleges and universities, outlining not only challenges but also highlighting some of the most promising responses to supporting a diverse student body."

New Understandings

The new understandings identified by our presidents and provosts take the form of lessons learned and acknowledgments of the contributions made by some of these chapters.

In her reaction to the chapter titled "Assessment of Student Learning Outcomes" by Kinzie and Cogswell, Letha Zook points out lessons she has learned from this chapter. She states that these lessons "center around three mandates for private higher education: identifying and assessing institutional student learning outcomes is essential, intentionality of curriculum is the path forward, and the scholarship of teaching needs to be the work of our faculty." Zook also regards the synthesis of research on the effects of pedagogy on learning outcomes as another major contribution of chapter 3.

Ross gained some possible new understandings from his reading and reactions to the chapter "Leveraging Learning Technologies at Liberal Arts Colleges and Universities" by Mayhew and Vassallo. Ross notes that some of the most successful online programs are at CIC member institutions. He contends that "it is worthwhile to learn from those independent institutions by studying their administrative structure and modes of delivery." Clearly Ross regards such possible learnings as important to independent colleges that elect to develop online programs.

A new understanding noted by Marcy comes from the research presented in Park's chapter titled "Student Demographics and Equity." Marcy contends that the changing profile of entering students affords an opportunity to reaffirm the mission of CIC member institutions. She posits that "many of our institutions were founded with a strong religious or values-based philosophy that challenged us to educate and elevate students in a spirit of inclusivity; today, we know that the percentage of underrepresented and low-income students at CIC institutions exceeds that of the rest of higher education. Our missions provide the framework for evolving in response to rapidly changing student demographics."

Conclusions and Next Steps

This book seeks to produce a type of conversation between scholars and practitioners as a means of identifying what we know about the independent college sector, how that research might be utilized by campus leaders, and what else we need to know to better equip these campuses and their leaders during what is an incredibly challenging period for smaller private colleges and universities. A reading of the book's contents, we believe, will shed some light on the state of the research to practice bridge between the scholarship of the higher education research community and the everyday realities of campus leaders. Some of what is revealed is agreement and some less clear. In either case, more work is needed. For example, our scholars and campus leaders agree on the importance of mission. As we note above, many scholars point to mission and identity as potential advantages for private colleges who seek more students and ways to improve the quality of learning on their campuses. Our president and provost authors agree with this perspective but also suggest that there may be more complexity to the issue because of differences in institutional resources or the availability of faculty who are prepared to teach on small college campuses. This agreement is illustrative: it suggests that higher education scholars would be wise to continue to do work on the importance of mission at private colleges and universities; the disagreement may mean that higher education scholars have misperceptions about what really goes on at small campuses.

The Association for the Study of Higher Education and the CIC will continue to work together to bridge the gap between what we know and what we need to know to produce more useful knowledge and better manage the hundreds of smaller private colleges and universities in the United States. This book is a good first step in that process because it illustrates specific areas where there are both strong support and gaps in the bridge. What we need to do is to identify other opportunities where scholars and leaders can share what they know and learn from each other. Scholars and practitioners are after many of the same things: better access for underrepresented students; more engaged students; contemporary teaching and learning practices that use technology to spur students' intellectual curiosity; and vibrant, inclusive campus environments. That's important but not enough; both communities need to be explicit and intentional in their efforts to continue building bridges.

NOTES

1. Hearn, Warshaw, and Ciarimboli, *Strategic Change and Innovation.*
2. Franklin Pierce University English Department. Sophomore Assessment Seminar.
3. Stetson University. "Change in Staffing Request Form."

REFERENCES

Franklin Pierce University English Department. Sophomore Assessment Seminar, Spring 2009. https://www.franklinpierce.edu/academics/ugrad/programs_of_study/humanities/english/docs/soph%20syllabus.pdf. Accessed on February 17, 2017.

Hearn, James, Jarrett B. Warshaw, and Erin B. Ciarimboli. "Strategic Change and Innovation in Independent Colleges: Nine Mission-Driven Campuses." Washington, DC: Council of Independent Colleges, 2016. https://www.cic.edu/r/r/Documents/CIC-Hearn-Report-2016.pdf. Accessed February 17, 2017.

Stetson University. "Change in Staffing Request Form." http://www.stetson.edu/administration/human-resources/media/Change%20in%20Staffing%20Request%20Form.pdf. Accessed February 17, 2017.

Contributors

John M. Braxton is professor of education in the Department of Leadership, Policy, and Organizations. His research interests center on the college student experience and the sociology of the academic profession. He has published over 100 publications in the form of articles in refereed journals, books, and book chapters. Of his books, six are full-length coauthored and seven are edited books. His full-length books include *Rethinking College Student Retention* (with William Doyle, Harold Hartley, Amy Hirschy, Willis Jones, and Michael McLendon), *Professors Behaving Badly* (with Eve Proper and Alan Bayer), *Faculty Misconduct in Collegiate Teaching* (with Alan Bayer), and *Institutionalizing a Broader View of Scholarship through Boyer's Four Domains* (with William Luckey and Patricia Helland). Professor Braxton serves as a member of the editorial board of the *Journal of College Student Retention* and served as the ninth editor of the *Journal of College Student Development* for seven years, from 2008 to 2015. He is also a past president of the Association for the Study of Higher Education.

Erin B. Ciarimboli is a doctoral candidate at the Institute of Higher Education at the University of Georgia. She earned her MA in Higher Education and Student Affairs from the Ohio State University and her bachelor's degree from the University of Kentucky. Before coming to the Institute for further graduate studies, she worked in student affairs at Kenyon College for eight years. Her research interests include the intersection of college access and policy, the sociology of higher education, and innovation and change in the independent college sector.

Cynthia A. Cogswell is a postdoctoral fellow for assessment and evaluation at Dartmouth College. At Dartmouth, her work focuses on assessing and evaluating campus efforts to enhance learning and classroom pedagogy. Her PhD is from Indiana University in Higher Education and Student Affairs. Through her research, Cynthia aims to enrich the national dialogue about student learning in higher education and regional accreditation in the United States. She is interested in understanding how institutions use the process of assessment to improve student learning, the relationship between institutions and accreditors, and supporting institutional improvement through regional accreditation.

Valerie Crespín-Trujillo is a doctoral student in the Educational Leadership and Policy Analysis Department at the University of Wisconsin-Madison. She currently serves on the board of directors for the Association for the Study of Higher Education as the graduate student representative. Her research interests include higher education finance and policy and how the two intersect to impact institutional behavior and student outcomes.

Daniel Custer is a PhD candidate in higher education at the Pennsylvania State University. He received his master of arts in higher education and bachelor's degree in biblical studies and adventure education from Messiah College. His research interests include institutional assessment, church-related higher education, and diversity in higher education. He currently serves as research analyst in the Office of Institutional Research at Messiah College.

Richard H. Dorman was the fourteenth president of Westminster College (Pennsylvania). He retired following the 2015–16 academic year. Dorman lead Westminster through the implementation of a strategic plan called "Advantage: Westminster," which won a bronze medal from the Higher Education Marketing Report in the nation's largest educational advertising awards competition. In addition to his role as president, Dorman served as president of the national Association of Presbyterian Colleges and Universities (APCU) and president of Pennsylvania Campus Compact. In 2013, Dorman coauthored the best-selling higher education management book *Leadership and Governance in Higher Education* along with Robert Hendrickson, Jason Lane, and James T. Harris.

Roger Drake is president at Central Methodist University in Fayette, Missouri. He arrived at CMU in 2013 after serving nine years as vice president for administration and finance at Lindsey Wilson College in Columbia, Kentucky. Drake teaches finance for the Council of Independent Colleges' New President's Program. He currently chairs the association of Independent Colleges and Universities of Missouri (ICUM) and the Council of Presidents for the Heart of America Athletic Conference. He is a member of the

Missouri Coordinating Board of Higher Education's Advisory Council. In his prior post, he served as a Special Reader in Finance for SACSCOC's Committee on Compliance and Reports.

Richard Ekman has been president of the Council of Independent Colleges since 2000. He previously served as vice president for programs of Atlantic Philanthropies and, in 1991–99, as secretary and senior program officer of the Andrew W. Mellon Foundation. Ekman is a recipient of the W. E. B Du-Bois Medal of Harvard University and is coauthor, with Richard E. Quandt, of *Technology and Scholarly Communication* (1999). His essays have appeared in the *Chronicle of Higher Education, University Business, Inside Higher Ed,* and *Washington Post*. Ekman earned his AB in history and PhD in the history of American civilization from Harvard University.

David Guthrie, PhD, is an associate professor in the higher education graduate program at the Pennsylvania State University, where he also currently serves as co-professor-in-charge. He is the author of two monographs, several articles and book chapters, and numerous presentations, and has previously served as a dean in both student affairs and academic affairs, a co-director of a multi-million-dollar grant focused on the theological exploration of vocation, and a campus minister. His intellectual interests include church-related colleges and universities, and connections among religion, society, and higher education.

Harold V. Hartley III is senior vice president of the Council of Independent Colleges, where he is responsible for CIC's Presidents Institute, the largest annual meeting of college and university presidents in the country, and other initiatives for college presidents. He also supervises CIC's data and research activities. In addition, he oversees the Network for Vocation in Undergraduate Education, a membership organization of 226 colleges and universities committed to supporting the intellectual and theological exploration of vocation among students. He earned a BA from Westminster College in Pennsylvania, where he serves as a trustee, and an EdD in higher education from Vanderbilt University.

James C. Hearn is professor and associate director in the Institute of Higher Education at the University of Georgia. He holds a PhD in sociology of education and an MA in sociology from Stanford University, and earned earlier degrees from Duke University and the University of Pennsylvania. Prior to initiating his academic career, he worked as an administrator at a small private college and as a policy analyst in a Washington, DC-area consulting firm. His research and teaching focus on postsecondary education organization and policy. In recent work, he has examined the emergence of new models for higher education governance and financing, organizational change and strategic adaptations in independent colleges, and faculty workforce issues.

Nicholas W. Hillman is an associate professor of Educational Leadership and Policy Analysis at the University of Wisconsin-Madison. Hillman's research focuses on postsecondary finance and financial aid policy, primarily as they relate to college access and equity. This work includes research on student loan debt, performance-based funding, and college affordability.

Jillian Kinzie is associate director at the Center for Postsecondary Research and the National Survey of Student Engagement (NSSE) Institute at Indiana University School of Education. She conducts research and leads project activities on effective use of student engagement data to improve educational quality, and serves as senior scholar with the National Institute for Learning Outcomes Assessment (NILOA) project. She is coauthor of *Assessment in Student Affairs* (2016), *Using Evidence of Student Learning to Improve Higher Education* (2015), *Student Success in College* (2005/2010), and *One Size Does Not Fit All: Traditional and Innovative Models of Student Affairs Practice* (2008/2014).

Mary B. Marcy is the ninth president of Dominican University of California. Prior to joining Dominican, she served as provost of Bard College at Simon's Rock and vice president at Bard College. She has worked in both public and private institutions of higher education. Marcy earned her DPhil and MPhil in politics from the University of Oxford. Her research focuses on women in American politics. She has also published extensively on issues of diversity, leadership, and strategy in higher education.

Matthew J. Mayhew is the William Ray and Marie Adamson Flesher Professor of Educational Administration at the Ohio State University. He is interested in how collegiate conditions, educational practices, and student experiences influence learning and democratic outcomes, including moral reasoning, pluralism, productive exchange across worldview differences, and innovation capacity. To support the study of college and its impact on student development and learning, Mayhew has been awarded more than $15.7 million in funding from sources including but not limited to the Andrew W. Mellon Foundation, the Fetzer Institute, the United States Department of Education, the Ewing Marion Kauffman Foundation, and the Merrifield Family Trust.

Charlie McCormick is the president of Schreiner University in Kerrville, Texas, where he previously served as provost and vice president for academic affairs. Prior to arriving at Schreiner, McCormick served as dean for academic affairs at Cabrini College in Radnor, Pennsylvania. His scholarly work focuses on folklore performances. Most recently, his work has focused on American women bullfighters from the early 1950s to the mid-1960s. He has made frequent presentations on the assessment of student learning, undergraduate research, and civic engagement.

Linda McMillin is provost, dean of the faculty, and co-chief operating officer at Susquehanna University. She has taught at Susquehanna University since 1989 and is also professor of history. Linda earned her PhD in history from the University of California, Los Angeles. Her undergraduate degree in theology and English is from Loyola Marymount University. She was the recipient of an American Council on Education Fellowship in 2000–2001. Linda has authored more than 25 articles, in both English and Spanish, and edited two books, *A New Academic Compact: Re-visioning the Relationship between Faculty and Their Institutions*, with Jerry Berberet (2002) and *Hrotsvit of Gandersheim: Contexts, Identities, Affinities and Performances with Katharina Wilson and Phyllis Brown* (2004).

Christopher C. Morphew is dean of the School of Education at Johns Hopkins University. He has also served as a tenured faculty member at the University of Iowa, University of Kansas, and University of Georgia, and as a Leiv Eiriksson Scholar at the University of Oslo. Morphew served on the executive board of the Association for the Study of Higher Education and co-chairs (with Hal Hartley of CIC) the ASHE-CIC collaborative project. He earned degrees from the University of Notre Dame, Harvard University, and Stanford University. His research agenda focusing on issues of institutional diversity has been funded by the National Science Foundation, the Ewing Marion Kauffman Foundation, the Ford Foundation, the Lumina Foundation, and the Research Council of Norway.

Julie J. Park is assistant professor of education at the University of Maryland, College Park. Her research addresses how race, religion, and social class affect diversity and equity in higher education, including the diverse experiences of Asian American college students. An associate editor of the *Journal of Diversity in Higher Education*, she is the author of *When Diversity Drops: Race, Religion, and Affirmative Action in Higher Education* (2013), an examination of how universities are affected by bans on affirmative action. Park earned her PhD in Education and BA at Vanderbilt University.

Laura Perna is James S. Riepe Professor and executive director of the Alliance for Higher Education and Democracy (AHEAD) at the University of Pennsylvania. She has served as president of the Association for the Study of Higher Education (ASHE) and vice president of the Postsecondary Division of the American Educational Research Association (AERA). She is currently (2016–17) chair of Penn's Faculty Senate. Her research uses a range of methodological approaches to identify how social structures, educational practices, and public policies can promote college access and success, particularly for groups that continue to be underrepresented in higher education.

Kevin M. Ross is the fifth president of Lynn University. During his tenure, the university implemented a redesigned core curriculum, received rankings as one of the most international schools in the country, and hosted the final 2012 presidential debate. The university also was recognized twice as an Apple Distinguished School and named one of the most innovative schools in the country by *U.S. News & World Report* for two consecutive years. Ross received his AB in English from Colgate University, MA in liberal arts from St. John's College, and doctorate in higher education leadership and policy from Peabody College of Vanderbilt University.

Marc Roy serves Albion College as the provost and professor of biology. He also serves on the board of directors of the American Conference of Academic Deans. Roy previously was the provost at Goucher College and the vice president for academic affairs and dean of the faculty at Coe College. Before becoming a chief academic officer, Roy was a professor of biology at Beloit College. He earned his BA from Lawrence University and his PhD in neurosciences from the University of Wisconsin-Madison.

Laurie A. Schreiner is professor and chair of the Department of Higher Education at Azusa Pacific University in southern California. Coauthor of *The Student Satisfaction Inventory*, as well as *Helping Sophomores Succeed* (2009) and *Thriving in Transitions: A Research-Based Approach to Student Success* (2012),

Schreiner is coeditor-in-chief of the journal *Christian Higher Education* and serves on the editorial board of *About Campus*. She has published research on positive psychology and higher education, engaged learning, sophomore success, retention, faculty development, and strengths-based approaches to teaching and advising. Most recently she has developed the Thriving Quotient as a holistic measure of student well-being.

Carolyn J. Stefanco is president of the College of Saint Rose in New York. After receiving a PhD in history from Duke University, she served as a faculty member and academic administrator at a wide variety of institutions, ranging from public research universities to private liberal arts colleges. Stefanco was resident director of a London Study Program and Senior Fulbright Scholar to the University of Zagreb in Croatia. She is a trustee of the American University in Bulgaria. Her research focuses on women and leadership in a global context, and she speaks and writes about many higher education issues.

Barrett Taylor is assistant professor of higher education at the University of North Texas. His research emphasizes the complex relationships between colleges and universities and their environments via topics such as academic science, evangelical Christian colleges, faculty work, and higher education finance and governance.

Stephen Vassallo is the assistant vice chancellor in the Office of Data Analytics at the University of Colorado Boulder. He oversees both the institutional research and data analytics functions for the University. He holds a master of public administration degree from the Wagner Graduate School of Public Service at New York University. His research interests include higher education finance and public policy and the intersection of student development theory, epistemology, and digital learning environments.

David Weerts is associate professor of higher education in the Department of Organizational Leadership, Policy, and Development at the University of Minnesota-Twin Cities. His research focuses on state-university relations, community-university engagement, and alumni giving, volunteerism, and advocacy. He currently serves as faculty liaison for the Private College Leadership Network at the University of Minnesota.

Cynthia A. Wells is associate professor of higher education and director of the Ernest L. Boyer Center at Messiah College. She authored the monograph

Realizing General Education: Reconceptualizing Purpose and Renewing Practice (2016). Wells has also been a contributing author to several texts, including *At This Time and in This Place: Vocation and Higher Education* (2015). Her scholarly interests include general education, common learning, and inclusive excellence. She completed her undergraduate work at Occidental College and her doctoral study at Ohio State University.

Letha B. Zook is an experienced administrator with over 18 years of progressive leadership responsibilities. She has served in leadership of physical therapy programs and as dean/provost at two universities. During this time she has worked with regional and specialized accreditation agencies for candidacy and continued program approvals, including physical therapy, pharmacy, physician assistant, teacher preparation, and other allied health professions. Zook is a magna cum laude graduate of the University of Pennsylvania with a physical therapy degree. She earned a master of science in pathokinesiology from New York University. Zook received her doctorate in applied physiology from Teachers College, Columbia University.

Index